Encounters With God

William K. Dorrance

Olympus Story House

CONTENTS

Preface   vii

Chapter 1: What Science Ignores   1
    Proof Of Psychic Abilities   3
    Proof Of Life After Death   9
    More Proof Of Life After Death   12
    Early Childhood Memories Of Previous Lives   12
    Deathbed Visions   17
    Near-Death Experiences   18
    Past-Life Regression   21

Chapter 2: What Christianity Ignores   31
    Empirical Evidence For Religious Beliefs   33
    Prophetic Revelation Inspires Revealed Religions   36
    Gnosticism   39
    Reincarnation In Early Christian History   41
    Worldly Perspectives And Agendas   46
    Inner Experience And Guidance   48

Chapter 3: An Examined Life   53
    Reflections Related To My Childhood   56
    Samadhi   58
    My Introduction To Christianity   62
    René Descartes's Influence On Science
        And Christianity   72

Chapter 4: After High-School   78
    The Hard Problem Of Consciousness   79
    Argument From Design And The Evolution Of Eyes   82
    God's Removal From Science's Concerns   88
    Emotions   90
    How To Live: Other-Centered
        As Opposed To Self-Centered   92

The Four-Way Test Of The Things We Think,
    Say, Or Do   101

Chapter 5: My High School Prayers Bear Fruit   **109**
    Fox Theater Practice–Related Experiences   111
    The Parapsychology Association Of Riverside (Par)   124
    Edgar Cayce   130
    Channeling And A Course In Miracles   133

Chapter 6: Nonduality   **143**
    "Universal" Experiences, And Esoteric
        And Exoteric Believers   146
    Nonduality   149
    "I Am That I Am"   152
    Perennial Philosophy, Perennial
        Or Ageless Wisdom, And Perennialism   156
    Sri Nisargadatta Maharaj   157
    Meditation   160
    My Second Church Sermon   168
    Adding Facts To Faith   168

Chapter 7: 1986   **177**
    Divination   179
    Anita Burns And Corona Light   185
    Phyllis Krystal   187
    Armand Marcotte   191
    Trudy Philpot Kieschnick   196
    Kathryn Leeman   198
    India And Sathya Sai Baba   201

Chapter 8: Experiences As A Devotee of
Sathya Sai Baba   **205**
    Back Home After Receiving Sai Baba's Darshan   209
    Condensed Transcript Of Talk
        By Dr. Michael Goldstein   212

Condensed Transcript Of Talk
    by James Sinclair   215
Isaac Tigrett: "My Story"   219
Providing Examples Of Ideal Health Care
    And Education   224
Sathya Sai Bookstores In Prasanthi Nilayam
    And Tustin, California   225
Sathya Sai Baba Center Of Cherry Valley   228
Body, Soul, And Person Or Jiva   231
Discovering And Learning From Those
    Who Achieved Self-Realization   234

Chapter 9: Left Out Odds And Ends   **243**
Seeing Dead People   246
The Truth, The Whole Truth, And …   247
Love   249
Locating And Experiencing Our Soul   250
An Odd, Spiritual-Dimension Look At History   252
Believe It Or Not   252
Dharma   253
Why Do Bad Things Happen To Good People?   255
Destiny   263
When Thoughts Marry Beliefs   265

For Further Study   **269**
Glossary   **272**
Endnotes   **277**
Contributors   **281**
About The Author   **283**

Written in appreciation of and
with the hope of sharing
God's grace.

PREFACE

Have you learned about everyone's underlying reality? Teachers must conform to cultural norms, and parents cannot teach what they do not know. Do you know that cultural psychology research across diverse cultures reveals the distinctive imprint of a person's culture on their attitudes and beliefs? When attitudes and beliefs pass from parents and teachers to children, "common sense," as Albert Einstein observed, "is nothing more than a deposit of prejudices laid down in the mind prior to the age of eighteen."[1] Despite their differences, the commonsense attitudes and beliefs of both science and Christianity oppose and suppress the information contained in this book. Their combined influence in the Western world ensures that almost everyone is either unaware of or misinformed about the information contained in this book. If you finish reading this book's culturally taboo content, you will realize it contains humanity's most important insights into the nature of everyone's reality.

Despite our immersion within them, we seldom notice the existence of air or gravity. A sudden guest of wind can remind us that we are immersed in air. Isaac Newton told a fellow member of the Royal Society that the inspiration for his law of gravitation occurred while watching an apple fall to the earth. Our physical senses are unable to inform us of something more relevant to our reality than air and gravity. Like experiencing a gust of wind or gravity's influence when lifting a heavy weight, I experienced, as a child and as an adult, what Eastern religions call **samadhi**—being immersed in God's love, light, and bliss. Words like samadhi, which contain concepts that are relevant to understanding this book, appear in **bold print** when first used and in the glossary. The experience of samadhi, which Eastern religions attribute to **God**'s grace, conferred upon me the awareness of being immersed within God's omnipresent awareness and love, but the experience is ignored by Western science and Christianity. I am writing this book to share a lifetime of accumulated empirical **evidence** that God, like air and gravity, is a confirmable, omnipresent reality.

While listening to a church sermon when I was thirteen, a voice (which I attributed to God) told me the three primary teachings of the world's divinely inspired religions. While reading Jesus's Sermon on the Mount when I was fifteen, I envied his audience's ability to experience a divinely inspired spiritual teacher. As I envied those who were born two thousand years ago, I realized that a planet with billions of people and an omnipresent god must have at least one Jesus-like person somewhere. I earnestly prayed to be led to a divinely inspired spiritual teacher.

Along with supportive scientific research and the illuminating but ignored experiences of others, this book contains the sequence of improbable experiences—as if controlled by an invisible, gravity-like power—which led me to a hypothesized Jesus-like teacher. The scientific research and the experiences of others would not be necessary if Western science and Christianity were not opposed to the concepts contained in this book. As a child with an atheist father, I realized my experiences were unusual and not likely to be understood or believed. Sharing my experiences necessitates writing a book because experiencing samadhi and God talking to me are as culturally unacceptable as when I first experienced them seventy years ago. Western science and humanity's understanding and acceptance of spiritual phenomena have not progressed because Western science ignores the evidence for nonmaterial, spiritual phenomena like God, **souls**, and an **afterlife**. To share my experiences, I must write a book to explain them because Western science suppresses evidence-based spiritual knowledge.

Confirmation bias, habitually defending and maintaining one's beliefs, transformed Western science into an atheistic discipline. Relative to the truth about something, we can be correctly informed, misinformed, or aware of or oblivious to our ignorance. Psychological studies find that confirmation bias affects everyone's ability to separate fact from fiction. I am writing about confirmation bias because the reader may not be able to understand and finish this book while defending and maintaining many of the Western world's attitudes and beliefs.

My **psychic** and **mystical** experiences, and those of countless others, would be impossible if human **consciousness** (awareness) was limited by a brain's plausible neurobiological capabilities. Despite Western science and philosophy's inability to explain the ability of physical brains to manifest nonphysical thoughts and experiences, Western science embraces and promotes atheistic assumptions as proven facts. Why would Western science, which is incredibly competent and successful at investigating the natural world, be less successful investigating spiritual concerns? Physicist Thomas Kuhn answered that question in his 1962 history of science, *The Structure of Scientific Revolutions*, which contains profound insights into the nature of science. His research revealed that similarly trained scientists embrace the same beliefs and understandings which he called a **paradigm**. "Normal" scientists, according to Thomas Kuhn, conform to their scientific community's paradigm. Each scientific community—such as anthropology, chemistry, and physics— focuses on a unique paradigm or body of knowledge. Thomas Kuhn found that scientific communities do not alter their paradigms by adding anomalies (findings which conflict with their paradigm's version of reality). A "revolution" in thinking within a scientific community must take place before anomalies can be incorporated into a new paradigm which contains previously ignored anomalies.

During the eighteenth century's portion of the **Enlightenment**, the scientific method and human intellect replaced revelation (God) as humanity's most reliable source of knowledge. A **materialistic** understanding of the universe (**materialism**) emerged, which assumed that nonmaterial, spiritual phenomena do not exist. Because of science's exclusively materialistic understanding of reality, nonmaterial phenomena like God, souls, and an afterlife are excluded from science's paradigms. In the twentieth century, modern scientists, "who prefer to solve their problems without recourse to God,"[2] began calling the evidence for God, souls, and an afterlife **"paranormal"** and **"supernormal"** phenomenon. Scientific communities and their journals discourage the investigation of "paranormal" phenomena. Schoolbooks, teachers, and boards must conform to norms established by atheistic scientific communities. Assuming "paranormal" phenomena do not exist within our phenomenal reality enables Western science to disregard the abundant evidence for God, souls, and an afterlife.

Phenomena either exist or they do not. The words "paranormal" and "supernormal" are not applied to dark matter and energy, consciousness, or anything that is mysterious except phenomena relevant to religious belief. Because materialistic science uses "paranormal" and "supernormal" to ignore the evidence for a spiritual component to reality, I use quotation marks to identify "paranormal" and "supernormal" as words coined to denigrate and avoid the evidence for God, souls, and an afterlife. A century of habitually applying "paranormal" to research findings which reveal consciousness's ability to transcend the assumed boundaries of time and space has enabled Western science to ignore overwhelming evidence of consciousness's independence from matter. The first chapter focuses on scientists and medical doctors with the courage to work outside science's restrictive paradigms. Their research findings refute the common assumption that "paranormal" phenomena are not amenable to scientific research.

Besides applicable scientific research, this book contains my experiences and those of others. Beliefs can be influenced by both reliable and unreliable sources of information. Empirical and antidotal evidence (instead of hearsay) guide scientific research. Confirmation bias is difficult to combat when learning about human experiences and abilities which conflict with our beliefs, but today's information age makes it possible to rationally investigate relevant human experiences and scientific research findings. To help you with your research, books and websites are suggested in the section labeled "For Further Study."

Isaac Newton, along with all the notable early contributors to the Scientific Revolution, was a devout Christian. Both Newton and Einstein were what Thomas Kuhn called "revolutionary scientists." Without their ability to think outside the boxes containing science's paradigms, they would not be among the greatest scientists who ever lived. They both wrote extensively about their spiritual beliefs without fear, like today's scientists and philosophers, of alluding to a higher power. In contrast to before the nineteenth century, when most scientists believed in God, surveys of contemporary scientists reveal that science has become an atheistic discipline. Ninety-three percent of those who responded to the National Academy of Science's August 1998 survey of biological and physical scientists identified themselves as atheists or agnostics. Only 7 percent expressed belief in a higher power. In contrast to the scientific community, 81 percent of the respondents to a May 2022 Gallup survey expressed belief in God. But 81 percent is down from 87 percent in 2017, and way down from 98 percent during the 1930s through the 1950s. Before assuming atheistic science and academia's influence have been desirable, we should look at the phenomena that science labels "paranormal" and ignores.

Atheism requires faith in science's eventual ability to explain how the brain's neurobiological processes enable us to be conscious of anything. Atheists must also ignore all the evidence to support belief in God, souls, and an afterlife. There is no way to explain away dovetailing evidence from multiple sources—early childhood memories of previous lives, near-death experiences, and past-life regression—harmoniously revealing that human consciousness exists before and after the birth and death of bodies and brains. The first chapter focuses on the evidence that science ignores and labels as "paranormal" phenomena.

"Researchers, who study how people resolve the uneasy feeling of holding inconsistent beliefs, note that most people would rather deny or downplay new, uncomfortable information than reshape their world view to accommodate it." The tendency to view one's opinions "through rose-colored glasses" enables people to maintain their beliefs without "feeling alarmed enough to reconsider [their] views. When doubts do creep in, instead of removing their rose-colored glasses, people dig in their heels even more."[3]

You would think that members of the academic and scientific communities would be above these human failings. But paradoxically, academic and scientific acumen makes matters even worse. Research in 2015, at Loyola University in Chicago, confirmed that those who perceive themselves to be experts are less open to new points of view. Scientists who cling to their opinions have difficulty grasping new ideas. This insight was expressed by Max Planck, the "father of quantum physics" and recipient of the 1918 Nobel Prize in physics, when he wrote, "A new scientific truth does not triumph by convincing its opponents and making them see the light, but rather because its opponents eventually die, and a new generation grows up that is not familiar with it."[4]

Nothing that I have written provides evidence for God, souls, or an afterlife, which is the primary theme of this book. But I hope that the above information will enable your mind to be less closed to ideas and information which conflict with your beliefs. For decades, the academic and scientific communities have refused to remove their rose-colored glasses while digging in their heels, ignoring the evidence contained in this book. If the academic and scientific communities did not stubbornly cling to dogma which conflicts with my experiences, I would not be writing this book.

Most people, I believe, would say that the most significant or meaningful experiences of their lives were not anticipated or sought after, but just happened. It was in that unexpected manner that samadhi, **astrology**, past-life regression, reincarnation, psychic experiences, **channeling**, **spirit guides**, **discarnate** spirits, the use of a pendulum for **divination**, the phenomena of **self-realization**, and an **avatar** (God in human form) were witnessed or experienced by me. Each one of these topics of possible interest, research, or experience conflicts with a materialistic understanding of reality. Anyone with positive experiences with these or related topics would be inclined to believe that the dismissal, ridicule, and ignorance of these topics by contemporary science and education is incompatible with the objective and curious mind which should be at the heart of both science and education.

This book contains words and concepts that are not commonly understood in the Western world. Because words often have more than one meaning, familiar words may have unfamiliar meanings. For example, self-realization in Western psychology refers to achieving the potential of one's character or personality. But in this book, it means one's usual experience of themselves is replaced with the consciousness of the spark of God that became their soul, achieving enlightenment, and fulfilling the ultimate purpose of human birth. Words like

atma, **jiva**, **maya**, and samadhi are not English words and probably contain unfamiliar concepts. Avatar, enlightenment, and self-realization may look familiar, but they express, in this book, concepts that the Western world ignores. If Western science and academia appreciated words like samadhi and self-realization, which refer to the direct experience of God, they would be capitalized.

Western science assumes that spiritual beliefs progressed from animism to the various organized religions, and science is the pinnacle of human understanding. The development of religions and the record of God's communication with humanity are assumed to be cultural creations. Yet, despite the diversity of religions, common themes exist in their original spiritual documents, which suggests a common source of inspiration. Reading this book requires a relatively small investment of time and effort to become aware of having a soul, continuing consciousness after death, and a conscious relationship with God. May my mundane to mystical life experiences, the more extraordinary experiences of others, and relevant but ignored scientific research inspire an appreciation of everyone's spiritual reality.

Chapter 1
WHAT SCIENCE IGNORES

*"There is no source of deception in the investigation
of nature which can compare with a fixed belief that
certain kinds of phenomena are impossible."*
—*William James*

Does your consciousness arise from your brain (which, along with your body, is born and dies) or "the breath of life"[5] (a soul, which is neither born nor dies)? Why were you born? Hindus believe you were born because, in your previous life, you died without realizing the consciousness of your soul. In the Western world, science ridicules and ignores research findings which suggest the possibility of souls and an afterlife. Science's exclusively materialistic understanding of reality influences the beliefs of even Christians. Harmonious understandings cultivate closed minds and ideological certainty instead of open minds, uncertainty, and wonder.

Responding to the Western world's lack of interest in his books, articles, and lectures on Eastern religions and philosophy, Alan Watts wrote *The Book on the Taboo Against Knowing Who You Are*, which was first published in 1966. An actual taboo does not exist, but Western culture discourages thinking of oneself as a spiritual being. More influenced by personal mystical experiences, Eastern religions and philosophy reveal a greater appreciation for the sense of unity, or oneness, within the diversity of creation. In the West, few people are knowledgeable of or even curious about Eastern philosophy and concepts like reincarnation, Karma, and liberation.

I have been blessed with a sequence of "paranormal"— the ignored and ridiculed evidence of our spiritual reality—

experiences which can be logically understood as God's answer to my high school prayers. Because my prayers were pleadings to be led to someone like Jesus, with divinely inspired wisdom, my experiences and the answers to my prayers are of relevance to everyone. I often resisted the answers I received because they conflicted with my "commonsense" understanding of reality.

We live in an age when religious faith is waning while the influences of scientific and technological achievements, products, and understandings replace spiritual concerns with an unending obsession with worldly interests and desires. Mystical experiences occur in all cultures and suggest a spiritual reality. But mystical experiences occur infrequently enough to be systematically eliminated from consideration as relevant aspects of our phenomenal reality. Paradoxically, Christianity has no more interest in the evidence for our spiritual reality than Western science. Because of ignorant, biased, and misleading understandings of religious concepts, only those with mystical spiritual experiences can distinguish fact from fiction.

Most Americans say religion is important to them, but in a 2019 Pew Research Center survey, which contained thirty-two fact-based, multiple-choice questions about religion, most of the over ten thousand respondents missed most of the questions and knew almost nothing about religions other than Christianity. Average scores for self-identified atheists surpassed average scores for self-identified Protestants and Roman Catholics. I am writing this book to provide the knowledge highly educated, intelligent readers need to be less likely, instead of more likely, to think of themselves as atheists. Because of a lifetime of experiences which encouraged and motivated me to write this book, I want to share with you the knowledge of where to look for empirically confirmable and rational answers to spiritual questions. Religious and spiritual understandings do not necessarily require faith in unsupportable myths and dogma.

Before sharing my experiences and commentary, which begin in chapter 3, we will look at human capabilities and experiences that suggest that consciousness does not conform to a materialistic understanding of reality. This chapter provides overwhelming evidence that few people—especially academically trained professionals—are exposed to or even know about. The research findings contained in this chapter suggest that consciousness is independent of matter, and we are spiritual beings. A brief look at abundant but ignored "paranormal" research findings reveals that ancient mystics had a better grasp of your reality than contemporary science.

PROOF OF PSYCHIC ABILITIES

For those who have had psychic or spiritual experiences, one experience is enough to be convinced that consciousness extends way beyond and outside the limits of our five physical senses. Physicist Russell Targ witnessed hundreds of psychic feats which, even from an observer's perspective, would be equally persuasive. In the preface to his book, *The Reality of ESP: A Physicist's Proof of Psychic Abilities* published in 2012, he wrote, "If it is possible for facts to convince a skeptical investigator of the reality of ESP, then I believe this book should do it." I also believe "[his] book should do it," and feel my best option for convincing skeptical readers is to encourage them to get and read *The Reality of ESP*. Hopefully, a synopsis of portions of the book will provide sufficient proof of "the reality of ESP."

Research shows that psychic ability, like musical ability, is not an extra ability that everyone does not have to some degree, which is why **parapsychologists** prefer to use **psi**, a word with other meanings, instead of **ESP (extrasensory perception)** to refer to psychic or "paranormal" abilities. Even though we all have some ability, most people do not believe they have psychic or musical talent. *The Reality of ESP* enables the reader to realize the psychic capabilities of those who are extremely talented.

When the CIA reviewed over twenty years of clairvoyant remote viewing research in 1995, they found that only 1 percent of those tested demonstrated significant remote viewing ability. Practice and training did not develop the ability.

In 1972, laser physicists Russell Targ and Hal Puthoff cofounded a remote viewing program at Stanford Research Institute (SRI) in Menlo Park, California. Obtaining both funding and approval for psi research can be a daunting task. Not only are psi phenomena inexplicable from a reductionistic point of view, but a perfectly timed sequence of several improbable events can be equally inexplicable. It is worth buying the book just to read, in chapter 2, the long sequence of serendipity which culminated in the initial funding by NASA and the CIA for SRI's ESP research program. SRI's ESP or psi research also received financial support from the Defense Intelligence Agency, Army and Air Force Intelligence, and others who provided $20 million for twenty-three years of psi research.

In 1972, Hal Puthoff became aware of Ingo Swann's participation in psi experiments conducted by Professor Gertrude Schmeidler at the City College of New York. Her published experiments reported that Swann was able to raise and lower the temperature of solid-state heat sensors within distant thermos bottles. Prior to Russell Targ joining Puthoff and Swann at SRI, Puthoff and Swann began the exploration of Swann's ability to see and influence things that were supposedly "secret and imperturbable." By psychically describing and influencing "an almost perfectly shielded, super-conducting magnetometer buried in a vault in the basement" of Stanford University's Varian physics building, Swann precipitated "the first of many governmental inquiries into" SRI's activities.

Several decades of psi research programs have shown that student volunteers with a positive attitude demonstrate statistically significant psychic ability; but, with boring and repetitive experiments, findings declined to chance expectations as students became bored. Even though most psi research programs have subtle results, over one hundred years of psi research has yielded billions to one statistical evidence of not only the reality of psi phenomena, but evidence of a nonphysical reality or dimension that is coexistent with our physical reality. In contrast to the limitations of our physical senses, ESP research found that electromagnetic shielding and distance—whether near or thousands of miles away—did not affect clairvoyant remote viewing test results.

SRI's secret Cold War psi research experiments did not obtain subtle findings. By making New York artist and gifted psychic Ingo Swann part of their initial research team, the two physicists were able to design their experiments to elicit profound and repeatable demonstrations of humanity's innate psychic ability. Unlike previous psi research programs, their psi research results did not decline with successive experiments. Instead of replicating previous experiments, which involved the telepathic transmission of familiar images, SRI's protocol consisted of a psychic remote viewer in a copper-screened, electrically shielded room with Russell Targ, who functioned as a facilitator for the psychic. After Targ and the psychic were in the electrically shielded room, a random number generator selected a target location for the other half of the remote viewing team, which consisted of Hal Puthoff and another team member. They drove as far as thirty minutes from SRI to one of sixty possible San Francisco Bay Area "target locations." One of the inexplicable findings was the ability of the remote viewer to describe target locations thirty minutes before Puthoff reached them. They all went to the target location to obtain feedback after the remote viewer finished describing the target, and Puthoff returned from the target location. *The Reality of ESP* has photographs of a few of the target locations and the drawings made by the psychic cloistered in the electrically shielded room with Targ. You can also find remote viewing examples on Russell Targ's website, https://espresearch.com/. Instead of helping, familiarity with the targets and their locations decreased the psychic's ability to make remarkably accurate drawings and descriptions. The psychic's drawings matched the photographs of the target locations as well as most people could draw something from memory. Often, the drawings looked like what most of us would draw when guided by a verbal description. The accuracy of the drawings was not influenced by the distance to the target or by electromagnetic shielding.

One of SRI's research programs, Project SCANATE, was developed in response to Ingo Swann's desire to explore the range of his psychic ability. He believed that he could describe any location by simply knowing its geographic coordinates. Over the telephone, the CIA provided the latitude and longitude, and upon being told the coordinates, Swann would close his eyes and begin describing what he saw in his mind's eye. As necessary, he opened his eyes to draw what he saw. On page 24 of the book is Ingo Swann's detailed drawing of "a super-secret National Security Agency listening post" located on the East Coast thousands of miles from Menlo Park, California. Swann's description and drawings were "correct in every detail." He provided not only the names of things like a flagpole, underground bunkers, buildings, a road, a fence, and several locations for trees; he provided their distances from each other and their orientation relative to north. It is impossible to refute *The Reality of ESP* without falsifying and denying evidence which proves the reality of psi phenomena and the nonlocality of consciousness.

The day after Ingo Swann received the coordinates, they were given to Pat Price, a retired Burbank, California, police commissioner, whose remote viewing ability enabled him to read the code words—"CUEBALL, 8-BALL, RACKUP"—

that were on file cabinets in the NSA listening post. He even supplied the name of the NSA facility. The coordinates given to Swann and Price were for the CIA agent's vacation cabin, which was a quarter of a mile from the NSA site. When two CIA agents came to SRI and asked Pat Price why he and Ingo Swann had accurately described the wrong location, Price said, "The more intent you are on hiding something, the more it shines like a beacon in psychic space." Subsequent successful demonstrations of psi's potential motivated SRI's funding during the Cold War.

NSA spacecraft "flybys" in 1973, 1974, and 1979 of Jupiter provided an opportunity to explore the range of remote viewing. On April 27, 1973, Ingo Swann, working with Russell Targ, began his "Jupiter probe." It only took three seconds for his psychic vision to reach the planet with these words: "There's a planet with stripes." Among Jupiter's previously unknown but confirmed features, which Swann described and drew, were faint rings around the planet, which were so difficult to see that they were not confirmed until six years later in 1979. Among the subsequently confirmed psychic feats of Ingo Swann were finding a downed Russian bomber in Africa, describing the health of American hostages in Iran, locating a kidnapped American general in Italy, and describing a Soviet weapons factory in Siberia and a Chinese atomic bomb test before it occurred.

It seems like I have rewritten *The Realty of ESP*, but I have merely skimmed over a few of the book's descriptions and insights into psi phenomena. Without Russell Targ's efforts, SRI's over twenty years of psi research may have never been declassified. In 1982, ten years after helping to start SRI's psi research program, Russell Targ left because "psychic spying for the CIA" lost its appeal when he could no longer publish SRI's research. You can read The Reality of ESP because Russell Targ was successful in declassifying

SRI's research. Besides *The Reality of ESP*, Russell Targ has written or coauthored eight books dealing with the scientific investigation of psi, how to do remote viewing, and Buddhist approaches to consciousness transformation.

I want to conclude this glimpse into SRI's research with their involvement with the 1974 abduction of UC Berkeley student and newspaper heiress Patricia Hearst. Aware of SRI's apparently not-so-secret research program, the Berkeley Police Department called SRI asking for help. To see if they could be of assistance, physicists Puthoff and Targ, along with Pat Price, drove to Berkeley. Thumbing through a loose-leaf mug shot book filled with hundreds of photos, Pat Price correctly identified one of the Symbionese Liberation Army's abductors with the words "That's the ringleader." Price was then asked where they could be found. Pointing north, Price replied, "They went that way. I see a white station wagon near a restaurant. It's across the highway from two large, white gas-storage tanks near an overpass." One of the detectives recognized the described location because it was close to where he lived. Within ten minutes, a police car reported finding the kidnapper's white station wagon. On page 59, Russell Targ wrote, "But because the Berkeley Police Department, the Alameda County Sheriff's Office, and the FBI did not cooperate with one another, all our work was fruitless." As police commissioner in Burbank, California, Pat Price used his psychic abilities to scan the city after crimes were reported to locate the criminals. I am sure that psychic ability can be appropriately and helpfully applied to activities other than catching criminals and spying on other countries.

Princeton Engineering Anomalies Research Laboratory (PEAR) at Princeton University also confirmed the reality of ESP by conducting their own remote viewing studies in 1978. In one PEAR study, the remote viewer "saw" the target location forty-five minutes before the other half of their remote viewing team arrived at the randomly selected target location. Like SRI's ESP research program, PEAR's 334 remote viewing trials confirmed the reality of clairvoyant remote viewing ability. Our physical senses and brain's capabilities obviously do not include seeing great distances or several minutes into the future. What enables even 1 percent of the population to demonstrate godlike clairvoyant ability? The answer is our underlying reality, or soul, and God. We are *spiritual beings* with souls that connect us with All That Is or God. Psi phenomena exist because we are spiritual beings immersed in God.

Psi phenomena imply that consciousness permeates and interconnects everything. The quantum mechanics world of subatomic particles also reveals the quantum interconnectedness or nonlocal (**nonduality**) nature of the universe. When physicist David Bohm proposed that quantum **nonlocality** and interconnectedness (entanglement) did not occur because particles mysteriously communicate with each other, but because they were aspects of a larger whole which coordinated them, he provided science's definition of religion's God.

The widespread realization that everyone and everything is interconnected, as taught by many religions, may inspire a greater sense of **empathy** toward others and peaceful cooperation among the world's inhabitants. Wars and the mistreatment of others are by-products of experiencing everything outside oneself as separate or "other." Where is the inspiration for not following the Golden Rule after realizing that everyone is an aspect of the same larger whole? Acceptance of the reality of psi phenomena could go a long way toward affirming, despite the scientific community's long-standing opposition, that matter is not the only reality.

PROOF OF LIFE AFTER DEATH

Dr. Gary E. Schwartz graduated Phi Beta Kappa from Cornell and received his PhD from Harvard University in psychophysiology. Prior to becoming director of the University of Arizona's Laboratory for Advances in Consciousness and Health, Dr. Schwartz was the director of Yale's Psychophysiology Center, co-director of Yale's Behavioral Medical Clinic, the director of Yale's Psychophysiology Center, and a professor of psychology and psychiatry at Yale University. Reminiscent of Russell Targ's "sequence of serendipity" which culminated in SRI's ESP research program, Dr. Schwartz experienced an improbable sequence of experiences that led to his controversial study of communication between psychic **mediums** and "dead people." After spending three years conducting and recording increasingly controlled scientific experiments with psychic mediums, Dr. Schwartz wrote *The Afterlife Experiments: Breakthrough Scientific Evidence of Life after Death.*

In response to habitual skeptics, Dr. Schwartz designed rigorously controlled and monitored experiments to determine if psychic mediums can communicate with the disincarnate souls of those who were previously, before their death, known by "sitters." A great effort was made to make sure the mediums did not know the identities of the sitters. The mediums were unable to see or communicate directly with sitters, who were limited to yes or no responses. Mediums were just as accurate when the sitters were using a muted telephone hundreds of miles away as when in the same room separated from the sitters by a screen. When transcripts of the experiments with sitters and mediums were scored for specific things like names, experiences, and descriptions, the statements made by the mediums accurately applied to no longer living acquaintances of the sitters. Often, the sitters were unaware of subsequently verified information provided by mediums, which ruled out assuming the mediums were merely mind readers. All the psychic mediums achieved high—as high as 95 percent—rates of accuracy.

The methodology used by Dr. Schwartz eliminated plausible explanations for his findings other than the ability of consciousness to continue after the death of the body, and the ability of psychic mediums to communicate with "dead people." The findings suggest that it is not unusual for the departed to maintain an active interest in the lives of those they left behind. Dr. Schwartz's research contradicts Western science's materialistic and atheistic understanding of consciousness's relationship with brains. The gap between secular and spiritual communities would narrow if Western science paid attention to "paranormal" research findings.

Transcendental, beyond ordinary or common, experiences and abilities are incredibly variable and numerous. The books in metaphysical bookstores contain thousands of human experiences, which would be impossible if we were not spiritual beings. Dr. Schwartz's research was concerned with psychic mediums, while SRI's psi research was primarily concerned with clairvoyance: psychically perceiving locations, objects, people, and physical events, and even precognition, or experiencing things before they happen. Among other psychic abilities or phenomena that Western science treats as taboo subjects are **aura** reading, automatic writing, energy medicine, psychic surgery, trance mediums, and psychometry.

Ingo Swann called our "monkey mind's" uncontrolled chatter *analytical overlay*; and he said that our mind's uncontrolled chatter not only blocks our ability to be psychically aware, but also influences our experiences and memories. The Hindu and Buddhist religions refer to our mind's *analytical overlay* influenced interpretation of the outer world as maya. Maya is an ancient Sanskrit word used to refer to the world we live in as an enticing illusion due to our obliviousness to the unity or oneness in creation's diversity. These ancient religions taught that we suffer needlessly because of maya, or ignorance of our true reality. In their most sophisticated forms, these religions taught the wisdom required to control instead of being controlled by analytical overlay. SRI's remote-viewing experiments and Dr. Schwartz's experiments suggest, just as the Hindu and Buddhist religions teach, that our physical senses' provided experience of separation between us and things is an illusion.

MORE PROOF OF LIFE AFTER DEATH

In addition to psi phenomena, there are several phenomena that suggest that our consciousness is independent of matter. I want to briefly cover four phenomena related to death. These topics may not be included in science's paradigms, but they have been well researched. Like psi, the topics and research findings conflict with entrenched Christian and scientific dogma. Early childhood memories of previous lives, deathbed visions, near-death experiences, and past-life regression are all distinctly different phenomena, but they provide logically consistent glimpses of consciousness taking place before the birth and after the death of human bodies. These phenomena refute reductionist materialism's ignorant claims, and they suggest that our consciousness preceded our birth and will continue long after the death of our body.

EARLY CHILDHOOD MEMORIES
OF PREVIOUS LIVES

In the 1950s, Ian Stevenson, MD, a University of Virginia medical researcher for fifty years, became interested in the possibility of scientifically investigating whether anything survives bodily death. In 1960, he became aware of young children who gave the impression that they remembered living and dying in a previous life. He reasoned that a two- to four-year-old child would be a good research subject because of the relative ease of distinguishing prebirth adult memories from a young child's probable experiences. He traveled around the world for forty years investigating over 2,600 young children with spontaneous past-life memories. In over 1,000 cases, the child provided enough specific details to positively identify the deceased person whose memories were contained within the mind of a young child. When possible, Dr. Stevenson examined relevant medical and autopsy records. By documenting and comparing each child's statements about their previous life with the actual circumstances and physical characteristics of the person described by the child, Dr. Stevenson accumulated prima facie evidence of young children with a recently deceased person's consciousness or memories. Even though Dr. Stevenson meticulously researched each case with detailed academic reports written for skeptical academics, his research findings, which are not compatible with science's atheistic paradigms, have been ignored and ridiculed by academic and scientific communities.

Chanai Choomalaiwong was one of the children whose memories of a past life were detailed enough to locate the described deceased person's surviving family. In 1967, Chanai was born in central Thailand with a bullet-size birthmark at the back of his head and a larger birthmark located above his left eye. Chanai's parents lived separately, and he lived with his maternal grandmother after his second birthday. When he was three years old, while pretending to be a schoolteacher, he said that in his previous life, "his" name was Bua Kai, and "he" was shot and killed while on his way to the school where he was a teacher. He told his grandmother that his previous personality's parents, wife, and children were alive at the conclusion of his previous life. Chanai begged his grandmother to take him to Bua Kai's parents' home, and he claimed to be able to show her where they lived. When he was less than four years old, Chanai and his grandmother went by bus to where Chanai said "his" parents lived. Chanai's grandmother was not familiar with Khao Phra or anyone who lived there. After leading his grandmother to a house in Khao Phra, they went in, and Chanai recognized an older couple as Bua Kai's parents. The older couple said

13

that they were the parents of a schoolteacher named Bua Kai Lawnak, who had been murdered in 1962. On subsequent visits, Chanai recognized other family members and objects that belonged to Bua Kai, and with impressive accuracy he answered questions about Bua Kai's possessions. Witnesses identified fourteen correct statements and only one incorrect statement by Chanai about Bua Kai's life and death. On one visit, Bua Kai's twin daughters asked Chanai if he recognized a man who had been one of Bua Kai's friends. In addition to recognizing the man, Chanai provided his correct name and described how, in his previous life, they had been best friends.

Learning about Bua Kai's life helped to understand his unusual death. He was not just a schoolteacher; he appeared to have been a part-time gangster with two guns, who, despite having three children and a pregnant wife at the time of his death, was upsetting the boyfriends and husbands of the women with whom he was having affairs. He was shot in the back of his head, where Chanai's bullet-size birthmark is located, while riding his bicycle to school. The bullet exited above Bua Kai's left eye, where Chanai's other birthmark is located.

Chanai's memory of his previous life is unusual in two respects. He was one of only a few whose past-life memories continued past the age of eight, and who remembered seeing the previous personality's dead body. When Chanai was eleven, he said, "I was not conscious when I died. Afterward though, I felt my soul leaving the body. I could see myself lying on the road. My legs were still twitching. My blood was running onto the road."

The above synopsis is taken from Dr. Stevenson's major work, *Reincarnation and Biology: A Contribution to the Etiology of Birthmarks and Birth Defects*, which consists of 2,268 pages in two volumes published in 1997 for medical professionals. The academic report of Chanai Choomalaiwong's past-life memories is one of 224 cases contained in the two volumes.

When possible, the case studies compare the child's birth defects and marks as shown on birth records with the previous life's autopsy records. Chanai's case is one of fourteen cases that involved entry and exit wounds that exactly matched the size and location of birthmarks.

Dr. Stevenson provided a shorter version of the above research for the general reader titled *Where Reincarnation and Biology Intersect.* The failure of Dr. Stevenson's research findings to significantly influence the Western world's attitudes and beliefs relates to the powerful influence of science's atheistic paradigms and Christianity's opposition to belief in reincarnation. Until one or more of Western science's atheistic communities become more open-minded, science is forced to ignore and claim to have evidence contrary to prima facie evidence that does not comport with prevailing and dogmatically held assumptions. The scientific and academic communities seem to be complicit with skeptics who manage to have their disparaging comments placed near and within research findings that would otherwise refute exclusively materialistic understandings of our reality.

Following in Dr. Stevenson's footsteps, Carol Bowman began to investigate the past-life memories of children in 1988. Her motivation was much more personal: her son's fear of loud noises and her daughter's fear of fire disappeared after past-life regression therapy. During past-life regression, her son reexperienced being killed by the blast of a cannon during the Civil War, and her daughter remembered being burned to death in a previous life. Parents with similar experiences contacted Carol Bowman after she shared her experiences on TV and radio programs. They provided her with hundreds of other children with past-life memories to investigate. Many of her cases involved children who remembered being a deceased relative instead of an unknown stranger, which suggests that souls have influence or choice in the selection of their next life.

Carol Bowman wrote about her experiences and research in *Children's Past Lives and Return from Heaven*. If it was traumatic, children tended to remember how they died in their previous life. Present-life phobias and health problems often disappear after past-life therapy enables children, as well as adults, to reexperience traumatic past-life memories. The best cases provide memories from previous lives that cannot be explained as coincidences or something that was overheard or inherited.

If this is a subject that you do not feel compelled to investigate by reading research findings, how about reading a *New York Times* bestseller: *Soul Survivor*, which tells the fascinating but true story of James Leininger. In Lafayette, Louisiana in 2000, two-year-old James Leininger began having reoccurring nightmares. His screams during the middle of the night puzzled his parents. Their desire to help their only child motivated them to discover the cause of their son's nightmares. To their surprise, they eventually realized that James was reliving the experiences of World War II fighter pilot James Huston after antiaircraft fire hit his plane in the battle of Iwo Jima. As you read the book, it becomes apparent that James Leininger was born with the memories, consciousness, and soul of James Huston.

Thousands of instances of prima facia "evidence having such a degree of probability that it must prevail unless the contrary be proved"[6] would add God, souls, and an afterlife to science's paradigms if science's atheistic disciplines were fair and impartial juries. If the above books on the past-life memories of children do not appeal to you, there are many other good researchers and books on the subject. If you are unaware of anyone who remembers a past life, it is because they, like you, have forgotten their early childhood memories. Just as amnesia about early childhood is normal, it is normal for children who remember a previous life to also forget the memories associated with their early childhood.

DEATHBED VISIONS

Deathbed visions, which are also called predeath visions, are another category of evidence for life after death. Deathbed visions are experienced and witnessed when the dying person is not too sedated with drugs to reveal what they are experiencing. Before the influence of modern medicine, people often died while appearing to see and converse with their departed friends and relatives. A previously anticipated part of the dying process, deathbed visions welcomed the dying person to the afterlife and provided comfort for those who loved them. Deathbed visions, in which the dying person appears to be seeing and conversing with deceased relatives as well as God and angels, strengthened the faith of those who witnessed them. But, thanks to modern science's dismissal of the possibility of souls and an afterlife, deathbed visions are treated as delusions with narcotics and tranquilizers.

In 1926, Sir William Barrett, a physics professor at the Royal College of Science in Dublin, was the first person to study and write a book, *Deathbed Visions*, about the experience of dying. Professor Barrett's interest in deathbed visions began when his wife told him about an apparent deathbed conversation between Doris and the spirit of her recently deceased sister. Because of concerns about Doris's health, no one had told Doris about her sister's death. Despite a person's fragile hold on life prior to death, Professor Barrett's research found that those who have deathbed visions appear to be fully conscious while experiencing peace and serenity.

Inspired by reading Professor Barrett's book on deathbed visions, Karlis Osis, PhD, (the director of the American Society of Psychical Research in New York) and the University of Iceland's Department of Psychology's Erlendur Haraldsson conducted a four-year study in the 1940s and additional studies in the 1960s and 1970s. They primarily based their research findings on questionnaire responses received from doctors and nurses who had witnessed deathbed visions. They wrote about their findings in *At the Hour of Death: A New Look at Evidence for Life after Death*. Their statistical analysis of deathbed visions found that people who die within an hour of their deathbed vision are almost twice as likely to be welcomed to the afterlife during their **apparition** as those who take longer to die. Despite the differences in the two culture's religious beliefs, when they compared replies from the United States and India on fourteen areas of comparison, they found very little difference in the two cultures' deathbed visions. They also found that none of the apparitions that welcomed the dying person to the afterlife were of a living person. It would be improbable for hallucinations, internally produced apparitions, to manifest as logically consistent phenomena within different people and cultures.

On page 95 in his book, *Closer to the Light*, Dr. Melvin Morse recalls his patient, June, who had a near-death experience during open-heart surgery when she was five, and at twenty-eight years of age experienced a deathbed vision. Despite knowing that she would probably die if her pacemaker stopped working, June was unafraid because her near-death experience revealed death to merely be a transition from this life to the next. On the morning before her death, June's dead sister's discarnate spirit said while appearing across the breakfast table, "June, it's time to go." Not wanting to share the experience with her husband, June called her aunt and uncle to share the experience and her conviction that she was about to die. Besides saying her final goodbyes, she told them not to tell and upset her husband. While sleeping that night, her pacemaker and heart quit working.

NEAR-DEATH EXPERIENCES

Near-death experiences (NDEs) are mystical experiences like deathbed visions, but the circumstances are not the same.

NDEs have been reported since the beginning of recorded history. Plato's *The Republic*, which was written about 380 BC, is concluded with a legend titled "The Myth of Er." Twelve days after being gathered up with (assumed to be dead) battle casualties, Er became conscious and described his afterlife experiences. *The Egyptian Book of the Dead* and *The Tibetan Book of the Dead* describe what happens after death and provide guidance in the afterlife. In the sixth century, Pope Gregory the Great collected NDEs to prove the reality of an afterlife. Most primitive and ancient cultures believed in survival after death because of firsthand and secondhand experiences with the phenomena covered in this chapter. Instead of being brainwashed with religious and scientific dogma like today's youth, firsthand and secondhand experiences guided beliefs prior to the development of organized religion.

Because of advances in medical science, especially following cardiac arrest, near-death experiences have become a much more common occurrence. Dr. Raymond Moody coined the term near-death experience (NDE) in his 1975 book, *Life after Life*. Within the scientific and medical communities, his book stimulated interest in the scientific investigation of near-death experiences. His book also helped to motivate the establishment of the International Association for Near-Death Studies, which publishes the *Journal of Near-Death Studies*.

Eighteen percent of those who survive cardiac arrest report NDEs. Regardless of the experiencer's religion or nationality, the event sequence is almost always the same. A greater number of NDE steps, as well as more profound experiences, are associated with longer lasting periods of clinical death. If you experienced a typical NDE with all the steps, you would have the following mystical experiences. After becoming unconscious, you will find yourself outside your body without experiencing the pain associated with the cause of your death. From your out-of-body vantage point, you will see and hear what is taking place near your brain-dead body. After failing to communicate with those who are attending to your body, you will pass through a tunnel toward a bright light. As a discarnate spirit immersed in God's light and love, you will experience peace and joy. At the end of the tunnel, you will be greeted warmly by deceased friends and relatives. If they do not direct you back to your body, you will experience a three-dimensional life review from your perspective as well as the perspectives of those who shared the experiences with you. When told to return, you will be sucked back into your body.

Your sense of reality will have changed after this profound mystical experience, and your NDE will become your life's most important experience. The welfare of others, nature, and spirituality will become of much greater concern to you, but material possessions and competing with others will no longer concern you. After experiencing the afterlife, you will have lost your fear of death. But if you survived cardiac arrest without having a NDE, research reveals that you will not experience the transformative changes associated with near-death experiences.

When a person finds themselves outside their body, the experience is called an **out-of-body experience** or **OBE**. When a person, whose body is not in a state of clinical death, has an OBE, they do not have the experiences associated with NDEs. Dr. Morse studied the NDEs contained in ten years of hospital records and conducted follow-up studies. His research found that NDEs are specific to surviving clinical death and are not related to overdoses of narcotics or any other aspect of being critically ill. NDEs were only found to be experienced by those who regained consciousness after their body experienced clinical death.

Those who report NDEs have met the criteria for clinical death. Among the criteria are the cessation of brain function (a flat EEG) and an inactive brain stem due to an absence of blood flowing to the brain. Within fifteen seconds of cardiac arrest, neuronal electrical activity in the brain ceases. Despite having brains that showed no electrical activity, NDE'ers report being able to see, hear, and have experiences like those of a fully conscious person. The most frequently reported and initial experience of NDEs is freedom from pain and feelings of peace and joy. The least common experience, a life review, is reported 13 percent of the time.

Near-death experiences often occur while the experiencer's vital signs are monitored in a hospital. Despite being unconscious with closed eyes and being legally brain-dead because of a heart that no longer pumps oxygenated blood, before NDE'ers transition to "the other side" of death, they can think, hear beyond the normal range, and see clearly even when blind since birth. While observing and being able to later describe what happens near their brain-dead body, NDE'ers have reported experiencing panoramic 360-degree vision and the ability to know what people are thinking. Thousands of Americans who have had NDEs are able to accurately describe subsequently verifiable events that took place in the operating room, in the waiting room, and in some cases several miles from the hospital. In other words, NDE'ers see without eyes, travel significant distances through walls, and remember it all without a functioning brain. When meeting deceased friends and relatives on "the other side," NDE'ers occasionally see people they did not know were dead, but they never report seeing people who are not deceased. NDEs provide evidence of an afterlife and the continuing existence of those who have died. NDEs unmistakably reveal that when "we" become a corpse, our true reality, a soul, lives on.

PAST-LIFE REGRESSION

Like most physiological variables, everyone is not equally hypnotizable, but you probably can experience one or more past lives while hypnotized by a past-life regression therapist. I have often been in the audience while a hypnotist attempted to hypnotize the audience members. For some reason, no one has ever hypnotized me. Most of the audience members succumb to the hypnotist's efforts and provide insight into not only the potential power of one mind acting upon another but of the normally unrealized capabilities of the human mind. Initially, the hypnotist screens the audience, looking for those with the greatest hypnotic suggestibility. The ease with which and the depth to which some people can be hypnotized is amazing.

In October 1952, Morey Bernstein, a Colorado businessman and an amateur hypnotist, noticed that twenty-eight-year-old Virginia Tighe (identified as Ruth Simmons in the book *The Search for Bridey Murphy*) fell into a deep trance during his house party demonstration of hypnosis. Mrs. Tighe's hypnotic suggestibility motivated Mr. Bernstein to wonder if he could induce her to experience a past life. He was motivated by British psychiatrist Sir Alexander Cannon's claim that hypnosis enabled more than a thousand of his patients to experience previous lives. On November 29, Mrs. Tighe gave Mr. Bernstein her consent to participate in a hypnosis experiment. With his wife and Mrs. Tighe's husband serving as witnesses, Mr. Bernstein asked Mrs. Tighe to go back in time and tell him what she saw when she found herself in another place and time. She initially connected with a past-life memory from 1806 when, as eight-year old Bridey Murphy, she was angry after receiving a spanking. Mrs. Tighe agreed to subsequent sessions, which were tape-recorded. Instead of ending when Bridey Murphy died in 1864 at sixty-six years of age, the tape recordings continued with descriptions of between-lives experiences until 1923 when Virginia Tighe was born. Hypnotized Virginia Tighe spoke with Bridey Murphy's Irish brogue and period-appropriate colloquial words and phrases. She sang period songs, demonstrated an Irish folk dance, accurately provided names and descriptions of places that no longer appeared on maps, and provided details about the crops grown in the region, the currency of the period, and Irish folklore and customs.

Prior to 1956, when Doubleday published Morey Bernstein's *The Search for Bridey Murphy*, scholars did not agree with and substantiate the details of Bridey Murphy's life. I do not recall seeing the book until a few years ago when I read it out of curiosity. But I do remember reading critical reviews when the book was first published. Not only was past-life regression an unfamiliar topic in the 1950s, but reincarnation (the rebirth of souls) is not compatible with Christianity's interpretation of the Gospels. Because of the book's taboo subject matter, it received enough skeptical reviews to become a bestseller. The book's notoriety brought it and the concept of reincarnation to my attention. I adopted the skeptical attitude of the book's reviewers, who probably knew little more than I did about reincarnation. It is human nature, especially when we are young, to absorb the attitudes of our culture and religion. Unfortunately, an opinionated mind screens out potential belief-changing ideas and information. How rare it must be to be blessed with Albert Einstein's ability to maintain objectivity as easily as most people embrace and cling to their beliefs.

It took the unfolding of an improbable sequence of events when I was in my thirties to inspire interest in reincarnation. For centuries, in the Western world, the concept of reincarnation has not been taught or understood by science or Christianity. Because reincarnation is an aspect of childhood memories of previous lives as well as past-life regression, and because Christianity's attitude toward reincarnation contrasts with Eastern religions, the next chapter will focus on reincarnation's place in Christian history.

I wish a few paragraphs provided you with the contents of several books because the topics in this book are the trees within a forest of phenomena that reveal the existence of an invisible world that Jesus called heaven. I am concerned about Western science's denial of the "trees" in our phenomenal reality. This book is concerned with revealing the "forest" by pointing out the "trees." Experiencing how the "trees" harmonize and relate to each other helps to reveal the larger reality from which they emerge or are an aspect. Anyone who really wants to can acquire an understanding and appreciation of the "trees." Even though the "forest" (God) is not beyond human experience, God is professed to be beyond human understanding. Among the ways of referring to the "forest," or God, are Creator, All That Is, and the Great Spirit.

Helen Wambach, PhD, was among the first to scientifically investigate past-life memories and reincarnation. Her initial motivation in the 1960s was to debunk the whole idea of reincarnation. She assumed that the past lives experienced by hypnotized volunteers could not possibly reliably correlate with known but obscure historical facts. Over a ten-year period, during which she accumulated over one thousand recorded interviews, she successfully regressed almost 90 percent of those who volunteered to participate in her research. Dr. Wambach asked each volunteer, while experiencing a past life, several questions such as their status, gender, race, clothing, footwear, utensils, money, housing, and the food that they ate. Each recorded session was compared with known historical facts. In all but eleven cases (less than 1 percent) the specifics of the volunteer's former life were logically consistent with known historical facts. The class or status experienced during hypnosis matched historians' estimates for the specific culture and time of their former life. Instead of recalling lives as famous historical figures, 55 to 70 percent experienced lives among the lowest classes. The clothing, footwear, food, and eating utensils reported by the volunteers were more accurate than could be found in popular history books. Obscure past-life details were invariably found to be correct, even when confirmation required obtaining knowledge which few historians possess. In 1978, her research findings were published in *Reliving Past Lives: The Evidence under Hypnosis*. Dr. Wambach began ten years of research with the goal of proving that reincarnation is a myth, but instead, she provided evidence supportive of belief in reincarnation.

Dr. Wambach's second book, *Life before Life*, published in 1979, looks at the time between the immediate past life and the current life of another 750 hypnotized volunteers. Among the findings of her between-incarnations research was discovering that souls have choices in their upcoming lives, and souls usually do not merge with a fetus until birth is imminent. She found that about half of her subjects experienced images (the answers to her questions) slightly before they heard her question. Brain waves (electroencephalograph) during hypnosis look the same as during a waking dream, which suggests similarities in the nature of the two experiences.

Like Helen Wambach, psychiatrist Brian Weiss was initially a skeptic. He graduated magna cum laude with a degree in chemistry from Columbia University and received his MD in 1970 from the Yale University School of Medicine. Because of a materialistically biased academic education, Dr. Weiss was surprised to discover how often past-life memories appeared to be the cause and the solution to patient difficulties that did not respond to conventional therapy. He discovered that hypnotized patients could provide explanations for their talents, fears, obsessions, and chronic behavioral, health, and relationship issues. His career abruptly changed when he discovered how much hypnotized patients revealed when asked, "Go back to the time from which your symptoms arise." Past-life regression clients can disclose more details than children with their limited vocabularies. In private sessions using past-life regression therapy, Dr. Weiss has treated thousands of patients. Working with large groups in experiential past-life regression workshops, he has found that about two-thirds are able to experience past-life memories and are frequently able to heal the emotional and physical symptoms that brought them to the workshop. Coincidence and materialistic understandings of our reality cannot account for past-life regression therapy's ability to heal emotional and physical symptoms.

The past-life memories of Dr. Weiss's patients have contained accurate names, home addresses, ship names, historical facts, military identification numbers, and numerous other details that provide prima facie evidence of a deceased person's memories. While hypnotized, Dr. Weiss's patients have spoken languages that were unfamiliar to them, and they have even spoken extinct languages.[7] Dr. Ian Stevenson studied several children and adults who exhibited xenoglossy, which is the ability to speak or write a foreign language without previous exposure to the language. He wrote *Xenoglossy*, which was published in 1974. One of the book's case studies involves an American woman who, under hypnosis, assumed the voice and personality of a man who spoke fluent Swedish. In her normal, not hypnotized, state of consciousness, she could neither speak nor understand Swedish. Dr. Stevenson's involvement with this study lasted for over eight years and involved linguists as well as other experts.

Dr. Weiss's hypnotized patients occasionally "channeled" their spirit guides and highly evolved souls, whose voices and thought patterns contrasted with those of the patients. During past-life regression, he found that the actual experience of death is described with the same sequence of events experienced by those who have near-death experiences. Dr. Weiss's books provide the experiences and insights of America's most popular past-life regression authority.

Psychologist Michael Newton was among the most noteworthy early researchers of hypnosis's ability to reveal the knowledge hidden within our unconscious mind. Initially a traditional therapist specializing in hypnotherapy with a skeptical view of supernatural phenomena and reincarnation, Dr. Newton's beliefs abruptly changed in 1968, when he accidentally led his patient to the realm between lives. Fascinated by his client's between-lives spirit world memories, and unable to find any books about what he called "spiritual regression," Dr. Newton spent decades quietly learning how to guide, *with the aid of the client's own spirit guides*, hypnotized clients to, in, and back out of the superconscious mental state required to reach the realm between lives. His research with thousands of clients revealed "the afterlife to be a realm of love, compassion, forgiveness, and justice"[8] *in which punishment and hell do not exit*. In the realm between lives, discarnate souls behaved as if they were "forms of light energy" that vary in development from beginner to very advanced souls. They communicated telepathically, were not confined within our linear experience of time, and they could alter their appearances to harmonize with the expectations of other souls. Spiritual development takes place by dealing with each incarnation's entirely different circumstances. In harmony with Dr. Stevenson's research, Dr. Newton found that "if a person's life is cut short prematurely, their soul often [reincarnates] within a short period of time."[9] This finding accounts for why so many of the confirmable prior lives in Dr. Stevenson's research, in which the deceased's friends and family were still living, ended traumatically.

Published in 1994, Dr. Newton's first book, *Journey of Souls*, was written after decades of researching the spirit world and reincarnation. Instead of using a telescope, microscope, or cloud chamber, he used hypnosis to reveal aspects of our phenomenal reality that exist outside our usual range of awareness. To share more insights and discoveries, Dr. Newton wrote *Destiny of Souls* and *Life Between Lives*, and he edited *Memories of the Afterlife*, which contains case studies submitted from around the world by hypnotherapists certified by the Michael Newton Institute. The Michael Newton Institute provided the first weeklong life-between-lives hypnotherapy training program. Because the proof of the pudding is in the eating, skeptics should consider reading Michael Newton's books or making an appointment with a certified hypnotherapist to experience the life-transforming insights and benefits of hypnosis.

Past-life regression is no longer a novel topic like it was when *The Search for Bridey Murphy* was published. Past-life and between-lives regression therapists and their books are readily available. For most people, mystical experiences just happen. They are not under our control or volition. The same can be said for early childhood memories of previous lives, deathbed visions, and near-death experiences. Past and between-lives regression, on the other hand, may enable you to safely prove to yourself that you are not subject to birth or death. The real you, your soul, is never-ending consciousness on a spiritual journey. The French Jesuit priest and mystic Pierre Teilhard de Chardin insightfully observed, "We are not human beings having a spiritual experience. We are spiritual beings having a human experience."

"No one has the slightest idea what consciousness is, despite it being the one and only thing any of us will ever personally know firsthand."[10] Early childhood memories of previous births and between-lives regression memories provide evidence that consciousness has access to not only the memories of this life, but also the memories from previous lives and the periods between them. Experiments with psychic mediums provide evidence of their ability to access the thoughts of deceased relatives. SRI's psychics demonstrated nonlocal awareness that extended for hundreds, even thousands, of miles. These phenomena suggest that human consciousness greatly exceeds reasonable expectations for a brain's neurobiological capabilities.

A computer's hardware provides little clue to its capability because a computer's capability is hidden within its software and wireless—radio waves—network connections. Our brains' software-like capabilities are hidden in complex neural networks. Supernatural experiences and abilities such as remote viewing, past-life memories, near-death experiences, and spirit communication suggest that our consciousness, like a computer, has wireless connections beyond our physical senses. Because it is not reasonable to believe a brain's "software" has prebirth memories or provides the abilities of psychics, supernatural abilities may be revealing the capabilities of consciousness instead of brains. Just as the phenomenal nature of the quantum world is not revealed in the world of classical physics, the capabilities and nature of consciousness are not revealed within atheistic paradigms.

I feel a sense of urgency to hasten changes within the Western world's scientific and educational communities. Exploring reality from a deterministic and mechanical (we are simply machines) perspective has been very fruitful. We have developed both wonderful and terrifying technological capabilities. But commensurate progress in humanity's ability to agree upon and implement appropriate principles upon which individuals and countries guide their actions has not occurred. A soulless and godless materialistic worldview inspires more concern for one's own self-interest than for this planet and its inhabitants. Because materialism is drummed into the minds of students at an early age, I fear that life on this planet will be destroyed because of science's atheistic paradigms.

Before science and religion went their separate ways, students were inculcated with their culture's religious beliefs. Belief in God, souls, and an afterlife has been replaced with today's scientific theories and technological achievements. When students are taught that belief in souls and life after death is unscientific, and that they are nothing more than recycled stardust, they are less likely to be concerned with values and the needs of others. Science should embrace and consider as part of its paradigms research into topics like those discussed in this chapter. By doing so, students would not be presented with a biased and deceptive portrayal of what science could say about their reality. Science and our educational institutions should reflect the research and discoveries of the last century, instead of maintaining the atheistic agenda of those who should have died off or lost their influence decades ago.

Chapter 2
WHAT CHRISTIANITY IGNORES

"Why do you see the speck that is in your brother's eye,
but don't consider the beam that is in your own eye?"
—Matthew 7:3

The first chapter's evidence for a spiritual or immaterial component to reality was written in the hope of motivating atheists to read this book in its entirety. Most of the evidence—especially early childhood memories of previous births, and past-life and between-lives regression—supports belief in reincarnation. Christianity has the same detached, skeptical attitude toward reincarnation as science has toward God and souls. I am not concerned about pointing out "the beam" in the eyes of scientists. No scientist is going to throw the baby (science) out with the bathwater, but Christian faith is not so stable or easily maintained despite the existence of both evidence and logic to support belief in God, souls, and an afterlife. Among the sources of evidence are the histories and contents of the world's religions (humanity's spiritual heritage).

The distinctive denominational beliefs of Christians encompass a variety of beliefs about God, Christ, and salvation. For many people, religion merely involves embracing the beliefs of other members of their faith. Christian sects often place a great deal of emphasis upon those beliefs that distinguish them from other religious groups. For those who want to feel part of and accepted by a sect, new and conflicting ideas are met with trepidation. But Jesus, as portrayed in the Gospels, was not concerned with what people believe. He was concerned with the thoughts, motives, and priorities that guide human behavior. Matthew 6:21, "For where your treasure is, there your **heart** will be also," reveals Jesus's insight that our heart, as opposed to our head, guides our motives and destiny.

Holding the beliefs of one's family, friends, and culture is not a praiseworthy achievement. Beliefs are as substantial as a mirage. A person can change their mind, beliefs, or opinions without changing themselves in any meaningful way. A person's character is altogether different. If a person changed from hateful and vindictive to loving and forgiving, their character would have changed in the tangible ways that concerned Jesus. For two millennia, Christianity has been reluctant to continue Jesus's efforts to motivate people to judge and correct their own personal failings. We tend to be unaware of and unconcerned about our shortcomings, and we dislike having them pointed out. It is not surprising that Christianity focuses upon beliefs despite Jesus's concern with the thoughts, words, and actions that reveal a person's character. Jesus probably extolled some behaviors while denouncing others because he wanted to motivate people to judge and correct their own thoughts and actions.

Teaching beliefs has enabled Christianity to become the world's most powerful political, economic, and religious institution in the history of Western civilization. Would Christianity be successful emphasizing Jesus's concern for not just following but going beyond Jewish law? The Torah, Judaism's most important text and the first five books in the Christian Bible, contains the Ten Commandments. The sixth Commandment in the Bible and seventh in the Torah is "you shall not commit adultery." In Matthew 5:28, Jesus said, "But I tell you that everyone who gazes at a woman to lust after her has committed adultery with her already in his heart." In Matthew 5:44–45, Jesus taught that we should "love [our] enemies, bless those who curse [us], do good to those who hate [us], and pray for those who mistreat [us] and persecute

[us], that [we] may be children of [our] Father who is in heaven." Only a saint would be inclined to love their enemies! Teaching that faith in Jesus's death and Resurrection leads to salvation is an easier sales pitch.

I am not writing this book to influence anyone's faith in Christianity or any other religion. I have no desire to lessen anyone's religious faith. By pointing out some of the ways in which God and our spiritual reality are revealed, I hope to refute the idea that God is merely a manifestation of human imagination. I am writing to point out that religions exist because of the divinely inspired words and actions of advanced souls like Jesus. I want you to dive deeper into your religion than a superficial understanding.

EMPIRICAL EVIDENCE
FOR RELIGIOUS BELIEFS

The first chapter looked at human experiences and abilities that were probably experienced during prehistoric times. Psychic abilities would be revered. Children who remembered previous lives provided empirical evidence for the concept of reincarnation or consciousness's ability to survive death and to be reborn. Deathbed visions suggested an afterlife between lives. Out-of-body experiences suggested and inspired belief in being a spirit residing within a body. Near-death experiences provided support for belief in the survival of and the transcendent nature of consciousness. Hypnosis and past-life regression were within the capabilities of the most primitive cultures. By simply accepting at face value all of life's experiences, instead of the Western world's culturally imposed ignorance and denial, religion can be an empirically and rationally based science. The researchers featured in the first chapter—Russell Targ and Hal Puthoff; Gary Schwartz; Ian Stevenson; Carol Bowman; William Barrett; Karlis Osis and Erlendur Haraldsson; Melvin Morse; Raymond Moody;

Helen Wambach; Brian Weiss; and Michael Newton—
provided proof beyond a reasonable doubt that "paranormal"
phenomena can be investigated scientifically. Quotation
marks signify that "paranormal" phenomena from a psychic
and mystic's point of view are common, *normal* experiences
and the most relevant clues to understanding consciousness
and the nature of our underlying reality.

The doctrine of reincarnation provides an explanation
for all the phenomena related to death discussed in chapter
1. Because Christianity's understanding of Jesus's life and
ministry is not compatible with the doctrine of reincarnation,
Christianity ignores and vehemently opposes the doctrine.
Western science also ignores and attempts to explain away
phenomena that are not consistent with a godless and
materialistic understanding of reality. Prior to being able
to rationally deal with the content of chapter 1, Western
science and Christianity must evolve beyond the influence of
centuries-old cultural beliefs.

Reincarnation was a common belief among early human
civilizations. It was believed by Egyptians, Celtic Druids, Greek
philosophy and religion, Norse mythology, Oceanic religions,
most Australian Aboriginal groups, and many African and
Native American cultures. American Indian medicine men
often claimed to remember their past lives. Reincarnation is
believed by all but one of India's ancient spiritual traditions.
Within Vedism (which predates Hinduism), **Brahman**ism,
Hinduism, Jainism, Sikhism, and most Buddhist traditions, the
primary spiritual teachings and goals revolve around achieving
enlightenment and liberation from repeated births and deaths.
Reincarnation is understood in a variety of ways by all these
religions because cultures separated by time and distance did
not understand or explain souls, the afterlife, or reincarnation
in the same ways. But similar reincarnation "myths" were
unlikely to arise prior to recorded history within widely

separated cultures unless the "myths" were inspired by empirical and antidotal evidence of consciousness's survival from one life to another.

In his 1871 book, *Primitive Cultures*, anthropologist Sir Edward Tylor coined the word *animism* for the oldest known belief system. Even though indigenous cultures had different myths and rituals, early anthropologists found that "primitive" people shared the same animistic beliefs about themselves and their environment. Unlike the modern dualistic sense that we are separate from our environment, animists experienced themselves as part of and not uniquely different from their environment. Like the experiences of a psychic medium, animists believed that most of the phenomenal world was infused with spirits or souls. Animals and plants, as well as natural forces, were believed to have conscious control over their actions.

Australia's Bishop Hilton Deakin found that, despite being "considered naïve and rudimentary prior to the 1950's," *primal* or Aboriginal religions are remarkably sophisticated. He found that members of primal religions have a deep sense of "their own spiritual existence and place in the universe;" they believe that "man is finite, weak and impure and stands in need of a power not his own;" and that they "can enter into relationship with this benevolent spirit world and share in its powers and blessings."[11]

While hunter-gatherer cultures relocated from one food source to another, they experienced themselves as an integral part of their environment. The concept of ownership of land—one's environment—was contrary to an animist's sense of themselves and reality. An animist's spiritual relationship with the environment was replaced with the concept of private property, which led to territorial groups and states and organized religions. From the European explorer's perspective, the animistic beliefs of Native Americans were primitive understandings of the nature of reality. The concept of dividing up and assuming ownership of the environment motivated westward expansion and the displacement of those with animistic beliefs. Contemporary beliefs about Manifest Destiny and the pursuit of the American Dream may not have resonated well with those of Jesus, who said in Mark 8:36, "For what does it profit a man, to gain the whole world, and forfeit their [soul]?" The animistic beliefs of Native Americans may have been more in harmony with Jesus's teachings than the beliefs of contemporary Christians.

In contrast to an animist's sense of merely being an aspect of the environment, followers of the Abrahamic religions are taught to believe they have a preferential status in God's creation. Throughout history, Christianity has promoted feeling unique and superior, at someone or something's expense, which has inspired some of history's worst atrocities. Instead of blaming religion or God for humanity's atrocities and shortcomings, the Bible (John 2:16) attributes the blame in this way: "For all that is in the world, the lust of the flesh, the lust of the eyes, and the pride of life, isn't the Father's, but is the world's." Religions raise spiritual awareness, but spiritual knowledge and wisdom are not appreciated or understood by minds focused upon worldly desires and concerns. In Matthew 6:24, Jesus expressed the conundrum as, "No one can serve two masters."

PROPHETIC REVELATION INSPIRES
REVEALED RELIGIONS

In addition to empirical evidence contributing to religious beliefs, religions are defined by the lives and teachings of their "divinely inspired" **prophet**s. I put quotes around "divinely inspired" because these words are a nonstarter from a materialist's perspective. I wrote this book in the hope of converting skeptical readers into believers in nothing more specific than an awareness that we are more than recycled stardust. I hope materialists will read long enough to adopt a more animistic perspective.

Religions preserve their history and traditions. Buddha's life and teachings provided the inspiration for Buddhism. Without the remarkable influence on Western civilization of Jesus's life, we would not have Christianity, and Islam would not exist without Muhammad. To maintain the teachings of those who inspired the world's religions, their teachings must be recorded, maintained, and passed down to subsequent generations. Without the continuation of divine inspiration and assistance, religions inevitably deteriorate because of humanity's worldly perspective and ignorance of its spiritual heritage (God's communications with humanity).

A democratic system of government may be the most prudent way for people to allow themselves to be governed, but religion's purpose is to promote spiritual awareness and the teachings of God's divinely inspired messengers. Those who maintain the world's religions should realize that God's wisdom should not be limited to past sources of inspiration. To preserve spiritual wisdom, contemporary sources of divinely inspired guidance are necessary.

The ancient world believed that God chose prophets based on their level of spiritual attainment. Prophets performed (or were given credit for performing) miracles to establish their supernatural level of spiritual attainment. The Talmud contains the teachings of thousands of rabbis. The Old Testament documents the lives of several major and minor prophets. The life and teachings of just one Hebrew prophet, Jesus, provided the inspiration for the Christian religion. Because the Hindu religion arose within many cultures and languages, Hinduism has thousands of allegories (gods and goddesses) for the characteristics of Brahman or ultimate reality. Major spiritual teachers within the Hindu religion, such as Rama and Krishna, are regarded as incarnations of

God: avatars. Some religions, such as the Jewish and Hindu faiths, have many providers of divine guidance, while other religions (Buddha: Buddhism; Jesus: Christianity; and Muhammad: Islam) primarily revere one source of inspiration.

Just as similar empirical experiences inspired belief in reincarnation for millennia, the similarities in ethical values taught by history's countless sources of religious inspiration can be explained by hypothesizing that true prophets reflect a common source of inspiration: God. Despite the differences among the world's cultures, very little difference exists within the ethical values taught by the world's religions. If you have been taught to focus upon the differences between religions, please google "the Golden Rule in world religions." Despite often being attributed to Jesus, the Golden Rule is expressed in a variety of ways within most religions.

Christianity emerged in a remote part of the Roman Empire during the first century among illiterate Jewish peasants. Jesus's ministry and miracles primarily took place from today's northern Israel to the mountainous regions south of Jerusalem among the Pharisees, who were the largest and the Bible's most mentioned Jewish group. The Pharisees believed in the ability of the dead, after the fulfillment of end-time prophecies, to rise from their graves and reunite with their souls. The beliefs of those who witnessed Jesus's ministry probably influenced their interpretation of Jesus's words and the New Testament's account of Jesus's life and ministry. Greek-speaking Christians wrote the Gospels from decades-old word-of-mouth stories passed down by the first generations to be influenced by Jesus's ministry.

During the last week of his life, Jesus joined with thousands of Jewish pilgrims traveling to Jerusalem to celebrate the Passover feast. Jerusalem's Jewish aristocracy, the Sadducees, managed the Temple and local affairs. The Sadducees responded to Jesus questioning their motives and moral fitness—pointing out "the beam that is in [their] own eye"—by encouraging the Roman governor, Pontius Pilate, to arrest and crucify Jesus for treason during Passover. The claim that Jesus was raised from the dead, Resurrection, provided the inspiration for the beginning of Christianity.

Christianity emerged among the Pharisees, Sadducees, and other Jewish groups. Early Christianity also consisted of many Christian groups with different beliefs about salvation, Christ, and God. The monotheistic beliefs of Jews and Christians contrasted with those of the Greco-Roman Empire's predominantly pagan population. Christianity is the only religion concerned with what people believe—"proper belief." What a person believes did not concern pagans and Jews, who were concerned with doing God's will.

The apostle Paul was Christianity's most influential missionary. He developed the idea that Jesus's Crucifixion and subsequent Resurrection led to the salvation of the world and the idea that Gentiles did not need to abide by Jewish laws. Despite the apostle Paul's success in creating a religion that focused on Jesus's death and Resurrection instead of his ministry, only 2 to 3 percent of the second and third centuries' primarily pagan population were Christians.

GNOSTICISM

Gnosticism is a modern name for one of the Christian sects that arose among other Christian sects during the first and second centuries. In Upper Egypt near Nag Hammadi in 1945, fifty-two Gnostic documents were found buried in a large earthenware vessel. These documents, which were copied on papyrus from first- and second-century documents, were translated and published as the Nag Hammadi Library. They consisted of expositions of religious doctrines, apocalypses (revelations), dialogues that Jesus apparently had with disciples after his resurrection, mystical reflections, and Gospels allegedly written by Jesus's disciples. Prior to this discovery of a time capsule of Gnostic documents, orthodoxy's early criticisms of alternative versions of Christianity provided all that was known about the existence of Gnosticism.

The Nag Hammadi documents reveal that the Gnostics were concerned with understanding their relationship with God. Gnosticism's primary concern was obtaining the knowledge (gnosis) required to achieve salvation. Gnostic writings, in harmony with Hinduism's ancient spiritual texts, describe how "divine sparks" (souls) are born into an "evil" material world from which they must learn how to escape by acquiring spiritual knowledge or gnosis. Gnostics believed that Christ, Jesus's spirit, gave them privileged, **esoteric** teachings between his Resurrection and ascension. Gnostics believed the secret spiritual truths revealed by Jesus would enable them to be set free from the "evil" material world. Jesus alluded to these secret teachings in John 8:32 with the words: "Then you will know the truth, and the truth will set you free."

Orthodox Jews and Christians believe that God is separate and apart, "wholly other," from the material world; but, in harmony with Eastern religions and the concept of nonduality, Gnostic writings describe the human soul and the divine as inseparable aspects of the same reality. The kingdom of God was understood by Gnostics to be an immaterial, spiritual dimension located both within and surrounding the material world. At the end of Saying Number 113 in the Gospel of Thomas, Jesus said, "The kingdom of God is spread out upon the earth and people do not see it." The Gospel of Thomas, which is the most famous document in the Nag Hammadi Library, contains 114 "secret sayings" of Jesus. Some scholars suspect that these secret sayings were written before Jesus was crucified. Many of Jesus's Gnostic sayings are like Zen riddles. Gnostic documents contain Jewish and Christian terminology, but Jesus is portrayed as a spiritual teacher, like a

Hindu guru, concerned with enlightenment instead of sin and redemption. The similarity between Gnosticism and Eastern religions suggests that Jesus, Buddha, and Hinduism's avatars reveal and reflect the same source of inspiration. Gnosticism's harmony with Eastern religions contrasts with Christianity's assertion that salvation is achieved through faith in Jesus's death and Resurrection. By the sixth century, orthodoxy's version of Christianity was the only Christian sect that was not declared to be heretical. By hiding them, a few "heretical" Christian sects, like the Gnostics, saved their documents for a future in which they might be appreciated.

REINCARNATION
IN EARLY CHRISTIAN HISTORY

You may be wondering, "With all the religions that embrace reincarnation, what happened to Christianity?" The answer to that question relates to neither empirical experiences nor Jesus's teachings. The answer relates to the ability of Christianity's orthodoxy, those in power, to determine Church doctrine. I wish religions could be evaluated after everything with a worldly (instead of a "divinely inspired") basis was stripped away. Just as adding one substance to another alters its nature, religions are debased by worldly perspectives and agendas.

There are many historical and contemporary sources of information about the doctrine of reincarnation. Reincarnation encompasses the belief that, prior to self-realization, we are the consciousness of our soul's **ego**-bound counterpart. Screened from our underlying spiritual reality, we construct our worldly sense of self-identification from the input from our mind's thoughts and our physical senses. To achieve karmic and spiritual growth concerns, divine sparks or souls can incarnate (be born male or female) within a multitude of possible life circumstances. Prejudice and discrimination exist because people do not realize that what they despise or mistreat may be their next life's reality. The doctrine of reincarnation teaches that life on Earth is comparable to going to school. We each have, in effect, our grade in school and the goal of achieving liberation (graduating) from an endless cycle of births and deaths.

Worldly life provides opportunities to make choices guided by our levels of wisdom and self-discipline or willpower. Divine sparks become wise old souls over the course of many lifetimes. The good as well as the bad karmic consequences of thoughts and actions provide souls with motivation and opportunity to achieve liberation from a repetition of births and deaths. Advanced subjects to master include reducing worldly desires and attachments as well as cultivating an all-inclusive love that recognizes that everything is part of God. Our motivations and actions influence our spiritual progress. Reincarnation philosophy assumes we have the ability and freedom, freewill, to choose (sow) our actions. Because our underlying spiritual reality, what we truly are, does not suffer, and because the spiritual purpose of human suffering is to encourage looking within to realize the consciousness of our soul, there is no conflict between human experience and a just and loving God. The apostle Paul, in Galatians 6:7–8, emphasized the cause and effect (Karma) aspect of reincarnation philosophy when he wrote, "… whatever a man sows, that he will also reap. For he who sows to his own flesh will from the flesh reap corruption. But he who sows to the Spirit will from the Spirit reap eternal life." The exercise of freewill requires using our intellect, or a higher state of consciousness than our ego's habitual inclinations. When we are doing our druthers, we are little different from an automaton. According to reincarnation philosophy, we develop the ability to experience compassion and empathy as we experience the pain and suffering of others as well as our own pain and suffering. Our level of spiritual consciousness evolves through the proper use of discrimination. Self-realization refers to realizing the consciousness of our soul instead of the perspective of our ego.

Souls in reincarnation philosophy are described as waves in the ocean of God's consciousness. In effect, each wave has two faces, like a coin. One faces toward God, while the other faces the world. The challenge for the side facing the world is to realize the ultimately unreal nature of their worldly perspective and to realize the consciousness of their soul, or, as explained in 1 Corinthians 3:16, "Don't you know that you are a temple of God, and that God's Spirit lives in you?" You may wonder why aspects of God would immerse themselves in illusion. A plausible answer to that question can be found by asking yourself, could God devise a better solution to His problem of spending eternity without being bored to death?

Past-life regression and between-lives regression reveal that souls who have known each other in previous lifetimes get together to plan and coordinate, with the assistance of spirit guides, their next lifetimes together. Each incarnating soul's incarnation is coordinated with the lives of other incarnating souls to favorably influence their karmic and spiritual growth concerns. Thousands of near-death experiences contain life reviews from the perspectives of those affected by the near-death experiencer's words and deeds. Helping a soul to process and learn from their previous life's experiences would be the most obvious (and possibly only) benefit of a life review. Without a subsequent lifetime in which to apply "life lessons," why would souls observe, from the perspective of others, their most recent life's words and deeds?

The Torah is a multilayered document with less well-known, deeper levels of esoteric teachings that include gilgul. Gilgul means "cycle" or "wheel" and refers to the recycling of souls, or reincarnation. Even though reincarnation was a tenet of belief within early forms of Jewish mysticism and is still believed by some Christians and Jews, neither religion encourages belief in reincarnation today.

Despite being officially banned during the fifth ecumenical council in AD 553, the concept of reincarnation has not been completely removed from the Bible. Among the Bible verses that deal with reincarnation are those that discuss Elijah's reincarnation as John the Baptist. During the ninth century BC, Elijah was an important biblical prophet credited with extraordinary powers and abilities. The Old Testament claims that Elijah brought a widow's dead son back to life, parted the waters of the Jordan River, ran faster than King Ahab's chariot, and caused jars of meal and oil to automatically refill during a drought. At the end of the Old Testament (Malachi 4:5), God said, "Behold, I will send you Elijah the prophet before the great and terrible day of Yahweh comes." God's announcement in Malachi is followed up in the New Testament (Luke 1:13–17) by the angel Gabriel, announcing:

> Do not be afraid, Zacharias, because your request has been heard. Your wife, Elizabeth, will bear you a son, and you shall call his name John. ... He will be filled with the Holy Spirit, even from his mother's womb. He will turn many of the children of Israel to the Lord their God. He will go before him in the spirit and power of Elijah.

"In the spirit and power" is an exact description of what happens during reincarnation because the spirit, but not the body, survives death to be reborn. On three different occasions in the Gospels (Mark 9:13, Matthew 11:13–14, and Matthew 17:12–13), Jesus told his disciples that Elijah's "spirit" was reborn in John the Baptist. James 5:17—"Elijah was a man with a nature like yours"—implies that the reincarnation of Elijah's soul several centuries later as John the Baptist was not an unusual or extraordinary event.

Because the Old Testament tells us that Elijah will prepare

the way for the Messiah, and John the Baptist prepared the way for Jesus, Jesus can be understood as the prophesized Messiah and John the Baptist as the reincarnation of Elijah. The above understanding of God's announcement in Malachi agrees with the beliefs of historians who believe that John the Baptist was born before Jesus and that Jesus's ministry began after his baptism by John the Baptist.

The Gospels also reveal that Jesus and his disciples believed in reincarnation. After seeing a man who was born blind (John 9:1–3), Jesus's "disciples asked him, 'Rabbi, who sinned, this man or his parents, that he was born blind?' Jesus answered, "This man didn't sin, nor did his parents; but, that the works of God might be revealed in him." Without a previous life in which to sin, a person could not be born blind because of their own sins. If Jesus's disciples did not understand and believe in Karma and reincarnation, they would not have asked this question; and Jesus, who was not bashful about correcting misunderstandings, would have corrected his disciples if he did not want them to believe in reincarnation and Karma.

At the beginning of the fourth century, Emperor Maximian persecuted Christians in the western part of the Roman Empire while Diocletian, the pagan emperor in the east, persecuted Christians in the eastern part of the Roman Empire. For almost ten years, edicts ordered the imprisonment of Christian clergy and the destruction of Christian documents and churches. Christians were tortured, starved, and killed in gladiatorial contests to amuse spectators. Thanks to Emperor Constantine, who reigned from 306 to 337, one version of Christianity experienced what may be history's most spectacular transformation. Instead of thinking it was all his doing, Emperor Constantine attributed his political and military success to Christianity's god. He began the transformation of

Christianity, one version anyway, into the Roman Empire's preferred religion instead of its most persecuted.

Emperor Constantine used his authority to support Rome's, orthodox version of Christianity. He created within the Church ecumenical councils, the position of a Christian emperor, and the concept of orthodoxy. He gave Rome's bishops wealth and property, and he built basilicas for them while encouraging Rome's bishops to suppress alternative versions of Christianity. A vindictive God under the Church's control enabled Christianity and the emperor to control people with fear. Instead of the Roman Empire continuing to persecute Christians, Rome's bishops eliminated the evidence for alternative, "deviant" versions of Christianity by destroying their theological treatises, Gospels, sermons, prayers, and letters. Rome's bishops determined the traditions of worship and Church doctrine, while the emperor enforced the bishop's (orthodoxy's) version of Christianity.

The miracle of Jesus's Resurrection is not significantly different from the after-death expectations of those who believe in reincarnation. Before they established centralized power and authority, orthodoxy had little influence on those who believed in reincarnation. Emperor Justinian's consolidation of Christianity within a single church canon and dogma during the sixth century enhanced Christianity's ability to intimidate and control people. The fifth ecumenical council, during Emperor Justinian's rule, banned belief in reincarnation. After alternative versions of Christianity and belief in reincarnation were eliminated at the end of the sixth century, Christians became dependent upon the Church for their salvation.

WORLDLY PERSPECTIVES AND AGENDAS

Today's Christianity retains orthodoxy's desire for power and control over converts. Control cannot be achieved by allowing people to think "God's kingdom is within you," as it says in Luke 17:21. The church assumed power and control over people by making God intimidating and inaccessible outside the Church.

Christianity has also been shaped by misunderstandings. For example, Jesus taught that sin, right and wrong, relates to how people treat each other; but Jews, Jesus's audience and apostles, believed right and wrong related to obeying Jewish laws. Jesus opened his heart to the needs of others and wanted us to do the same because "… they may all be one; even as you, Father, are in me, and I in you, that they also may be one in us; that the world may believe that you sent me."[12] If Jesus was not one of God's messengers or prophets, would his brief ministry inspire several versions of Christianity and the writing of many Gospels?

The idea of evil is unique to the Western world. Zoroaster and the Zoroastrian religion are credited with the concepts of two (evil and good) opposing forces, a Messiah who triumphs over evil, and the resurrection of the dead after the fulfillment of end-time prophecies. Scholars believe Judaism was influenced by the Persians and by Zoroastrianism during their Babylonian captivity. During their captivity, they experienced the use of religion by Babylonian and Persian leaders to persecute dissent and to establish national unity. Ancient Persian beliefs were passed from Judaism to Christianity to Islam. They helped to make possible the atrocities inspired by "Christians": the Crusades, the Inquisition, the witch craze (the execution of between 80,000 and 100,000 mostly elderly women), the genocide of Native Americans, and the Holocaust. The concept of a god of love coupled with heaven and a sadistic god coupled with hell has survived all these years because converts can be frightened into obedience, and nonbelievers can be dehumanized into scapegoats. Zoroaster's influence on the world's two largest religions helps to explain their success as well as thinking the world would be a better place without religion.

The eighteenth century's Enlightenment period profoundly changed the West's perception of religion. During the Enlightenment, human reason was glorified, while the divine realm was marginalized as metaphysics, supernormal, and myth. Since the Enlightenment, Western academics and even Christian writers have assumed that religion progresses from primitive to sophisticated. But those who bother to study the history of the world's religions and read their ancient spiritual texts realize that time and "human reason" negatively impacted revealed religions.

INNER EXPERIENCE AND GUIDANCE

The Bible, or any spiritual text, conveys only as much benefit or meaning as the understanding ability of the reader. In Matthew 13:13, Jesus said, "Therefore I speak to them in parables, because seeing they don't see, and hearing, they don't hear, neither do they understand." Much more important than reason or intelligence to understand religious texts is an inner experience of divine truth. When acknowledged, the synchronicity of mysterious coincidences suggests an invisible spiritual component to reality. We experience thoughts and words as our own, even though their appearance is unanticipated. Have you ever wondered about the origin of "your" thoughts and words? Even though psychic and mystical experiences suggest the brain's ability to function as a receiver/transmitter, consciousness is assumed to only arise from brains. Can divine guidance play a role in understanding spiritual texts that do not necessarily reflect worldly perspectives and understandings?

For those who are not aware of experiencing divine guidance, I want to share what Pharrell Williams said on *CBS Sunday Morning* on April 13, 2014, during an interview with Anthony Mason. While reflecting on his achievements, the music producer, writer, and singer said, "It's not all you! It can't be all you! Just like you need air to fly a kite: It is not the kite. It's the air!" To appreciate the air, the flip side of our worldly perspective, it helps to realize that unanticipated thoughts provide guidance and influence our destiny. Unfortunately, as Jesus lamented above, not everyone has progressed far enough on their spiritual journey to appreciate "the air." Logic and intelligence cannot take the place of actual experience. As the archbishop of Canterbury, Saint Anselm (AD 1033–1109), put it, "Who does not experience, will not know. For just as experiencing a thing far exceeds the mere hearing of it, so the knowledge of him who experiences is beyond the knowledge of him who hears." If most clergymen personally experienced God's love, the devil and a god of wrath and vengeance would exist only in history books. Everyone, but especially clergymen, should realize that competence in spiritual matters requires actual spiritual experience.

In the Western world, people do not talk about experiencing God—"the air." Eastern religions are not concerned with beliefs. They are concerned with the direct experience of God, samadhi and self-realization, during which God's light and love replaces a person's egoic sense of themself. It may surprise you to learn that Catholic saints drink from the same spiritual well and have the same religious experiences as mystics and holy men from every spiritual tradition. Saint Catherine of Sienna (1347–1380), a Roman Catholic mystic and spiritual writer whose description of experiencing mystical union with God ("I am That I am; thou [referring to her egoic sense of herself] art that which is not") describes what Hindus call samadhi. Saint Catherine of Genoa (1447–1510) was an Italian Roman Catholic mystic who selflessly attended to the needs of the sick and poor. Writing about the direct experience of her soul (samadhi), she wrote, "The soul, when purified, abides entirely in God; its being is God." In her autobiography, the Spanish mystic and Roman Catholic Saint Teresa of Avia (1515–1582) wrote, "The soul is entirely transformed into the likeness of its Creator

– it seems more God than soul." Saint Veronica Giuliani, a seventeenth-century Capuchin convent nun, was so devoted to Jesus that, in 1694, her devotion manifested as stigmata wounds corresponding to Jesus's crown of thorns, and in 1697, as five additional wounds that corresponded to Jesus's Crucifixion wounds. Her bishop put her under constant observation until convinced that her stigmata wounds were authentic. After experiencing the supreme ecstasy of mystical union with God, she wrote in her diary her conviction that, "Outside God nothing has any existence at all."

The above quotes taken from the writings of Catholic nuns correspond exactly with the samadhi insights and descriptions provided by all religious traditions. Nuns, as well as monks, take vows of poverty, chastity, and obedience. They may live very strict, contemplative, and cloistered lives. These spiritually focused Christian lifestyles are associated with life experiences that are like those experienced in Buddhist monasteries, which emerged in the fourth century BC, and by Hindus who renounce worldly desires. Buddhists and Hindus believe that freedom from personal worldly desires leads to freedom from the cycle of death and rebirth. Christian religious disciplines lead to the same spiritual outcomes as those of Eastern religions. Because there are many cultures and languages, there are many versions of revealed religion.

Despite being slaves for hundreds of years in Egypt, wealthy Hebrew merchants and landowners owned slaves. Because of the tendency for those who are wealthy and powerful to feel superior and to oppress those who are less fortunate, in Matthew 19:23, Jesus said, "A rich man will enter into the kingdom of Heaven with difficulty." The hijacking of Jesus's religion, the one he tried to inspire, by Rome's emperors and bishops enabled Christianity to become the world's largest religion. But Rome's emperors and bishops did not share Jesus's view of oppressing others. Jesus's life and sermons promoted compassion, empathy, and a conscience to guide behavior instead of conforming to laws made by those in power for their own benefit. Instead of Jesus's teachings, love and concern for everyone, Christianity maintains Rome's emperors' and bishops' concern for the rich and powerful. In 2022, if Christianity maintained Jesus's concerns, would the S&P 500's chief executive officers receive on average 272 times as much as an employee receiving a median salary? Culture and religion should reflect the concerns and teachings of God's messengers, like Jesus, instead of the concerns of the rich and powerful.

I wrote the first chapter in the hope of encouraging science to embrace instead of denying the existence of "paranormal" phenomena. I wrote this chapter to suggest, just as the Gospels do, that Jesus and his disciples believed in reincarnation. This chapter's secondary goals are to explain how and why reincarnation became anathema to Christianity, and my belief that religions evolve from empirical experiences, revelation, and worldly perspectives and agendas. My desire was never to adversely impact anyone's religious faith.

Science cannot seem to evolve beyond materialistic understandings of reality while refusing to consider the possibility of God, souls, and an afterlife. I do not know how Christianity can evolve beyond maintaining that it is "the one and only valid revelation of the one living God." Christianity's fictional story about Jesus, instead of his teachings, has made Christianity incompatible with the concept of religious pluralism. Eastern religions embrace other religions as additional spiritual teachings, and do not, like Christians, assume the superiority of their religion.

Who are you, and why were you born? Neither Western science nor Christianity appreciate these questions in the same way as Jesus, Gnosticism, and Eastern religions and philosophies. I am writing this book to share experiences (mine and those of others) which reveal who you are and why you were born.

"Religions are many, but God is One."
—*Sathya Sai Baba*

Chapter 3
AN EXAMINED LIFE

An unexamined life is not worth living.
—Socrates (470-399 BC)

When I began writing this book, *An Examined Life* seemed like the perfect title. As the book developed, *Encounters with God* became more descriptive of the book's content, but Socrates's famous quote resonates with my book-writing motivations. When I examine my life, as Socrates recommended, my experiences suggest that, not only does God answer prayers, but He must also be able to influence our thoughts, words, actions, and experiences. Not only was I led through a series of improbable experiences to God in human form, but answers to spiritual questions seemed to be revealed to me in response to my high school prayers. In the 1950s, I was under the impression that all religions believed they were the one true religion. The experience of samadhi—which, at least, feels like the direct experience of God's love—implies, just as many Bible verses proclaim, that God "is not far from each one of us. For in Him we live, move, and have our being."[13] Christianity's self-serving claim of a favored relationship with God led me to believe I was born into a culture of spiritual morons. After experiencing samadhi, I assumed the direct experience of God's love was common enough that, with billions of people on our planet, at least one living person must have divinely inspired wisdom or knowledge. Something prompted me when I was a high school sophomore to read the Gospel of Matthew's Sermon on the Mount. As I read the words of Jesus, I envied those who were in his presence two thousand years ago. I read something that made me think I could find a contemporary Jesus-like person in India. Fortunately, after a few days, I realized leaving home without finishing high school and optimistically expecting to find someone like Jesus was impractical. I allayed my desire for a divinely inspired spiritual teacher by giving the problem to God in several heartfelt prayers. Karmic destiny and God hearing and responding to my prayers are the only explanations I can think of for the experiences that I want to share in this book. I do not have the imagination to make up experiences that give credence to the clichés "truth is stranger than fiction" and "there are no accidents."

I want to present ideas and experiences chronologically as I experienced them. Initially, rejected ideas were often proven to me as if through God's grace and persistence. Hopefully, I will present ideas that you do not agree with. Except for an inflated ego, what would be gained by avoiding experiences and ideas that conflict with your beliefs? I hope you are a spiritual seeker and are open to exploring new ideas.

By remembering and reflecting on our experiences, we can acquire greater insight into our underlying reality. We all have beliefs we assume to be true. According to the Danish philosopher Søren Kierkegaard, there are two ways to form false beliefs: "One is to believe what isn't true; the other is to refuse to believe what is true." Our beliefs are influenced by our unique past experiences and the ideas that we have embraced. We interpret information so that it confirms our beliefs while ignoring information that does not support our beliefs. We readily embrace ideas that enhance our self-esteem and those that harmonize with what we want to believe. If you have raised children, you know that we come into this world with preprogrammed personalities. Our delusional tendency to persist in believing whatever we believe is a normal habit of human minds. Others may have different beliefs, but we assume they are wrong, and we are right. With reflection, we become aware of thinking and behavior patterns or tendencies that we did not consciously choose. We tend to be oblivious to tendencies or blind spots that are obvious to others. In the Socratic dialogues, the protagonist, Socrates, reveals the path to wisdom by uncovering blind spots and inconsistencies. While I am sharing my life experiences and those of others, my hope is that you will recall with fresh insight your own relevant experiences. From the perspective of bottom-up creation or evolution, our behavior patterns and life experiences would have physical-world or materialistic explanations. The experiences that I want to share suggest that consciousness is an intrinsic, causally influencing feature of reality, and not simply the by-product of neurobiological processes in our brain, as is widely taught and believed. Mystical experiences and improbable coincidences, not probable from a materialistic perspective, prove to me that matter is not the only reality. By writing this book, I hope to add God, souls, and an afterlife to science's paradigms.

Our culture discourages spending time in self-examination and reflection by keeping us preoccupied with worldly interests, demands, and desires. Capitalism encourages people to have unending desires that are easily but only temporarily satisfied with each new purchase. Any possible nonmaterial or spiritual aspect to our reality is obscured when all our concerns relate to the physical world. It would be radical in our culture to believe, like Socrates, that "an unexamined life is not worth living."

Materialist science says that you have no reality beyond that of a body-mind organism that was born and hopes to die of old age. I want to share experiences which imply that you have an underlying nonmaterial, divine reality. This reality existed before you were born and will continue after the death of your body. It is hidden by your self-image, worldly hopes, fears, plans, and desires. My pointers may be unconvincing, but please be patient. Only one pointer ultimately needs to give rise to an epiphany that lifts the veil of illusion cast by your mind.

REFLECTIONS RELATED TO
MY CHILDHOOD

The sequence of events that led to my motivation to write this book can be traced back to the death of my father's mother when he was four years old. When my father's mother, Lucy, died of pneumonia in 1924, she left three children between ten and fifty-two months of age to be raised by their father with his mother's assistance. Nine months after Lucy died, her father died while working alone in his soda water factory. His obituary described him as "a staunch member of the Catholic Church." Dad's widowed grandmother, Maria, wanted her daughter's children to be raised as Catholics. When Dad was eleven years old, Maria contacted Dad's father and told him that she wanted to raise her daughter's children. As the oldest child, my dad was sent 152 miles to Alexandria, Minnesota. In Alexandria, Maria told my dad that she saved him from going to hell with the rest of his non-Catholic family. Dad did not appreciate Maria's efforts to make him a God-fearing Catholic with regular church attendance. He developed such a strong hatred for religion that, for the rest of his life, he could not think about religion, especially the Catholic religion, without getting visibly upset. By expressing and demonstrating his unhappiness, Dad motivated Maria to return him to her daughter's family.

My oldest spiritually significant memory had nothing to do with my dad or his hatred of religion. Even though it was a very ordinary experience of childhood, it had a profound and lasting influence on me. The experience took place in 1949, when I was seven years old, and the first episodes of *The Lone Range* could be seen on Thursday evenings. At the home of a second-grade classmate was one of the first televisions in our neighborhood. Until we had a television, I was at his house every Thursday evening. In addition to the Lone Ranger and his horse, Silver, I was captivated by the exciting ending to Rossini's overture to

William Tell accompanied by these words: "A fiery horse with the speed of light, a cloud of dust and a hearty 'Hi Ho Silver!'"

Along the eight-block route to school, I walked by a toy store whose window display contained a realistic-looking copy of the Lone Ranger's gun and holster set. I became obsessed with wanting the gun and holster set. I told my mom about the object of my affection, but it cost twenty-seven dollars. In 2025's inflation-adjusted dollars, I was asking for a $365 gun and holster set. Mom said that, because it was so expensive, its purchase depended on my ability to raise the money. At that time, as I recall, the tooth fairy's rate of exchange for a tooth was a dime. Suddenly, I was getting fifty cents, and my baby teeth could not fall out fast enough. Mom thought of extra chores for me to do to raise the money. Within a month or two, I purchased the gun and holster set.

That weekend, I paraded up and down the neighborhood showing off my fast draw and ability to twirl a gun around my finger. I felt like the most super-special kid who ever lived ... until Monday morning on my way to school. The toy store's window display contained an even more realistic and desirable gun and holster set for only twenty-two dollars. I was devastated. Instantly, my gun and holster set lost its magic. I contemplated restoring my inflated sense of myself by buying another gun and holster set. As I thought about my emotional responses, I began to feel foolish as I realized that the pride I had felt as I paraded up and down the neighborhood was based on an illusion. I realized my inflated self-image was based on the false assumption that I had the world's most desirable gun and holster set. Thoughts about buying another set enabled me to realize that my emotional responses— feelings of superiority and pride of ownership—were illusions. That realization enabled me to realize what most people never do: our sense of self is an illusion. We can identify with and believe our thoughts and emotions, or we can be observing witnesses to our thoughts and experiences as they arise. I acquired the ability to shift my consciousness from my ego to that of a relatively detached, objective observer.

Learning to be the witness to your thoughts and emotions, instead of being swept away by them, is the initiation to realizing consciousness has levels of awareness. Why would intelligent people continually reshape their feelings about themselves based upon peripheral or irrelevant factors? A person's clothes, car, job, relationships, golf score, and how well their favorite sports teams are doing could not possibly have anything to do with their fundamental reality. Why would those things affect how people feel about themselves, unless they have never taken Socrates' advice and examined their responses to life's experiences. Do people live in an illusion that they have never thought to investigate?

SAMADHI

Hindu, Buddhist, and Zen cultures encourage becoming aware of a more objective perspective than one's ego. The Western/Christian world that I grew up in provided little encouragement for contemplation, introspection, or meditation. I assumed (or was taught) that our culture had the answers to life's questions, and I merely needed to accept, learn, and follow them.

Despite being born in a Christian culture, I had another childhood experience suggestive of Hindu and Buddhist cultures. But the experience is so incongruous with Western beliefs that I have never revealed having the experience to anyone. As a child, I became aware that people with different experiences of reality were put in sanitoriums. This book feels like a necessary context within which to share my experiences. My hope is that I can write a book that enables others to understand my experiences.

Samadhi is the Sanskrit term for this other childhood experience. Spiritual practices associated with the experience of samadhi exist within all religions. Judaism has Kabbalah practice. Christianity's various methods of contemplating God—vocal and silent prayer, with and without the rosary—have often been rewarded with the experience of samadhi. The unique spiritual practices of Islam's Sufis can also be rewarded with an experience of samadhi. In the Hindu and Buddhist religions, samadhi is achieved through God's grace, prayer, and practices to quiet the mind. Samadhi, which is experienced by individuals within all cultures and religions, is the direct experience of becoming, for a moment anyway, the love, light, and bliss of God.

I suspect that I know of no English word for samadhi because of Christianity's influence on culture and language. Despite experiencing samadhi as a child, I did not come across a reference to the experience until I was in my forties. References to samadhi attribute the experience to God's grace. My efforts to foster the experience have always been without success. Samadhi was not experienced as my or my sense of self's experience. My earliest memory of samadhi took place in my father's garden when I was twelve years old, and the last two took place beside my own garden when I was forty-two and forty-four. Because I (my self-awareness) disappeared when samadhi occurred, I do not recall what I was doing in the gardens or even whether I was standing or sitting. I became the energy of light and love, which was both flowing in and radiating out in all directions. Self-awareness was obliterated by the intensity of experiencing being light, love, and bliss. We think of love as a feeling, but during samadhi, love is experienced as flowing white light and an all-embracing energy, like the electricity that powers our cities. When I last experienced samadhi, butterflies and hummingbirds flew around me as if I was a flower. I do not believe neurochemicals in my brain, or my imagination can account for samadhi. Samadhi is purported to be the direct experience of and the realization that everything is interconnected and sustained by an unappreciated power that is as different from our worldly experience of love as sunlight is different from candlelight.

When the experience of samadhi ended and my usual consciousness returned, an awareness of love's energy and omnipresence remained. I assumed that the unseen basis of the phenomenal world and God's omnipresence was revealed in and accounted for my experience of samadhi. I was almost fifty years old when I first heard someone describe their experience of samadhi. I agreed with his description of the experience, but he assumed he merely experienced his soul, which he compared to a coin with his soul on one side and God on the other.

The experience of samadhi has a timeless aspect to it that prevents any sense of knowing how long it lasts. My absorption in being light, love, and bliss always ended with my usual consciousness thinking, "How did 'I' get here, and how can 'I' stay here?" It seemed as if I, the ego self, played no role in the experience. The ecstasy of bliss is way beyond any normal human experience. When I heard descriptions of heaven as a child, they always sounded as if heaven would rapidly become a boring hell. But, after experiencing samadhi, I assumed that the bliss I experienced during samadhi was the eternal bliss claimed for heaven. Samadhi can be understood as a direct experience of God, or one's own divinity or soul. Jesus expressed this insight with these words: "I and the Father are one." Jesus was alluding to his spiritual Christ consciousness and not our usual egoic or worldly sense of ourselves.

After experiencing samadhi in my forties, I drove into the San Bernardino Mountains and meditated on a large boulder next to a small but rapidly flowing stream surrounded by tall pine trees. Just like my childhood obsession with a gun and holster set, I was obsessed with the bliss of samadhi. If, through some magic, I could have left this life and returned to that blissful state forever, I would have done so, even though it would have meant abandoning this life's relationships and responsibilities. That was the only time I can recall thinking in a self-destructive, addictive manner. Fortunately, I soon realized that samadhi was like most of the experiences I want to share with you in this book; it expanded my awareness of reality's facets, but it was not a goal or skill that I experienced encouragement to pursue.

Are you inclined to be skeptical of reports of anything that lies outside the bounds of established science? I have a knee-jerk tendency to be doubtful of the "paranormal" experiences of others. Because God's grace has allowed me to experience things that materialistic science has difficulty confirming and explaining, I have become less skeptical.

Are you inclined to believe that samadhi is a brain-generated experience? It is difficult to use brain imaging technology to test mystical states of consciousness, but studies that have been done suggest that mystical states of consciousness correspond with an overall decrease in brain activity. The frontal lobe (which helps coordinate thoughts with physical behaviors) and the parietal lobe (which is the brain's attention area) decrease their activities. If the brain was responsible for the experience of samadhi, I would expect a huge increase in brain activity. These experimental results correspond with my sense that our soul as well as our brain contribute to our experiences and sense of self-identification.

Human ingenuity and the scientific method have given us the scientific and engineering achievements we enjoy. Consider the possibility that science has yet to discover an energy field that is comparable to gravity and electromagnetic energy in its significance. Instead of assuming "paranormal" phenomena are bogus or illusions, does it not seem possible that reality has mysteries that science has yet to acknowledge and investigate? The first chapter's scientifically researched and documented evidence for consciousness's nonlocality, souls, and an afterlife suggests that contemporary scientists are either ignorant of the first chapter's research or lack the open, curious mind appropriate for scientists.

MY INTRODUCTION TO CHRISTIANITY

When I was young, Dad occasionally made angry, derogatory rants about religion, but I do not remember Mom mentioning the subject until I was about ten years old. She must have gotten up the courage to get Dad's permission to provide her children with a more balanced presentation of religion. While putting me to bed one evening, she taught me my first prayer. It was the popular eighteenth-century children's bedtime prayer:

Now I lay me down to sleep,
I pray the Lord my soul to keep,
If I should die before I wake,
I pray the Lord my soul to take.

Despite my dad's hatred of religion, without hesitation, I embraced believing that I had a soul and a relationship with an omnipresent god. In youth, we are all too willing to believe in Santa Claus, the Easter Bunny, and the tooth fairy. These are not long-lasting relationships, but the pages of this book reveal that everyone's longest lasting and most important relationship is with God. I hope the reader appreciates (or will, after reading this book) their relationship with God. The opportunity of impregnating gullible young minds with a spiritual identity is, in my opinion, a precious opportunity not to be missed. The evolutionary biologist and prominent promoter of the "new atheism," Richard Dawkins, does not share my opinion. He wrote in his book, *The God Delusion*, "Faith can be very, very dangerous, and deliberately to implant it into the vulnerable mind of an innocent child is a grievous wrong." His opinions reflect his "very, very dangerous" faith in Western science's exclusively materialistic understanding of reality. For his point of view to be valid, not just some but all mystical or spiritual experiences would have to be delusions. Instead of being tolerant of the beliefs of others, he wages war against religion with Hitler-like fanatical hatred.

Religion deals with dimensions or aspects of reality and levels of experience that are not amenable to being explained or investigated using the reductionist approaches of science. Even though science can explain what things are and what they do, science has difficulty answering "why" questions. Science cannot tell you why you were born or the *meaning* or *purpose* of your life. Despite being unable to see beyond a purposeless existence while maintaining its atheistic paradigms, Western science unintentionally and intentionally wages war against religion.

An April 19, 2013, survey of America's senior Protestant pastors conducted by Nashville's Lifeway Research found that 70 percent believe "Christians have lost or are losing the culture war" with Western science. In his hostile critiques of religion, Richard Dawkins picks the low-hanging fruit. The view of creationists that the Earth is only a few thousand years old is an example of easily criticized, low-hanging fruit. In this book, I will cover the high-hanging fruit that Richard Dawkins is unaware of or ignores. There are far more good examples of a nonlocal, causally influencing, nonmaterial, "spiritual" or divine component to our reality than can be covered in one book.

If spiritual and religious beliefs have, at least in part, arisen from "divine" influences, and if we have a soul and a mysterious relationship with "God," then faith, values, character, and acquired "wisdom" play a role in our "soul's" spiritual and worldly journey. All parents have the challenge of guiding young, impressionable children toward being a credit to their family and culture. Raising children is less challenging in a community with desirable shared values. It is axiomatic that desirable character traits and behaviors are motivated by belief in an omnipresent personal God concerned with how we treat others.

Unfortunately, both historically and even today, too many cultural and religious beliefs are examples of Richard Dawkins's low-hanging fruit. Instead of being guided by and embracing Jesus's concern for how we treat others, Christianity, during most of its history, has actively promoted religious intolerance and the persecution of those who do not conform to the "values" of Christianity's rich and powerful members. In the United States, well into the nineteenth century, a married woman was her husband's property because the Church's rich and powerful men appreciated the Bible's concept of coverture more than Jesus's teachings. During the exploration and development of the New World, embracing and preaching the Golden Rule may have prevented the development of slavery. But Christians, and even members of the clergy, wanted to own slaves. To justify slavery, Christian pastors used Colossians 3:22. Before and after the Civil War, Southern pastors claimed that white supremacy was sanctioned by God. Prior to the civil rights movement, racist sermons were common in Southern states. Interracial marriage did not become legal in all fifty states until 1967's *Loving v. Virginia*. Christianity continues to reflect and promote intolerant attitudes instead of Jesus's compassion and concern for everyone. Instead of embracing the reproductive health concerns of women, and the concerns of gays and lesbians, many "Christian" communities embrace prejudice and discrimination.

Sometime before I became an adult, my consciousness assimilated my parents' and culture's filters. I can remember when I experienced the perspective of a child without an adult's filters and ulterior motives. I fully appreciated the enthusiasm, spontaneous joy, open and trusting nature, and sense of wonder of childhood. I also remember becoming aware that, during their preteen years, children lose touch with their "inner child" and acquire the cultural programming of adults. I remember looking at adults and thinking with considerable dread, "Am I going to become like them?" From this memory, I know what Jesus was referring to when he said, "Most certainly I tell you, unless you turn and become as little children, you will in no way enter into the kingdom of Heaven."[14]

Neuroimaging research supports my childhood observation of profound changes taking place in our brains as we transition from childhood to adulthood. Research shows that "the overall metabolism in the brain begins to decrease – probably from the age of 11 to 20" when neural connections are pruned to establish the primary connections of adulthood.[15] People with psychic, artistic, and creative abilities do not seem to have lost touch with their "inner child."

When I was nine years old, we moved to a new home built on a third of an acre of rock-infused dirt. My dad gave me a quarter for every wheelbarrow load of rocks from our yard that I deposited outside the backyard's chain-link fence. When I smashed the larger rocks together, they frequently broke into two pieces with fossils on each half. The fossils usually resembled ferns. I wondered how long it would take for ferns to evolve and become encased in sediment that would become a rock. Because suitable conditions for rock creation did not exist in our backyard, I wondered what previous circumstances made the rocks, and I wondered what events enabled the rocks to end up in our yard's dirt with smooth, rounded surfaces. It was apparent to me that more time than I could comprehend was required to account for the rocks. In the Cascade Mountains, not far from where I am now living, you can find lava that flowed out from the bottom of the ocean and over time rose with the mountains to over eight thousand feet above sea level. I could provide better indicators for the Earth's age if I studied geology, but I want to suggest that neither education nor sophistication is necessary to realize that God and creation have coexisted for billions of years.

While growing up in San Diego, I frequently went to the San Diego Zoo. I was surprised to learn Darwin's *On the Origin of Species* introduced the concept of evolution only a century before my birth. Because of the ease of noticing the similarity among the zoo's monkey, wildcat, and antelope species, evolution seemed like a self-evident explanation for plant and animal variety and variation. Survival of the fittest through natural selection may be a self-evident fact, but it is not self-evident that evolution plays more than a minor role in creation. From my childhood experiences with fossils and samadhi, I knew that the source of manifestation and its manifested creation were inseparably connected over eons of time. John Glenn, the first American to orbit the Earth, told The Associated Press, "I don't see that I'm any less religious by the fact that I can appreciate the fact that science just records that we change with evolution and time. It doesn't mean it's less wondrous, and it doesn't mean that there can't be some power greater than any of us that has been behind and is behind whatever is going on."[16] Creation and evolution are simply the same thing, looked at from different points of view.

In addition to teaching me to pray, when I was ten years old, my mother began to take my seven-year-old brother, Jerry, and me to a Central Congregational church. She dropped us off and picked us up after the conclusion of Sunday school. This was a Sunday ritual for the next three years. My Sunday school teachers provided my first awareness of people selflessly giving others their time and knowledge. If you can think of no other reason to take your children to Sunday school, exposure to positive role models is more than enough reason. Christianity and the Bible, as I experienced them in Sunday school, were always positive experiences.

During this three-year period, when I was ten to thirteen years of age, I spent a week during the summer at the YMCA's Camp Marston near Julian in San Diego County.

By memorizing several Bible verses and going through an initiation ceremony at Camp Marston, I became a Blue, Brown, and Gray Ragger. The Bible study that we did in Sunday school and the Bible verses that I memorized enabled me to realize that Jesus's samadhi-like level of spiritual consciousness was not a brief experience like mine. Jesus obviously had continuous access to knowledge and power from which he performed miracles. Not only did Jesus describe samadhi's primary revelation with the words "God's kingdom is within you,"[17] but his words and deeds provided insight into the reality that Jesus spoke from and about. While reading Jesus's words in the Bible, I was envious of his contemporaries' opportunity to experience Jesus. Jesus could not have been any clearer that he wanted to wake people up to their reality and potential when he said, "Most certainly I tell you, he who believes in me, the works that I do, he will do also; and he will do greater works than these ..."[18]

When I was in middle school, I became aware of a very bewildering communication problem: unintended and unkind words, which did not feel like something I would say, popped out of my mouth. Facial expressions revealed the insensitive nature of my words. For several months after getting in bed at night, I critically reviewed the day's events in the hope that unkind words would quit popping out of my mouth. When this strategy did not seem to be working, for several months before talking, I previewed in my mind what I wanted to say. As I got older, saying things that I later regretted became less common. I am sharing this perplexing aspect of experiencing being me because of its relevance to an experience I will share in chapter 5.

Before the minister began his sermon on Sunday mornings, the children and teenagers in the congregation left for their youth group meetings. I heard a sermon on the radio, when I was in the eighth grade, that seemed incongruous with my understanding of Jesus's ministry. I wondered what the Central

Congregational Church's adults believed. The next Sunday, instead of leaving before the sermon began, I stayed. I quickly became upset when the minister described God as vindictive and remote, like a king in his castle. The experience of God's all-embracing love (samadhi) made it impossible to attribute jealousy, wrath, or vengeance to God, or to think of God as separate from creation. It seemed as if everything the minister said conflicted with my experiences. My experience of an omnipresent god of love contrasted with the minister's god, who provided heaven for those in agreement with him and hell for those outside the sound of his voice. As the congregation's ticket to heaven was receiving a privileged status, I thought about the Australian Aborigines I had read about in our next-door neighbor's *National Geographic* magazines. I assumed the Aborigines' remote location prevented them from hearing about Jesus and becoming Christians. The Aborigines were as much part of God's creation as Christians, and, based upon my understanding of the *National Geographic* article and my experience of samadhi, the Australian Aborigines' understanding of God greatly exceeded that of the minister. It seemed to me to be incongruous for an omnipresent god of love to have a heaven for Jesus's followers and a hell for everyone else.

The minister claimed, during the sermon, that only people had souls. He justified this belief by saying that the intellectual and emotional capabilities of people were superior to the rest of creation. My personal experiences informed me that my dog had a rich emotional life, and that I could not rationally have an exclusive claim to a soul based on a claim of relative intellectual superiority. During the sermon, I recalled reading (possibly in another *National Geographic* article) about comparative brain sizes. I do not remember numbers from that 1950s article, but more recent sources provide brain weights for sperm whales of 18 pounds, 12 pounds for elephants, 3.5 pounds for dolphins, and only 3.1 pounds for humans. I remember specifically recalling research with dolphins that showed they are highly intelligent. Relative to most animals' overall brain size, a dolphin's and our neocortex, which is responsible for cognitive ability, are large. It struck me as presumptuous to assume that humans, who do not have the largest brains, were the most intelligent and exclusively warranted a soul. While the minister was talking, I also thought about the running speed of a cheetah, the strength of a gorilla, the ability of birds to fly, a dolphin's superior swimming ability, and my dog's love. It seemed as if the minister wanted to say things that conflicted with my experiences and understanding of the Gospels. The sermon and the thought that the congregation probably agreed with the minister caused me to feel isolated and alone with my beliefs.

To attract and maintain church members, a minister's sermons must resonate with the attitudes and beliefs of parishioners. The minister's sermon resonated with the congregation by appealing to human tendencies: human egos appreciate feeling superior to the rest of creation and getting a free ticket to heaven. You would think sermons that conflict with scientific understandings and Jesus's life and teachings would negatively influence Christianity. But "nothing succeeds like success," and Christianity has succeeded very well by promoting ideas that appeal to human egos and create a fear-based dependency upon the church.

During the sermon, I heard a short sermon in my head that I attributed to God. For obvious reasons, I have been reluctant, until now, to tell anyone about this inner sermon. It was not like experiencing my own thoughts. I heard an authoritative male voice from an invisible source. It sounded like God was sitting on my right side as He talked to me. Usually, when I get messages (which I attribute to my spirit guides), they are quickly forgotten, like a dream. To retain them, I must immediately write them down. What was unusual about this inner sermon was that for twenty years

I had perfect word-for-word recall. I wish I had the good sense to write it down when I had word-for-word recall. My recollection of what I heard were the spiritual teachings or commandments of Jesus in the Gospel of Mark. My inner sermon emphasized in the same order the three concepts stated by Jesus in Mark 12:29–31:

> Jesus answered, "The greatest [commandment] is, 'Hear, Israel, the Lord our God, the Lord is one: you shall love the Lord your God with all your heart, and with all your soul, and with all your mind, and with all your strength.' The second is like this, 'You shall love your neighbor as yourself.' There is no other commandment greater than these.

In my inner sermon, "the Lord our God, the Lord is one" was elaborated upon and was the first commandment. Unfortunately, Christianity's founding fathers did not recognize that Jesus's "first commandment" contained two concepts. Not recognizing or emphasizing the first concept, "the Lord our God, the Lord is one" [for all of creation], has had a very negative impact upon both Christian and human history. When most people did not travel far from where they were born or appreciate other cultures, it is easy to understand why they would think of God as their own. But today, when we live in a "global village" visible from outer space as a small dot, such an ignorant and egocentric perspective is reprehensible. If Jesus's words—"the Lord our God, the Lord is one"—were embraced by Christianity, the perspective of samadhi would prevail, and Christians would have a less egocentric understanding of God. My inner sermon's second Commandment was about loving "God with all your heart," and the third was about loving "[others] as yourself." These three Commandments seemed quite harmonious with my understanding of Jesus's ministry but did not seem to be part of the minister's understanding.

When Mom picked my brother and me up after church, I did not want to return and risk reexperiencing feeling all alone with my beliefs. I told my mother, "I agree with Dad; I do not want to ever again go to church." It was not until I was forty years old that I risked reexperiencing feeling isolated and alone with my beliefs by attending a church service.

A brief glimpse of God, samadhi, and the inner sermon do not provide significant guidance or wisdom. If the divinely inspired prophets, who provided the prophetic revelation for the world's religions, could get together at the same time for a seminar, I am sure that they would give a harmonious presentation. But, after many centuries, a diversity of languages, cultures, and dogmas has made religious beliefs a muddled mess that would be difficult to sort out without assistance. When I was in high school, I spent a couple hours in the library looking for a book that would sort it all out for me. Not knowing exactly what I was looking for, or even if there were books that would be helpful, I gave up. No matter how perfect for my purposes a book might be, I would not have been able to appreciate or relate to it. I had absorbed too many contemporary cultural attitudes and beliefs to be able to distinguish "truth" from fiction. I became mad at God for allowing me to know of His existence but not providing me (or anyone else, it seemed) with adequate guidance. Eventually, I realized that it was not just OK for religions to be a muddled mess, but desirable. If our underlying spiritual reality was not a mystery, there would be no opportunity for God to play hide-and-seek. Spending eternity with nothing to do—no game, no drama, and no mystery—would make eternity seem like an eternity.

During my first two years of high school, when I prayed for assistance with my life's spiritual journey, I vacillated between being angry at God for leaving me up a creek without a paddle, and pleading for God to row, row, row my boat gently down the stream of life. My prayers expressed my anger with God as I pleaded to be led to someone with divinely inspired wisdom. A glimpse of what I assumed was the basis of Jesus's inspiration enabled me to assume that, among the billions of people on the planet, there must be at least one Jesus-like person. For a few years, I thought I would stumble upon something that harmonized with the three Commandments contained in my inner sermon. When nothing turned up, I forgot about God, and I became absorbed (like most of humanity) within the material world.

RENÉ DESCARTES'S INFLUENCE ON SCIENCE AND CHRISTIANITY

The belief from the minister's sermon that I found to be the most surprising and upsetting was the idea that only people have souls. Where did that idea come from, and why did it resonate with the congregation? Before I begin the next chapter, I want to look up the origin of the idea that only people have souls.

The idea can be traced back to René Descartes, who was the father of modern philosophy, analytic geometry, and scientific theory with his *Discourse on the Method*. Descartes lived from1596 to 1650. His mechanical or mechanistic theories of life and his belief that only people have souls became fundamental elements of Western philosophy. By merely doubting his own existence, Descartes assumed that he had proven his existence as a "thinking entity." He also assumed that he was only aware of the thoughts and feelings of people because animals "have no thoughts." If Descartes ever had a pet, I suspect that he never paid attention to it; yet his arrogant and ignorant speculations were (and still are) profoundly influential.

The French philosopher regarded animals as not just "thoughtless brutes" but as machines instead of organisms. Apparently unaware that human speech requires the ability to make a variety of sounds, which is a *physical* ability lacked by other animals, Descartes assumed our "nonmechanical" and "nonphysical" minds made human beings uniquely intelligent and conscious. Somehow, Descartes's ignorant assumptions passed through three centuries of Christian sermons to that 1950s sermon.

I suspect that othering—the human tendency to mentally classify others as "not one of us"—added to the appeal and influence of Descartes's theories. Classifying nonhumans as "machines," instead of as organisms, may stem from the human tendency to regard others as inferior and to mistreat them. Slavery and genocide are examples and evidence of this human tendency. Descartes's ideas changed Western science and religion's understandings of nature. Instead of thinking of living things as organisms, Descartes's theories enabled living things to be thought of as machines. In addition to science, the concept of machines appeals to Christianity because machines suggest the necessity of a designer or God.

René Descartes's ideas stimulated two competing theories of life: living organisms versus machines. The most influential theory has been Descartes's machine or mechanical theories from which science has removed "rational souls" and spirits. Science's understanding of reality is more disturbing than my 1950s sermon because science no longer gives people credit for having souls. Today's scientific communities believe that an exclusively materialistic understanding of reality will eventually enable atheists to explain our existence. Science's paradigms do not contain or even permit God, souls, or the concept of an afterlife because the proponents of vitalism— who observed that *living organisms*, unlike machines, are *alive*—lost their debate with those who embraced a materialistic, we-are-machines, understanding of reality.

Research in recent decades has proven that Descartes's assumptions about animals were wrong. We now have some insight into the intelligence and emotional experiences of other animals. Books and media appearances by Koko, a 280-pound lowland gorilla born in 1971 at the San Francisco Zoo, made her the most famous animal to learn sign language. With the support of the Gorilla Foundation, Koko lived most of her life in Woodside, California. Koko understood approximately two thousand English words, and she communicated with more than a thousand gorilla sign language words. According to Koko's handlers, like a loving, caring person, she liked to be hugged, and she mourned her first cat's death for many years.[19]

Prior to the Scientific Revolution, and especially Descartes's influence on Western science's attitudes and beliefs, living things were *organisms* with souls. Ever since the Scientific Revolution, our ability to reason has replaced the human soul as humanity's most significant attribute. What could possibly explain Western science maintaining to this day the Scientific Revolution's understanding of *organisms*, and ultimately us, as soulless machines? Why has mainstream science discouraged research relevant to souls or anything that could refute Descartes's ignorant speculations about living things? If science applied the scientific method to the "paranormal" phenomena preserved in metaphysical bookstores, science would have a much less ignorant understanding of our reality.

You would think that scientists would apply the scientific method to their own theories. But according to Thomas Kuhn (briefly written about in the Preface) the history of science reveals that scientists, like theists, do not question their own dogma. Thomas Kuhn became fascinated by the history of science after receiving his PhD in physics in 1949. In 1961, when I was a freshman at the University of

California, Berkeley, Thomas Kuhn became a full professor in the philosophy department. The following year, his influential book, *The Structure of Scientific Revolutions*, observed that most scientists work within what he called a "paradigm."

Because, according to Thomas Kuhn, scientists assume phenomena that do not conform to their paradigm's version of reality do not exist, he called famous scientists "revolutionary scientists" because their careers expanded their scientific disciplines' understanding of reality. To keep their jobs or be published in scientific journals, most scientists—what Thomas Kuhn called "normal scientists"—must conform to their scientific disciplines' versions of reality. Scientists, according to Thomas Kuhn, ignore "paranormal" phenomena or "anomalies" because they are taught to believe rationality only exists within their paradigm's version of reality. Scientists assume anomalies will eventually be explained within their paradigm's version of reality. Since the influence of Descartes and the Scientific Revolution, there have been times when new discoveries or theories motivated scientific communities to undergo a "scientific revolution," during which previously ignored "paranormal" phenomena or anomalies were incorporated into a new paradigm.

After the Scientific Revolution, scientists assumed we live in a predictable universe guided by discoverable and understandable laws. But unpredictable quantum systems and Albert Einstein's validated relativity theories reveal a universe that is radically different from the understandings of the eighteenth-century scientists who replaced God with human intellect.

Using neural imaging technology in the 1980s, psychologist Benjamin Libet demonstrated that our brain's neurons, which control our muscles, light up before the cognitive parts of our brain. His research found that, 95 percent of the time, we physically do things before and without apparent thought.

Did his research find evidence that we are mere machines, like René Descartes's "thoughtless brutes," or *evidence* that the brain does not contain the awareness and thoughts that occur before and during physical movement? Did Benjamin Libet find *evidence* that our conscious awareness, *consciousness*, takes place in something, like a soul, which is not contained within brains and science's paradigms?

How bizarre that Europe's "intellectual movement"—which glorified human reason but concluded that we are soulless machines—is referred to by the same word—enlightenment—used by mystics to refer to the spiritual insights that free a person from their ego's perspective and the cycle of rebirths. From the perspective of Eastern religions and mystical traditions, it is not our ability to be "intelligent and conscious" that makes humans, and only humans, unique; it is our ability to transcend our ego and achieve *enlightenment*. Enlightenment, self-realization, and liberation, which have similar meanings, will be discussed in later chapters.

Descartes's concept that living things are merely machines inspires today's assumption that man-made robots will eventually have consciousness. The belief that consciousness emerges from brains, like sweat from sweat glands, leads to the assumption that, with increased complexity, computers will become conscious. Many science fiction books and movies promote this assumption with lovable robots with human-like awareness. Who would not enjoy having *Forbidden Planet's* Robby the Robot, or *Star Wars'* R2-D2 and C-3PO, or my favorite, Wall-E. On the other hand, if you have seen the 1968 Stanley Kubrick classic 2001: *A Space Odyssey*, you know that computers or robots with consciousness, like nuclear energy, would have the potential to destroy what God created. In the fictional story, a depressed, sentient, spaceship-operating computer is more concerned with "his" survival than the people aboard the spaceship.

Cryonic preservation of a person's brain assumes that the brain contains a person's memories and the ability to have conscious experiences. The business of cryopreservation of brains, which has been going on since 1967, is another example of people believing that consciousness arises from matter. Despite a century of accumulating empirical and antidotal evidence which suggests that we are spiritual beings with souls, Western science persists in assuming that consciousness arises from physical matter. Machines and computers perform the capabilities that people incorporated into their design and construction. Magical thinking is required to think that increased complexity within matter leads to nonmaterial consciousness and self-awareness. Human consciousness does not necessarily come equipped with empathy, compassion, or concern for others. History and the evening news document the existence of people whose souls have yet to acquire these indicators of a desirable level of spiritual growth. The phenomena discussed in this book would not exist if consciousness arose from separate and independent locations in time and space (brains) instead of God's internet-like network of souls.

Chapter 4
AFTER HIGH-SCHOOL

We live in a fantasy world, a world of illusion.
The great task of life is to find reality.
—*Iris Murdoch (1919-1999)*

After junior high school, until I was thirty-three years old, my life experiences were probably typical of those experienced by atheists and agnostics: I had no unusual or "paranormal" experiences suggestive of a nonphysical, spiritual reality. My high school prayers and religious or spiritual experiences no longer concerned me. After graduating from high school, I spent the next six years going to the University of California, Berkeley. Initially, I studied architecture, but I switched to optometry after realizing I did not enjoy long hours of drawing and drafting.

Berkeley was an interesting place to be in the 1960s. Besides witnessing the nonviolent beginning to a decade of student activism, I took classes from Nobel laureates like my organic chemistry professor, Melvin Calvin, who received the 1961 Nobel Prize in chemistry for discovering the equation for photosynthesis, which reveals how plants convert the Sun's energy into chemical energy. Photosynthesis is another one of those things without which life as we know it would be impossible. The necessity of photosynthesis is obvious, but does this alchemy really have a chance of being manifested by a blind *chance and necessity* process?

One of my most interesting patients at the school of optometry was Donald Glaser, who received the 1960 Nobel Prize in physics for his invention of the bubble chamber to investigate the structure of matter. He was the first of fewer than ten patients, in my career as an optometrist, to read all the twenty-ten letters, and the only patient whose glasses I changed by such a minuscule amount.[20] Despite having twenty-ten vision, Dr. Glaser insisted his glasses needed to provide clearer vision. He responded to an imperceivable (for most people) prescription change as if it dramatically improved his vision. Extraordinary scientific achievements may sometimes require extraordinary, even "supernormal," abilities.

THE HARD PROBLEM OF CONSCIOUSNESS

Life experiences, which I attribute to God's grace, guide this book's inspiration and content, but my academic education at UC Berkeley's School of Optometry provided remarkably serendipitous insights into the enigmas of consciousness and perception. Our ability to have visual experiences or any first-person conscious experience is every bit as mysterious and inexplicable as any topic covered in this book. Contemporary philosopher David Chalmers is best known for identifying our ability to experience such things as colors, tastes, and smells as "the hard problem of consciousness." For materialistic science, conscious experience is as inexplicable as the appearance of the genie when Aladdin rubbed his lamp.

Our experience of seeing and the actual way seeing takes place are so different that, when I tried to explain it to my patients, my efforts usually seemed to cause more confusion than understanding. Because Western science's understanding of human perception harmonizes with the ancient Eastern religious concept that our experience of the phenomenal world is simply an illusion, hopefully I can write a lucid explanation. Ancient Hindu scriptures say that because everything is God, the only way for God to manifest as the separate and diverse manifestations of creation is through a veil of illusion or maya. Western science tells us that our physical senses merely provide the illusion of directly experiencing an external world.

Because we never perceive the world directly, seeing (representational realism) is a lot more complex than our illusion of looking out at and seeing our surroundings. Light reflects off the objects before us, passes through each eye's cornea and lens, and focuses an inverted image on the inside, back surface (or retina) of each eye. The optic nerves, which attach to the back of each eye, transmit information from the retina's light-receptive cells to our visual cortex, which is at the back of our brain. The visual cortex inexplicably conveys the neural input from our retina to our conscious mind, enabling us to see. What we see is an internally created representation of the image formed on our retina. We do not actually see what is before us any more than we see "in the flesh" actors and actresses while watching a movie. When you wake up from a dream or see what is in your "mind's eye," you know that what you experienced was created in your mind. Even though our perceptions while awake with our eyes open are also internal creations, we assume, *naive realism*, our perceptions accurately simulate an external reality. But, after three decades of studying perception, Donald D. Hoffman, professor of cognitive science at the University of California, Irvine, claims that our perceptions do not accurately reflect our reality. Disentangling the observer from the observed and figuring out the nature of reality should keep scientists scratching their heads for the foreseeable future. I just wish that they would quit assuming they know enough to ignore—as if it was unimportant—the evidence for God, souls, and an afterlife.

Our other senses work the same way. The sounds that we hear, what we taste and smell, and even our tactile experiences are created within our brain and consciousness from the information conveyed from our sensory receptors. Our experience of feeling with our fingertips, tasting in our mouth, hearing with our ears, and seeing with our eyes are all illusions. We have no ability to directly experience anything.

Because our network of sensory receptors and nerves cannot transmit actual colors, tastes, smells, or sounds; how (and how accurately) what is out there becomes our conscious experience is a profound mystery. For those who do not want to allude to God, a correlated mystery is the improbability of chance and necessity (which would not know there is a world out there to be experienced) manifesting complicated, indirect, and mysterious abilities that enable machines to experience an external world.

Despite decades of research and effort, science has been unable to find where consciousness arises within the brain or provide plausible explanations for how the brain manifests consciousness. Despite these failings, the fact that injury to the brain affects consciousness motivates the assumption that consciousness must arise from brains. The same logic applied to a broken radio without being aware of radio stations and waves leads to the assumption that a radio's sounds originate from within the radio. Ignorance of radio stations and waves leads to the same ignorant assumptions or false logic as ignorance of souls and God. Ignorance of souls, our fundamental reality, leads to assuming consciousness is created in brains instead of filtered through brains. The denial of the existence of radio stations and waves prevents the realization that a radio functions as an intermediary, a receiver/transmitter, between radio stations and listeners. For centuries, science's orthodoxy has dogmatically adhered to its materialistic understanding of reality by insisting upon ignoring and denying the evidence for a nonlocal attribute of consciousness that links and influences all forms of life.

Not all scientists have been reluctant to give star status to consciousness. Max Planck, who is known for his quantum theory and as the foremost genius of twentieth-century physics, wrote in his *Scientific Autobiography and Other Papers* a possibly accurate description of God when he wrote,

As a man who devoted his whole life to the most clearheaded science, to study matter, I can tell you as a result of my research about atoms this much: There is no matter as such. All matter originates and exists only by virtue of a force which brings the particles of an atom to vibrate and holds this most minute solar system of the atom together. We must assume behind this force the existence of a conscious and intelligent mind. This mind is the matrix of all matter.

Hopefully, the day will come when science, as well as education, will catch up to Max Planck's inclination to "assume behind" all matter lies "a conscious and intelligent mind" that "is the matrix of all matter." I believe that God and consciousness are likely to always remain outside complete human comprehension. Hopefully, the day will come when God is discussed and acknowledged by science as casually as consciousness. They may be one and the same.

ARGUMENT FROM DESIGN AND THE EVOLUTION OF EYES

Arguments from design for the existence of God focus on aspects of nature whose existence seems implausible without an intelligent designer or God. Nature's beauty and complexity suggest intelligent design instead of evolution theory's mindless chance and necessity. Things exist to fulfill a purpose; hearts exist to pump blood, and eyes exist to see. The fulfillment of purpose is logically associated with design and creation, but not with a mindless process. Arguments from design are easily made because beauty and complexity exist everywhere in nature. Ancient religious scriptures suggest that God's existence and influence are revealed within the natural world. Because beauty and complexity appear everywhere in nature, anyone can use the tools of science (empirical evidence and logic) to provide evidence for God. Arguments from design enable religion to be based upon evidence and logic, while Western science persists in assuming blind chance and necessity readily manifest impossibly long sequences of fortuitous mutations. Science's refusal to acknowledge the evidence for God, souls, and an afterlife motivates my desire to share Arguments from design that occurred to me in optometry school.

At the conclusion of my second semester of human physiology, the professor said we knew more about human physiology than most medical doctors. I hoped he was exaggerating, but I did know enough to marvel at the complex design and execution requirements necessary to create human beings. Unless our brain, heart, lungs, stomach, intestines, liver, kidneys, and other organ systems work perfectly and in harmony with each other, we have health problems that may bring our life to an end. Western science's rudderless evolutionary process—evolutionary naturalism—provides no plausible explanation for the coordinated design and creation of all the parts necessary to create living, breathing, reproducing organisms capable of simultaneously maintaining all their interdependent organ systems in a state of equilibrium.

Eyes have often been compared to man-made things like clocks and cameras, which obviously could not evolve by happenstance and obviously would require an intelligent, conscious creator. To focus clear images on the back surface of our eyes, the living cells that form each eye's cornea and lens must be clear, like glass. During our first four decades of life, our eyes can focus on a wide range of distances. Only blind faith in evolution theory readily embraces its ability to account for such perfect solutions to the challenging design and execution requirements of eyes. While studying my optometry books, I ran across three aspects of eyes for which evolution theory is not applicable because the necessary sequence of fortuitous mutations requires prior knowledge of the problems to be solved and how they can be solved.

One of the aspects of eyes that suggests the need for an intelligent and creative problem-solving ability is the hyaloid artery. The anterior segment of the eye (lens, iris, ciliary body, and cornea) is nourished by blood vessels that travel from the back of the eyeball, under its outer spherical shell (sclera), all the way to the iris. It takes ten weeks after conception for these blood vessels to reach the anterior segment. If the anterior segment had to wait ten weeks for blood and oxygen, the cells in the anterior segment would die. A faster means of supplying blood to these cells must exist, or the baby will be born blind. The faster means is a blood vessel called the hyaloid artery, which runs in a straight line, instead of in a circuitous route, from the back of the eye to the back of the lens. The arrival of iris blood vessels at ten weeks gestation indicates the establishment of the anterior segment's regular circulation, which makes the hyaloid artery superfluous. After saving the anterior segment, the hyaloid artery breaks up, leaving only small remnants of its previous existence. If the hyaloid artery remained in the middle of the vitreous, it would interfere with vision. It seems highly improbable to me that evolution's "chance and necessity" can manifest fortuitous and timely engineering solutions like a temporary artery.

Another optometry book discussed the size and density of the human fovea's light-receptive cells, which are called cones. The fovea is the portion of the retina that provides the best vision. Cone size and density are comparable to the number of pixels or image quality of a digital camera. The peak density of cones in the human fovea, about 180,000 per square millimeter, limits or determines a person's best possible acuity. Another chapter of the optometry book discussed light's inability to be focused perfectly because focused light forms a diffraction pattern, which limits the image quality or best possible visual acuity. I experienced a profound sense of awe when I read that the diameter of the human eye's diffraction pattern's central maximum is the same as the diameter provided in a previous chapter for the fovea's light-receptive cells. My optometry book did not comment on how perfectly our eye's cone diameter enables us to achieve our best possible acuity: Smaller cone diameters would not provide better vision, and larger diameters would prevent achieving our theoretical best acuity.

I consider our vision to be adequate for our needs; but birds, especially birds of prey, would not be able to survive with our visual abilities. Birds need to fly swiftly between branches and find their prey at great distances. If we could fly between branches, they would be indistinct blurs that we would have difficulty avoiding. Because birds process visual information much faster than humans, they easily see and avoid flying into branches. The visual capabilities of birds (along with reptiles and fish) also surpass ours because the colors that they experience are extrapolated from four, instead of our three, locations on the visual spectrum. Birds of prey can see and follow small animals or fish at distances that are four times farther away than can be seen with twenty-twenty vision. They can see ultraviolet (UV) light and experience greater contrast between shades of color. To see so much better than we do, birds of prey must have smaller, more compact light-receptive cells and a correspondingly smaller diffraction pattern. To achieve a smaller diffraction pattern, birds of prey must have pupils and eyes that are bigger than our eyes. It seems impossible for birds that weight less than fifteen pounds to have bigger eyes than a two-hundred-pound man, but they do because their design requirements make it an absolute necessity. While we have less than 200,000 cones or pixels per square millimeter, birds of prey have a million. To compensate for larger pupil sizes, their corneas and lenses are clearer than ours. To improve vision by reducing aberrations, birds of prey can appropriately modify the shapes of their lenses and corneas. Just like humans, the cone and diffraction pattern sizes for birds of prey are in the same size range or "pixel" size.

A bird of prey that needed glasses would not be able to find food and would starve to death after leaving the nest. For birds of prey, failure to achieve perfect focus is not an option. To achieve perfect focus, the eye's optical elements—cornea and lens—must match up perfectly with the distance to the retina at the back of the eye. The focal length for people-size eyes averages about twenty millimeters. When light rays, which come from far away, focus before reaching the retina, the eye is myopic, or nearsighted. Myopia is the most common eye problem or difficulty in the world. Focusing only one millimeter in front of the retina reduces visual acuity to about 20/400. Legal blindness begins at 20/200 vision, which means a focusing error of only one millimeter diminishes vision beyond what is considered legally blind.

Most biological variables have a wide range of normal measurements. A person can be significantly less than five feet tall or over seven feet tall and be perfectly normal. Most biological variables, such as height, form a bell-shape curve when many measurements are plotted. Most measurements are similar and form the top portion of the bell, and the smaller and larger measurements form the sides and bottom of the bell-shape curve. Only unusually small or large measurements would normally be a cause of functional or health concerns. But, for an eye to see clearly, focusing must be perfect.

How is it possible for eyes with varying sizes and corneal curvatures to consistently achieve perfect focus? When I was a student, no one could answer that question, but the name of the process for achieving perfect focus, emmetropia, is emmetropization. Research using tree shrews, monkeys, and chicks revealed choroidal and scleral mechanisms that compensate for artificially induced focusing problems. The alterability demonstrated by the eyes of chicks, as would be expected because of a bird's vision requirements, was remarkable. The need for a feedback mechanism that monitors and corrects focusing problems was the third requirement for creating eyes that I believe exceed rational expectations for science's evolution theory.

The emmetropization process reminds me of my difficulty backing up a trailer when my daughter moved to Florida. After renting a U-Haul trailer and attaching it to my daughter's car, I helped her move her possessions into the trailer. While driving from California to Florida, the first time, and each subsequent time, that I tried to back up was a nightmare. When the back end of the trailer veered to the left or right, I invariably made the situation worse. I never did figure out how to back up a trailer. Backing up a trailer merely involves appropriately turning a steering wheel; but, for an eye to achieve perfect focus, the front as well as the back surface curvatures of the cornea and lens and the spacing and index of refraction of the optical elements must harmonize perfectly. Relative to guiding eyes toward emmetropia, backing up a trailer is easy.

The eye's three impossibly difficult design and execution challenges for evolution theory (which occurred to me when I was an optometry student) were the hyaloid artery, a perfect match of cone size with the diffraction pattern's central maximum, and emmetropization. Billions of years to "get it right" are of no help when survival-dependent developmental attributes require improbably fortuitous and timely sequences of mutations. Evidence for the sequential development of organisms does not mean those developmental changes occurred without divine guidance. Unassisted evolution, without the well-planned and executed moves of the "divine chess player," only makes sense with a naive and superficial understanding of the complexity of nature's design and execution requirements. The assumption that brains manifest consciousness and evolution theory accounts for everything's origin and development should be treated as refutable hypotheses instead of proven facts.

I wrote about Arguments from design, especially those related to the exacting requirements of eyes, because it is not rational to believe solutions to several complex design problems can be simultaneously and reliably manifested by a mindless mechanism. Western science ignores the significance of Arguments from design by uncritically and dogmatically embracing its materialistic understanding of reality: evolutionary naturalism.

GOD'S REMOVAL FROM SCIENCE'S CONCERNS

By making the Sun, instead of the Earth, the center of our solar system in 1543, Nicolaus Copernicus changed God's perceived relationship with humanity, and he provided science with the first of two discoveries that facilitated the removal of God and souls from science's understanding of reality. In 1859, Charles Darwin provided science with a materialistic explanation for the evolution of life with his book *On the Origin of Species*. His survival-of-the-fittest theory of evolution provided a mindless mechanism to account for the Earth's many and variable forms of life. A random universe cosmology developed during the nineteenth century as Darwin's ideas combined with those of Copernicus and the mechanistic theories of René Descartes. Among the atheistic philosophies inspired by science's random universe cosmology are existentialism, positivism, Marxism, Freudianism, and more recently, the "new atheism" of Richard Dawkins and others.

Neither relocating humanity from the center of the universe nor a mindless chance and necessity explanation for in-species variation rationally justify such a bold move, but Western science has not looked back since turning away from God. To maintain its atheistic paradigms, Western science must habitually ignore Arguments from design and "paranormal" phenomena.

While working on communication satellites in 1964, two Bell Laboratories scientists detected cosmic background radiation. Physicists identified the low-level "noise" coming from every direction in the universe as the fourteen-billion-year-old echo of creation's "Big Bang." Evidence for the Big Bang theory, which harmonizes with the Bible's version of creation, motivated physicists to look for alternative explanations for the universe's creation. Their discovery of just-right-for-our-existence values and ratios for the universe's fundamental physical constants and forces provided the inspiration for the Anthropic Principle. According to the Anthropic Principle, the fundamental physical constants are the precise values necessary to create a universe with living organisms. The formation of stars and galaxies and the evolution of eyes would be impossible if the relative strength of the four fundamental forces were slightly different. Obviously, we do not live in a random universe, and Western science should rethink its random universe cosmology, and stop criticizing and ignoring the evidence for God.

Despite discovering that the universe, in harmony with Arguments from design, was precisely designed to create life, Western science continues to assume Darwin's theory of "natural selection" is more than a partial explanation for evolution. Scientific communities have not responded well to evidence for the universe's abrupt beginning, as described in the Bible, and evidence for a universe precisely designed to enable our existence.

The Anthropic Principle forced scientists to confront the improbability of chance and necessity manifesting a universe that is just right for our existence. You would think that those with atheistic and materialistic worldviews, those who maintain science's paradigms, would look at the Anthropic Principle's implications and become less rigid in their opposition to acknowledging the evidence for God, souls, and an afterlife. But, as pointed out in the preface, research shows that "most people would rather deny or downplay new, uncomfortable information than reshape their world view to accommodate it." In an obvious effort to ignore the Anthropic Principle's implications, physicists are obsessed with William James's 1895 concept of a "multiverse," or many universes. If we live in one of zillions of universes, without God's help we could beat the odds and live in a precisely designed universe that is just right for our existence. Mired in nineteenth-century understandings of reality, today's scientific communities use the concept of a multiverse to avoid "[reshaping] their world view to accommodate" the significance of the Big Bang theory and the Anthropic Principle.

EMOTIONS

During my teens through my twenties, my emotional life was more vivid and varied than in subsequent years. There is a huge variety of emotions without which life would be less interesting and meaningful. Emotions can guide us toward and away from people and experiences, and color our thoughts and experiences. Our visual system, which uses colors to represent the different wavelengths of light in the visual spectrum, can be used as an analogy for the way emotions color our experiences. Grass is green because our visual system assigns the color green to the wavelength of light reflected by grass, and not because the colors we experience necessarily correspond with actual attributes of the visual spectrum or our environment. In other words, the colors that we experience help us to appreciate our surroundings but may not correspond with "reality." Similarly, our emotional responses are powerful but problematic influences upon our understanding of "reality."

I am inclined to believe that each of us experiences, with varying levels of intensity, a limited sampling of an abundance of possible emotions. My inclination was confirmed in 2017 by a UC Berkeley study, led by Dacher Keltner, PhD, that updated psychology's long-held assumption that human emotions are limited to six categories: happiness, sadness, anger, surprise, fear, and disgust. Instead of only six, the study found twenty-seven distinct categories of "feelings" by adding up all the feelings reported by hundreds of people. The study concluded that human emotions are "richer and more nuanced than previously thought."[21] As an example of the size of our emotional pallet, in response to the same set of circumstances, a person might experience individually or in combination guilt, embarrassment, or shame. These emotions feel or color the perception of our circumstances differently. Most emotions are associated with a unique set of physiological changes in our body that, depending upon the emotion, can have positive or adverse effects upon our health. I find it much easier to imagine that emotions exist as a prod to and indicator of spiritual development (soul evolution) than as an aid to survival of the fittest or human evolution. How can a bewildering array of emotions, our most problematic and powerful cause of self-deception, be of assistance to human survival and evolution? But emotions are a good indicator of and stimulant to spiritual growth.

If we are not feigning our emotions, they are spontaneous, unintended (not a product of our will) responses that may not provide desirable assistance relating to and understanding our circumstances. What I imagine to be older, wiser souls are more likely to experience tolerance, humility, generosity, compassion, and love. The emotional responses of older souls have positive health benefits relative to young souls who are more likely to experience intolerance, pride, greed, envy, anger, and hate. Because emotions can greatly add to the joy of living, as well as make our lives so miserable that life becomes unbearable, it makes a lot of sense, both from worldly and spiritual points of view, to replace undesirable tendencies with those virtues that religions have recommended for thousands of years. I believe that a greater effort should be made by school districts to teach children the consequences of desirable and undesirable character traits, values, and emotional responses. John Adams, the second president of the United States, wrote, "There are two educations. One should teach us how to make a living, and the other how to live." Of the two, "how to live" is the most important, but the most neglected. Children should be taught to be exemplary human beings. By teaching children "how to live," which involves understanding and controlling emotions, they will live happier, healthier lives.

HOW TO LIVE: OTHER-CENTERED
AS OPPOSED TO SELF-CENTERED

As I reflect on my college and US Air Force experiences, I realize they are not relevant to this book's theme. Because I want to focus only on experiences and topics that may inspire insight into a spiritual dimension or reality, I am forced to skip ahead to my initial experiences as a self-employed optometrist. In April 1971, I purchased an optometry practice located in the Fox Theater Building in downtown Riverside, California. After purchasing the fifty-year-old optometry practice, I purchased another optometry practice located in Edgemont. Because of a fire and a lack of appropriate rental space in Sunnymead, the practice was recently relocated to Edgemont. The communities of Edgemont, Sunnymead, and Moreno formed the incorporated city of Moreno Valley in 1984. Rental rates and home values in Edgemont, located under the flight path of planes landing at March Air Force Base, were extremely low.

Up to this point, unbeknownst to me, I led a rather sheltered life. The students I knew in high school valued education and wanted to go to college. The students at Berkeley came out of the same mold, but extremely bright students were the rule instead of the exception. The US Air Force's high standards continued to shelter me from people whose actions or circumstances led them to the bottom of the socioeconomic ladder.

During my formative years, I was taught that everyone would be successful if they worked hard enough. This widespread and destructive myth leads to the assumption that people are totally responsible for their lives. With inflated egos, successful people are often unappreciative of the circumstances and blessings that enabled their success, while those who struggle without success are left with no one to blame but themselves. The experiences I want to share happened in an economically depressed neighborhood; but, if my destiny involved working for a morally bankrupt corporation, I could be writing about everything that is diabolical when people and organizations benefit themselves at the expense of others.

There must have been a grapevine for con artists, who put out the word that there was a naïve, new optometrist in town. It seemed as if every disreputable person within several miles found their way into my office. During my first few months as a self-employed optometrist, I was frequently bamboozled out of just compensation for my services. Office policies, which recognize that not everyone can be trusted, had to be established. For the first time in my life, I became aware of people who lacked the character traits to be good employees, parents, or citizens. Preoccupied with their own wants and needs, they seemed to be oblivious or indifferent to the needs of others. Fortunately, my first year of practice was an aberration, and I again became oblivious to human behavior that inflicts pain upon others.

An elementary school nurse told me that she noticed three inappropriately dressed and hungry (no breakfast) siblings arriving late to school. When she went to their home, she discovered that the refrigerator contained lots of beer but no milk for the children. I will never forget the beautiful lady in a wheelchair, who could not be toilet trained or taught how to walk or talk because her father, when she was a baby, had banged her head against the wall until she quit crying. In addition to severely brain-injured adults, my patients included boys, who lived in a home with other boys, whose mothers did not want to raise them. I remember the tears of a lady who cried as she told me how her adult son had stolen her retirement savings. As I examined their grandchildren's eyes, grandparents told me how their daughters had abandoned the children to their care. Even though life reviews during near-death experiences reveal that nothing escapes God's awareness, I became aware that most of the physical and mental injuries inflicted upon others occur outside the awareness of our criminal justice system. I became depressed for the first time in my life. Being a human being became a source of shame instead of pride.

Fortunately, my depression did not last long. From the first Tuesday that I owned the Edgemont practice, and every Tuesday for the next six months, when I tried to leave for lunch, my savior was in the waiting room insisting on taking me to lunch. His name was Bill Markham. I assumed that he was a salesman, but to my surprise, he provided my first exposure to service activities and organizations. Bill took me to a meeting of the Moreno Valley Rotary Club that Tuesday, and every Tuesday for six months before asking if I wanted to join Rotary.

Unlike those whose actions brought on my depression, the Rotarians were among the most prominent and successful members of the community. Among the eighteen members were the school district's superintendent, assistant superintendent, high school and junior high school principals, an elementary school principal, the civilian community's only physician, one of the community's two dentists, and Bill Markham, who owned the area's only hardware store. The Rotarians were among the most respected members of the community, but what most impressed me about them was the selfless (other-centered as opposed to self-centered) way they conducted themselves. Prior to meeting the Rotarians, my experiences had not included selfless people and activities. They filled me with a sense of awe and restored my ability to feel good about being a human being.

The extreme range of character traits that I experienced during my first few months in practice mystified me. Heredity and life experiences did not satisfactorily explain how one person can be indifferent to the needs of others, while another person seems more concerned with others than with themself. What would be the explanation for a few of my patients and the Rotarians being so incredibly different? Because most people lie somewhere between these two extremes, it is easy to not be aware of those who are at the extreme ends of the character spectrum. I wanted to identify with the Rotarians, but their selflessness was not a conscious choice. People do not choose to be loving and caring or insensitive to the needs of others. Why are there saints as well as sociopaths? Is there something beyond nature and nurture? What accounts for the extreme ends of the character spectrum?

The contrast between those who were concerned about and those who were indifferent to the needs of others stimulated thoughts about happiness and human tendencies and values. Our culture encourages us to pursue the fulfillment of our desires. But my experience with Rotarians suggests that success and happiness are found by acknowledging and fulfilling expectations and opportunities—especially opportunities to serve others—as they arise. As children, it means obeying our parents; as students, it means doing our assignments to the best of our ability; and, as adults, it means fulfilling our responsibilities. The Rotarians lead successful lives because, when they were young, pleasing their parents and teachers was more important than doing what they wanted to do. In leadership positions and as business owners, they were concerned with the needs of their employees and those they were in business to serve. As husbands (women were excluded from membership in Rotary until 1987), their primary concern was the needs of their wives and children. The Rotarians were role models for John Adams's advice about knowing not only "how to make a living," but also "how to live."

Rotary has two mottos: *Service above self,* and *He profits most who serves best.* Neither motto made any sense to me. I was taught to believe that diligence and hard work were the secrets to a better life for everyone. No one told me that selflessness is a virtue, or that we benefit ourselves as we benefit others. I grew up with no role models for Rotary's mottos. What impressed me the most about the Rotarians was the motivation behind their Rotary membership. Empathy and concern for others motivated Rotarians to combine their time, talents, and money to serve those living in distant countries as well as their own neighbors.

God's involvement was not overt, but it occurred to me that God may have arranged my self-absorbed patients in juxtaposition to my first awareness of people who appeared to be more concerned with the needs of others than with their own needs. Without my continued involvement in Rotary, I would not have experienced the transformative influence of serving others. The primary beneficiaries of organizations like

Rotary are their members, because service activities open the hearts of those who serve. When I acquired an understanding of reincarnation philosophy, I realized the Rotarians were old souls who had developed empathy and concern for others by experiencing, during many lifetimes, their own physical and emotional challenges. Service activities and organizations are the best places to find role models for "how to live."

The contrast between the Rotarians and my self-absorbed patients provided insight into the importance of being able to see with humility and empathy beyond oneself. In 1944, Viktor Frankl—an Austrian neurologist, psychiatrist, and Holocaust survivor—experienced similar revelations as a prisoner in Germany's Auschwitz concentration camp. He "noticed that prisoners who were able to see beyond themselves and help others often stood the greatest chance of day-to-day survival." Viktor Frankl's personal insights, research, and books (such as *Man's Search for Meaning*) inspired others to investigate "the role of meaning and purpose in human life." His research, as well as "a fairly large body of scientific studies, suggests that … we thrive when we are working for some greater good." Researchers Jeffrey Froh and Robert Emmons found that children who readily experience gratitude are "better able to see beyond themselves."[22]

Robert Emmons, the world's leading scientific expert on gratitude, wrote, "Some people suffer from a condition known as excessive entitlement: They feel they deserve more than others, a disproportionately greater amount of a particular good beyond what would be considered appropriate. They are dissatisfied with whatever they receive, whether it is pay, promotion, or praise." I attribute the depression that I initially experienced as a sole proprietor to excessive entitlement personalities and the physical and mental pain they inflict without regret. Professor Emmons wrote that "gratitude reduces excessive entitlement" and "produces higher levels of positive emotions that are beneficial in the workplace such as joy, enthusiasm, and optimism; and lower levels of the destructive impulses of envy, resentment, greed, and bitterness."[23]

Materialism is a word that can be used to refer to two completely different concepts. I have used the word materialism to refer to the belief that all things in nature, even our consciousness, are solely the results of physical, material, interactions. Materialists, in this context, believe that consciousness is created and maintained by matter. In this section of this chapter, I am using the word materialism to refer to the human trait of being preoccupied with possessions. Materialists, those concerned with the number and quality of their possessions, assume success and happiness are associated with possessions and money. Decades of research consistently find that materialistic people are less likely to experience empathy and concern for others, and they are less likely to have meaningful relationships with others. Their lives are more likely to be associated with anxiety, depression, and unhappiness.

An inevitable feature of capitalism is the continual bombardment of potential consumers with advertising messages that equate happiness and social status with consumption. Our country's preoccupation with consumption is promoted by corporate strategies that seek perpetual growth. Promoting consumption depletes limited resources while increasing materialism, competitiveness, selfishness, anxiety, depression, and unhappiness. Is it any wonder so many of my Edgemont patients led unhappy, dysfunctional lives?

Fortunately, we live at a time when several years of groundbreaking scientific research exists to guide us in our search for happiness. Among the most prominent experts on happiness is Sonja Lyubomirsky, who received a million-dollar grant to conduct research on the possibility of perpetually increasing happiness. The information in the following three paragraphs is derived from her books, *The How of Happiness* and *The Myths of Happiness.*

Based upon studies with identical twins, 50 percent of a person's long-term happiness is genetic. We attribute our moods and happiness to our circumstances, but research finds that a person's happiness has only a 10 percent correlation with the day-to-day circumstances of their life. The research finding for everyone to appreciate is that over 40 percent of a person's happiness relates to things that are under their control and can be learned. These habits of thinking and being relate to a person's attitudes and motivations. Happiness is associated with experiencing gratitude, concern for others, and altruistic endeavors.

Experiencing gratitude makes us happier in several different ways. When we acknowledge our life's blessings and take pleasure in them, we derive the most happiness from them. Those with an optimistic, positive attitude have less difficulty dealing with life's unpleasant and stressful circumstances. Grateful people are aware of and appreciate their life's blessings, are more likely to help others, and are less likely to be materialistic. Regardless of their life's circumstances, those who readily experience gratitude tend to have lower resting blood pressure, and to experience better sleep and fewer illnesses because they have stronger immune systems, and experience fewer aches and pains. They also tend to be more positive, likable, and happy.

A growing body of research reveals that volunteering provides the same benefits as having an attitude of gratitude. Altruistic endeavors provide a sense of purpose and are associated with being more resistant to stress and inflammation, having better physical and mental health, and living a longer, happier life. Now that science has evidence for the benefits to society and its inhabitants for prosocial skills like gratitude and empathy, John Adams's advice about learning how to live should be part of every child's school curriculum.

I would not know, without appropriate personal experiences and research, that grateful hearts tend to be happy hearts, while hearts that are ungrateful and yearn for the things of this world tend to be unhappy. I would not know that the best way to prevent children from becoming entitled brats is to teach them the teachable, prosocial skill of gratitude. And I would not know that dozens of studies have shown that gratitude combats feelings of entitlement.

If you were raised in a religious household, chances are good that you were exposed to these concepts as a child. The Bible is filled with praise and encouragement for an attitude of gratitude and concern for the interests of others. Thanksgiving, Christmas, and Easter are celebrations inspired by gratitude. With respect to the things of this world, Jesus said, "Beware! Keep yourselves from covetousness, for a man's life doesn't consist of the abundance of the things which he possesses."[24] The Golden Rule, "As you would like people to do to you, do exactly so to them," encourages people to anticipate and fulfill the needs of others. The apostle Paul wrote, "In everything give thanks, for this is the will of God in Christ Jesus toward you."[25] He also wrote that "doing nothing through rivalry or through conceit, but in humility, each counting others better than himself; each of you not just looking to his own things, but each of you also to the things of others."[26]

Both the Old and New Testaments are saturated with encouragement for an attitude of gratitude and selflessness. Islam's holy Koran (14:7) states, "If you are grateful, I will give you more." The sacred books of Islam's mystical branch, Sufism, contain chapters devoted to developing gratitude. Ancient Eastern religious teachings focus on freeing the mind from worldly concerns and opening the heart. Buddha is believed to have condensed his teachings into one sentence:

"Nothing whatsoever is to be clung to as 'I' or mine." Hinduism's Mahatma Gandhi wrote, "The best way to find your self is to lose yourself in the service of others."

Because I was not raised in a religious household and did not experience altruistic service activities before joining Rotary, I did not know about the personal benefits to those who serve others and readily experience gratitude. The Rotary motto—*He profits most who serves best*—and the personal benefits of having "an attitude of gratitude" are not, at least in my opinion, logical or intuitive. Without appropriate instruction or experience, how would anyone know of the profound benefits to those who readily experience gratitude and selflessly serve others? Evidence for "supernormal" prophetic revelation is suggested by the similarity of the prosocial skills or ways of thinking and being taught by those who inspired the world's major religions. Unfortunately, this insight, like Arguments from design and the Anthropic Principle, is unlikely to change the dogmatically held atheistic biases of Western science, philosophy, and academia.

THE FOUR-WAY TEST OF THE THINGS WE THINK, SAY, OR DO

During the first few decades of my life, I was perplexed by the absence within Christianity of ethical guidance commensurate with the capabilities of the universe's creator. Thousands of years ago, the Ten Commandments' "thou shalt nots" may have sufficed, but they are too specific to provide guidance for a variety of circumstances. The Golden Rule made up for the Ten Commandments' failings, until I realized how different one person can be from another.

During the summer of 1964, I worked as the swimming pool lifeguard at the same San Diego County YMCA camp that I attended as a child. During a boys' camping session, I went to Julian for lunch with a carload of cabin counselors.

One of the counselors read a love letter written to him by one of the boys in his cabin. Another counselor boasted that he and a couple other sailors, when he was in the US Navy, lured gay men to a remote location in San Diego's Balboa Park and beat them up. Until that moment, I was completely unaware that people could be romantically attracted to members of their own sex. The "othering" problem of homophobia was also completely new to me. Compassion and concern for the boy's welfare were conspicuously absent from the conversation. Without the counselors facing their own consequences if they abused the boy, his letter could have led to his physical injury.

This experience comes to mind because, while experiencing the content of the boy's letter and the counselor's comments, I was thinking how incredibly inappropriate the Golden Rule—"As you would like people to do to you, do exactly so to them"—was and always will be for this boy. Because everyone marches to the tune of their unique drummer, providing ethical guidance may be difficult, but surely not for God, the drummer who plays the tunes. My inclination to believe that God should provide us with flawless ethical guidance revealed my inclination to think of myself as a human being instead of as a spiritual being. If, as the first chapter suggests, our consciousness exists before our birth and after our death, and arises from spirit instead of matter, then we are spiritual beings in need of developing inner guidance by becoming spiritually conscious and developing a conscience (encounters with God's disapproval) by experiencing the effects upon others and the consequences of our actions.

During my initial introduction to Rotary, the Rotarians took pride in teaching me about Rotary and sharing their Rotary experiences. The previous section of this chapter, *How to Live: Other-Centered as Opposed to Self-Centered*, discussed the wisdom contained in Rotary's mottoes: *Service above self*, and *He profits most who serves best*. The other gem the Rotarians expected me to memorize and apply in both my personal and business life was Rotary's Four-Way Test. Unlike my initial response to Rotary's mottoes, the Four-Way Test made perfect sense to me. It was the ethical guidance I expected from Christianity. The thought occurred to me that God had finally updated the Western world's ethical guidance.

Herbert J. Taylor is given credit for the Four-Way Test, but his autobiography confirms my assumption that the Four-Way Test required the Providence of God. The following information and quotations come from his book, *The Herbert J. Taylor Story.* "In 1930, in the grim days of the Great Depression, millions of men were out of jobs, companies were going bankrupt everywhere you looked; even banks were failing." A local bank's vice president, who believed Mr. Taylor could save Club Aluminum Products Company (CAPC) from bankruptcy, persuaded Mr. Taylor into working fewer hours for his employer so that he could serve as CAPC's president and hopefully save the jobs of CAPC's 250 employees.

Before resigning from his current job, taking a cut in salary to $6,000 from $33,000 a year, and personally borrowing $6,100 to help CAPC with its financial problems; Mr. Taylor "did a lot of praying ...asking the Lord for guidance" before being convinced he "was being directed by God." Mr. Taylor wrote, "At that time, it was quite apparent that I was the only person convinced that the company could be saved. I was convinced because the Holy Spirit told me so." As a Christian who wholeheartedly strived to do God's will, Mr. Taylor believed "things can work out well for you if you place yourself in the hands of God's wisdom and let yourself be guided by His will in even the most difficult circumstances."

Because CAPC's competitors had good products and employees, Mr. Taylor believed CAPC needed something that was superior to its competitors. He decided it should be the character and dependability of their employees. "What we needed was a simple, easily remembered guide to right conduct – a sort of ethical yardstick – which all of us in the company could memorize and apply to what we thought, said, and did in our relations with others."

Mr. Taylor searched through many books for the right words to guide the employees, but the right words eluded him. He then did what he often did when confronting problems he did not know how to solve: he leaned over his desk and prayed. After a few moments of prayer, he "looked up and reached for a white paper card. Then [he] wrote down ... [what he] called The Four-Way Test of the things we think, say, or do."

1. Is it the *truth*?
2. Is it *fair* to all concerned?
3. Will it build *good will* and *better friendships*?
4. Will it be *beneficial* to all concerned?

Mr. Taylor thought about the Four-Way Test for a few months while applying it in several business situations. After satisfying himself that he and others could live up to the Four-Way Test, he presented his ideas to the company's department heads. When they applied the test to advertising copy, words like "better," "best," "greatest," and "finest" were removed from their advertisements. Eventually, all employees were expected to memorize and use the Four-Way Test. Establishing a tool that encourages concern for truth, fairness, goodwill, friendship, and mutual benefit improved CAPC's relations with its competitors, customers, and among its employees. "This combination of God's help, The Four-Way Test – which came in answer to prayer – good people, and good products enabled us to cancel our $400,000 debt in five years. We paid it off with interest – every single dollar of it!"

Mr. Taylor was president of Rotary's first club from 1939 to 1940, and president of Rotary International from 1954 to 1955. In 1942, one of Rotary International's directors asked Mr. Taylor if Rotary could use the Four-Way Test "to promote Rotary's objectives of high ethical standards." The test soon became a central and prominent part of Rotary as clubs around the world promoted the use of the Four-Way Test of the things we think, say, or do.[27]

Imagine the impact on human civilization if everyone throughout the world was taught the Four-Way Test and was expected to revere truth, fairness, and concern for the welfare of others. These are the values taught by Jesus but not unequivocally expressed within Christianity. Individuals, politicians, and corporations get away with flagrant abuses of ethical concerns because, in part, they were never given and are not held accountable to clear expectations. The following two paragraphs provide examples of the consequences for America's citizens when people and corporations are not given and expected to follow ethical guidelines.

In 1994, the "Cigarette Papers" provided evidence of the tobacco industry's false statements and distortions of their own research about the addictive nature of nicotine and the health consequences of smoking. A September 16, 2015, *Inside Climate News* exposé—"Exxon: The Road Not Taken"—revealed decades of Exxon's false and misleading representations of their own research on the connection between fossil-fuel consumption and climate change. A November 2016 *JAMA Internal Medicine* article titled "Sugar Industry and Coronary Heart Disease Research: A Historical Analysis of Internal Industry Documents" reveals that, since the early 1960s, the Sugar Association systematically manipulated medical research findings, legislators, and public opinion to protect its economic interests. Their goal, which corrupt politicians helped them to achieve, was to obtain the federal government's assistance in motivating Americans to increase their sugar consumption by eating less fat. Clear "rules of the road," like the Four-Way Test, could have prevented the sugar industry from using the tobacco industry's tactics of hiding research findings which should be shared with medical doctors and their patients. An April 2014 JAMA Internal Medicine study—"Added Sugar Intake and Cardiovascular Disease Mortality among US Adults"—found that, relative to those who consume the least added sugar, those who consume the most are almost three times as likely to die from cardiovascular disease.

If the application and use of the Four-Way Test had prevented lenders from providing subprime loans to unqualified homebuyers, the Four-Way Test may have prevented the 2007 subprime mortgage crisis and the worst recession since the Great Depression. Aided and abetted by a morally bankrupt corporate culture, Wall Street corporations bundled risky mortgages into sure-to-fail mortgage-backed securities to sell to their own clients. After making suckers out of their own clients, Wall Street firms added insult to injury by short selling the securities. When circumstances encourage deplorable, self-serving behavior, belief in God, an afterlife, and an ethical guide like the Four-Way Test may prevent humanity from causing its own destruction.

Baby food may convince those who do not believe that the education system and parents need to do a better job of teaching desirable human values to children. After the 2019 investigative findings of Healthy Babies Bright Futures found toxic metals in 95 percent of the baby food available in grocery stores, Congress launched an investigation. Baby food was found to have up to 91 times the arsenic, 177 times the lead, and 69 times the cadmium levels allowed in bottled water. Toxic metals can cause devastating and permanent damage to a baby's developing brain. Despite the consequences to society and their customers, the congressional investigation found internal company documents that revealed baby food manufacturers knowingly selling contaminated baby food to unsuspecting parents.

When matter—me and my company or industry's self-interest—is all that matters, as exemplified by the above companies and industries, "The End – the fulfillment of goals and desires – Justifies the Means." Instead of being guided by the-end-justifies-the-means, wouldn't desirable ends for "all concerned" be achieved more equitably if corporate America was guided by concern for truth, fairness, and mutual benefit: the Four-Way Test? Widespread adoption and use of the Four-Way Test would prevent the consequences of deplorable human behavior. Because the Four-Way Test has no religious association, it could be incorporated into elementary school curricula. Imagine living in a society in which everyone has been taught to value and expect from others honesty and concern for others.

"Religions are many, but God is One."
—*Sathya Sai Baba*

Chapter 5
My High School Prayers Bear Fruit

Most of my life I look back on and
I don't see how that really happened.
I would say that about most of my life.
—*Joan Baez*

In the previous chapter, I skipped over experiencing downward causation: empirical evidence that "thoughts are things ... that we send forth to fill the world with good results, or ill."[28] After graduating from San Francisco's Hastings law school in 1970, my brother, Jerry, took the California Bar Examination while staying with our dad in San Diego. Despite living one hundred miles from San Diego, I coincidentally was at Dad's when Jerry took the bar exam, and a few months later when Jerry learned he'd passed the bar exam.

When Jerry returned to Dad's home after completing the grueling bar exam, he complained that his back itched. Taking his shirt off revealed why: across Jerry's upper back were five or six large, raised red welts. Nothing Jerry tried brought relief from the discomfort caused by stress hives until the letter arrived informing Jerry that he passed the bar exam. Supportive of Henry van Dyke's conjecture, those raised red welts disappeared that evening. Is Henry van Dyke's speculation—"Thoughts are things" that "build our future, thought by thought, for good or ill"—true? Did the stress of passing the bar cause Jerry's hives? Despite the coincidental evidence, it did not seem plausible to me that stress could manifest as raised red welts. During the 1970s, I frequently encountered ideas that required persistent exposure, which I attribute to God's grace, before I related to them with anything other than skepticism or disbelief. The French writer and philosopher Michel de Montaigne beautifully captured in *Essays* "my" experiences and insights with these words:

> It is a stupid presumption to go about despising and condemning as false anything that seems to us improbable; this is a common fault among those who think they have more intelligence than the crowd. I used to be like that once, and if I heard talk of ghosts walking, or some other tale I could not swallow, I would pity the poor people who were taken in by such nonsense. And now I find that I was at least as much to be pitied myself.

Those who are inclined to regard Henry van Dyke's speculations about thoughts as "**occult** nonsense" and "pseudoscience" may be surprised to learn that accumulating scientifically gathered evidence suggests that the influence of our thoughts greatly exceeds commonsense assumptions. Harvard Medical School's special health report, *Living Longer, Living Better*, covered four studies that suggest that optimism significantly improves health. During the 1960s, the University of North Carolina gave 6,959 entering students a comprehensive personality test. During the next forty years, 476 died for a variety of reasons. The most pessimistic students, relative to the most optimistic, were 42 percent more likely to be among those who died. Two Dutch studies obtained similar results. Researchers in another study tracked 545 elderly men who were cardiovascular disease-free when they were tested in 1985 for dispositional optimism. During the next fifteen years, optimists were 55 percent less likely to die from cardiovascular disease. A study of 726 football fans during two NFL seasons, published in the August 7, 2013, issue of *Psychological Science*, found that the day after the game, the fans in the losing team's city ate more saturated fat and calories than usual, while fans in the winning cities consumed less saturated fat and fewer calories. Previous studies found that traffic fatalities, heart attacks, domestic violence, and alcohol-related crimes increased in cities whose NFL teams lost. These and other studies show that our thoughts "fill the world with good results, or ill."

FOX THEATER
PRACTICE–RELATED EXPERIENCES

My two optometry practices provided completely different life experiences. After almost six years, I relocated the Edgemont practice to Sunnymead and notified all my patients, including my Fox Theater practice patients, about the new practice location. Initially, the Fox Theater practice generated most of my income, but the Moreno Valley practice became too busy to continue both practices. Even though experiences related to the Fox Theater practice led to the answers to my high school prayers, finding a buyer was as unlikely as when the previous owner essentially gave the fifty-year-old optometry practice to me to get rid of it.

In the suite to the left of my Fox Theater practice's suite was a boutique specializing in 1960s-style clothing for teenagers. During the lunch hour, I occasionally stepped into the boutique to talk to Gail, the boutique's owner. Gail told me that, one evening each week, she and four or five other women met at Hazel Denning's home to be concurrently hypnotized and regressed by Hazel to experience their previous lives. Gail described past life experiences that she believed to be the explanation for this life's idiosyncrasies and phobias. She attributed this life's fear of swimming pools to a past-life memory of drowning in ancient Egypt. Gail described realizing, while experiencing past-life memories, that the souls of the people in her past-life memories are the souls within this life's friends and family members. Gail said her "soul group" had assembled prior to their current lives to plan and coordinate their current incarnations. While encouraging me to attend the monthly meetings of the Parapsychology Association of Riverside (PAR), Gail said Hazel Denning was PAR's primary founding member.

Does Gail's understanding of her experiences at Hazel Denning's home seem preposterous to you? It did to me. A critical review of *The Search for Bridey Murphy*, which I read when I was in high school, provided my only awareness of the concepts of reincarnation and past-life regression. No matter how often or confidently Gail told me about her experiences at Hazel Denning's home, my "commonsense" prior programing or skepticism of unfamiliar concepts prevented me from being able to relate to Gail's ideas and experiences.

If we are members of soul groups, as Gail suggested, our lives are preplanned and directed outside our conscious awareness. Our reality would literally be as Shakespeare wrote, "All the world's a stage. And all the men and women merely players" who are oblivious to their underlying true reality. This is a counterintuitive understanding of our reality that harmonizes with Eastern religions and philosophy as well as migration phenomena.

The migration of monarch butterflies is one of many examples of phenomena whose initiation and continuation would be easier to explain if "all the world's a stage" and God is the director. In the fall of 1975, researchers in Canada tagged monarch butterflies before they left for their winter "nesting" location. Two months and over two thousand miles later, the tagged butterflies arrived at specific fir trees in Mexico. In subsequent experiments, the tagged monarch butterflies were relocated and released hundreds of miles east so that their usual flight path (or heading) would take them to the middle of the Gulf of Mexico. As if guided by a divine copilot, the flying insects made appropriate course corrections and arrived at their usual "nesting" location in Mexico. While monarchs living east of the Rocky Mountains migrate to fir trees in Mexico, monarchs living west of the Rocky Mountains migrate to and hibernate on eucalyptus trees located in and around Pacific Grove in California. During February or March, monarch butterflies come out of hibernation, mate, and migrate back north and east to where they emerged from their life cycle's chrysalis stage. Staying where they hibernate is not an option because of a lack of desirable food, milkweed plants, for the caterpillar portion of their life cycle. The life cycle of a monarch butterfly becomes inexplicable when you learn that they hibernate in the very same tree each year despite transitioning through four stages: egg, caterpillar, chrysalis, and butterfly. Each autumn, a new generation of monarch butterflies heads south and west to hibernate in the tree used by the butterfly that laid the egg that produced the caterpillar that became the chrysalis from which they emerged. How do monarch butterflies migrate thousands of miles on a journey they have never taken before to a specific tree they have never seen before? Materialistic, "it's in their genes," explanations are at least as implausible as believing monarch butterflies are directed by, as written in Ephesians 4:6, "one God and Father of all, who is over all, and through all, and in all."

If consciousness arises from brains, how can the migration of monarch butterflies continue from generation to generation with new brains for each migration? If consciousness arises from brains, how can children have confirmable previous-life memories?

Not long after I became aware of Gail's experiences at Hazel Denning's home, Hazel's husband, Burl Denning, came in to get his eyes examined. I met Mr. Denning when I went to the Bank of America to enable my patients to use their credit card. Because he seemed like a levelheaded, conservative banker, I asked Mr. Denning, after the eye examination, what he thought about his wife's unusual activities. He said his hobby was selling Shaklee products, and despite saying that he did not pay attention to Hazel's interests, he said, "One of my wife's friends, with nothing more than my birth information, described me in an astrology report more insightfully than I could have written." His reply surprised me because I did not expect a rational person to have anything positive to say about astrology. It was intuitively obvious to me that the relative positions of celestial bodies could not possibly correlate with anything about anyone.

My first wife and I became separated in the summer of 1975 and divorced the following summer. The transition from married to divorced provided insight into the fragile nature of our self-image. Our life's circumstances, relationships, possessions, and memories mysteriously combine to create our "I am" sense of autonomous reality. Despite embracing and discarding circumstances, roles, and relationships while passing through childhood, adulthood, and old age, our "I am" sense of self persists until an event, like a divorce, shatters our "I am" touchstone and reveals the insubstantial, imaginary or unreal nature of our self-image. Because a person's self-image is no more substantial than thoughts and beliefs, after my divorce I was able to—unlike Humpty Dumpty—put myself back together again. I experienced this difficult chapter in my life through the fog of depression.

In early 1976, I began dating. The first three women I dated were enthusiastic proponents of the same book: *Linda Goodman's Sun Signs.* I was astonished that seemingly intelligent women believed a person's birth date could reveal anything about them. The concept was simply preposterous. Despite having opposing views on astrology, the first woman that I asked out was a remarkably serendipitous choice. On our first date, she said she had been planning on asking me out. She was a previous airline stewardess and a graduate student in psychology. Asking her out had nothing to do with her knowledge of psychology, but that was because I did not anticipate benefiting from her insights as I struggled to understand and embrace my life's new circumstances. Being in a relationship reduced my loneliness and depression.

After six weeks of dating, I was appreciative of our relationship and was looking forward to our date on Friday. To avoid a parking ticket, after spending the morning examining patients in Edgemont, I had to park four blocks from the Fox Theater building. In my mind's eye, as I walked to the Fox Theater Building, I saw a red-and-blue trimmed airmail envelope, with my handwritten name on it, floating in a fluffy, pink cloud. I immediately knew the content of the letter, the unwritten thoughts of the writer, and the letter's location behind my office door.

Except for when I am asleep and dreaming, I do not experience seeing anything in my mind's eye. People report a wide range of differences in their ability to experience vivid mental images, but my usual inability to experience mental images may be unusual. The extraordinary clairvoyant experience—instant awareness of a letter, its contents, and its significance—caused my heart to beat so fast and forcefully that I felt like I was having a heart attack.

When I got to the office, I unlocked the door, picked up the mail, sat at the receptionist's desk, and looked without success for the anticipated letter. While wondering about my amazing but apparently spurious experience, I looked up and noticed a heavy curtain hanging just above the floor next to the door's mail slot. I thought, "The letter may have passed through the mail slot after the mail was delivered and been diverted under the curtain." With renewed anxiety, I reached under the curtain and found the red-and-blue trimmed envelope with my handwritten name on it. The letter's contents were exactly as I somehow instantly knew: "Our relationship is taking up too much of my time; Our Friday date is off; Do not call me; I will call you." My brief encounter with clairvoyance also revealed that she had no intention of calling. As a footnote to this letter, I could describe the letter found under the curtain as a carbon copy of my original, psychic reception of the letter's contents. In chapter 7, I will introduce you to someone who receives all their correspondence in the same manner I received this letter. They do not even bother to read their mail because "it's just a carbon copy."

Seeing a pink cloud with a letter in it is the only time in my life that I can recall seeing a mental image when I was not sleeping. Having my first and only clairvoyant experience served two purposes: It motivated me to look for and find the letter; and it enabled me to know that, even if some people are merely pretending to be psychic, being psychic is a real possibility.

After I started to date the third lady in a row who raved about Linda Goodman's book on Sun signs, during my lunch hour I saw the book in a used bookstore's window display. I purchased the book, and that evening, I wrote descriptions of five people whose birth dates and personality characteristics I felt I knew. I then read Linda Goodman's descriptions. Her description of my Sun sign was remarkably insightful and accurate. I identified with everything Linda Goodman wrote about my Sun sign, but I did not identify with the other Sun sign descriptions. Linda Goodman's Sun sign descriptions captured each of the five people more insightfully than what I had written. She even made me aware of things about myself that I was oblivious to until I read her book. I expected my experiment to confirm my "commonsense" assumption that a person's tendencies could not possibly correlate with their birth date. But the opposite happened, suggesting that I should be more skeptical of my "commonsense" logic.

Three years after my experiences with Sun signs, Beverly, who only knew me as another student in one of PAR's classes, asked if I would provide her with the date, time, and place of my birth so she could calculate my natal chart and tell me all about myself. A few weeks after I provided Beverly with the contents of my birth certificate, she provided me with an eleven-page, single-spaced astrology report. In this book's third chapter, I wrote about a "perplexing aspect of experiencing being me." I was astonished when I read Beverly's accurate description and explanation for the "unintended and unkind words which [...] popped out of my mouth." She wrote, "It must be very confusing ... to have Aries Rising. He can't understand why or when he annoys people by being aggressive and forceful. His Aries impulsiveness will show occasionally and truly bewilder his true nature."

Beverly conferred upon me her time, talent, and my own personal astrology report. I was amazed how much can be predicted and explained from a person's birth information. Skeptics, who dismiss astrology and other "occult nonsense," lack personal positive experiences with the phenomena. My experiences with astrology revealed that common sense and logic are poor substitutes for actual experience. Not only did my experiences suggest that astrology is a form of divination that mysteriously works, but my sequence of experiences with astrology appear to be too well choreographed to merely be a sequence of coincidences.

Since I was in my thirties, I do not recall meeting anyone who was interested in astrology or my Sun sign. Even though astrology makes as much sense to me as wave-particle duality and entanglement, Linda Goodman's book and Beverly's astrology report suggest to me that much of what we experience as our sense of self—our personal peculiarities or tendencies— is imposed upon us. But how? Is astrology's premise true? Are we like puppets controlled by strings connected to the Sun, Moon, and planets? Or are our strings connected to something else whose influence astrologers reveal with a remarkable degree of accuracy? The implications of astrology combined with the doctrine of reincarnation suggest that, with each incarnation, "we" can be molded, like moist clay, with proclivities suited to each incarnation. While reading Beverly's accurate description of my peculiarities, it occurred to me that, if astrology (puppets on strings) is true, my sense of autonomy is an illusion. These speculations are easily embraced when applied to someone whose thoughts and actions are consistent and predictable.

During 1976, when I began dating and occasionally talking with Gail next door, I had an experience that was too extraordinary to be believable, but I am going to share it with you anyway. The Church of Religious Science near Fairmont Park is about a mile from the Fox Theater. Prior to this experience, I was unaware of New Thought churches like Religious Science. Just before I was ready to go home on a Saturday morning, the Church of Religious Science's minister, Reverend Madalyn DeGrace, arrived to pick up her glasses. After delivering her glasses, I locked the office door as we left together. I drove home and heard the phone ringing when I entered the house. Anxious to write Sunday's sermon when she arrived at the church, Reverend DeGrace immediately discovered that one of the temples on her new glasses was not attached. Unable to use the glasses, she obtained my unlisted phone number from a member of her congregation employed by the phone company. When I answered the phone, Reverend DeGrace asked me to drive back to my office to fix her glasses. Not more than fifty minutes after we left together, I unlocked the door, entered, and stood dumbfounded looking for a leak in the ceiling. Precisely placed puddles of what I assumed to be water surrounded, without touching, all the objects on the glass surface of the receptionist's desk. Reverend DeGrace walked through the open door and asked what I was so concerned about. After I showed her the blobs of liquid on the desk and pointed out to her that other than the Fox Theater's manager,

I had the only key, she acted as if seeing mysterious blobs of liquid was an ordinary event. She said, "Things like this happen to me all the time. Once, when I was sewing, I picked up my scissors, cut the thread, and put the scissors back where I picked them up. The next time I reached for my scissors, they were not there! To this day, I have not found those scissors."

After I fixed her glasses, she handed me the book in her hand and said, "A man in the congregation loaned this book to me. It should give you some insight into this experience. After you finish reading it, bring it back to me at the church so I can return it." The book was the first nonfiction book on "paranormal" phenomena that I ever read. I was unaware of the existence of books about human experiences and scientific research that Western science ignores because the phenomena, like Arguments from design, are not compatible with science's atheistic paradigms.

Before continuing with my experiences, I want to attempt to clarify terms with variable and confusing meanings and understandings. The branch of philosophy concerned with the nature of reality is called metaphysics. I am not interested in philosophy's abstract themes and speculations. I am writing this book to elucidate the evidence for reincarnation and your spiritual reality. The word metaphysics is often used to apply to phenomena labeled "paranormal" and "supernormal," to exclude them from "the furniture" (content) of Western science's understanding of reality. I dislike the terms supernormal and paranormal because they imply the phenomena being referred to are not normal. I put quotation marks around paranormal and supernormal because the phenomena would be included within science's understanding of our phenomenal reality if science wanted, with an open mind, to investigate and understand them.

Metaphysical fiction, like science fiction, can range from possible speculations to complete nonsense. Metaphysical fiction and bogus claims can make separating fact from fiction impossible for those who lack personal esoteric experience with the phenomena covered in this book. In the same way that expertise with mathematics and music is dependent upon aptitude and experience, only those with aptitude-dependent relevant personal experiences and abilities can competently relate to and evaluate "paranormal" and "supernormal" phenomena.

The ceiling did not have a leak, and the mysterious appearance of blobs of liquid on the desk's glass surface never occurred again. The extraordinary nature and timing of this experience and the clairvoyant experience with the letter could not have happened by chance. Improbable, yet perfectly synchronized, events must have meaning beyond mere coincidence. I believe these and future experiences are God's responses to my high school prayers. The clairvoyant experience with the letter revealed the reality of psychic phenomena and abilities. Finding and reading that letter transformed me from a disinterested skeptic to someone anxious to attend a meeting of the Parapsychology Association of Riverside. The mysterious physical phenomena of precisely placed puddles on my desk happened within days of my one and only clairvoyant experience. These experiences redefined or expanded my understanding of our phenomenal reality and directed my curiosity toward phenomena that Western science ignores.

The book lent to me by Reverend DeGrace, *Arigo: Surgeon of the Rusty Knife*, documents the observations of American doctors and tells the story of a Brazilian peasant who was a trance-guided surgeon-healer for over two decades. While in a trance guided by the spirit of a German doctor, Arigo merely needed to look at people to make accurate diagnoses, even of blood pressure. His ability to cure health problems, which the local doctors said were incurable, brought thousands of patients to his door. While in a trance, Arigo successfully performed surgeries with unsterilized kitchen knives and pocketknives. With verbal commands, he stopped the flow of blood, and he wrote sophisticated medical prescriptions without medical or pharmacological knowledge. Without the benefits of anesthetics and antibiotics, his patients seldom experienced pain or infection. Motion pictures made by Brazilian and American doctors documented Arigo's surgeries and ability to cure cancer and other potentially fatal diseases.

I wondered what a Brazilian healer had to do with mysterious blobs of liquid on my desk. Eventually, I realized Arigo and my "paranormal" experiences were examples of phenomena that Western science files under metaphysics: topics to be ignored, ridiculed, or confined within abstract, theoretical philosophy. My clairvoyant experience with the letter and the mysterious puddles on my desk do not lend themselves to scientific research. Only those blessed with "paranormal" experiences receive the benefit of knowing with certainty that they really happened. But not all metaphysical phenomena exceed science's grasp. Remarkable people like Arigo and the investigators in this book's first chapter provide examples of "paranormal" phenomena that lend themselves to scientific research and verification. But, for centuries, Western science has dogmatically insisted upon disregarding "paranormal" phenomena. I assume Western science ignores and disparages metaphysical research findings like those in this book because the findings violate basic limiting assumptions or principles that have been drummed into the minds of scientists for decades. I cannot help but associate the three monkeys—who "see no evil, hear no evil, and speak no evil"—with the scientific community's longstanding refusal to see, hear, or speak other than disparagingly of phenomena that do not comply with materialistic understandings of reality. "Paranormal" phenomena fill the pages of thousands of books that provide an immense quantity of empirical evidence that the "evil" that science refuses to acknowledge is the evidence for humanity's nonphysical, spiritual reality.

121

Western science's elevation of the natural sciences and marginalizing of metaphysical phenomena appear to be a fait accompli. All the marginalized subjects contained within this book's first chapter and the broad category of metaphysics contain overwhelming but ignored empirical evidence that consciousness survives death and transcends matter. Genesis 2:7 says, "Yahweh God formed man from the dust of the ground and breathed into his nostrils the breath of life, and man became a living soul." Genesis 3:19 points out, "For you are dust, and you shall return to dust." What insanity motivates Western academia and science to focus exclusively upon the dust when the only thing that is of lasting concern to anyone is "the breath of life" that "became a living soul"?

My father liked to say, "You will never get out of this world alive." Of course, our body is made of "dust," but our consciousness, as the first chapter's content reveals, transcends the "dust" of our bodies. If, like my father, you believe you have no reality beyond the birth and death of your body, you are not going to believe in souls and consciousness's independence from the birth and death of bodies and brains. Why do you ignore the evidence—children who remember previous lives, near-death experiences, and past-life and between-lives regression—for consciousness's ability to get out of this world alive? What question could be more important to answer correctly than, "Who or what am I?" Am I simply this physical body that will return to the dust of the ground, or a spiritual being influencing with every thought, word, and deed a future that follows physical death? Western science's apparent a priori assumption that the answer to this question is beyond its grasp or concern is perplexing in view of the harmonious, abundant, and readily available evidence for a nonphysical, spiritual reality.

When I returned *Arigo: Surgeon of the Rusty Knife* to Reverend DeGrace, she insisted I borrow another book.

As I returned subsequent books that she loaned to me, I occasionally took a few of the pamphlets displayed in the lobby. I learned that the New Thought Movement began in the United States during the nineteenth century. Philosophers, authors, and religious denominations emerged with similar beliefs concerning God's omnipresence and the ability of thoughts to influence our health and life experiences. Instead of mindlessly adhering to centuries-old religious dogma, the New Thought Movement integrated religion and empirical science with spiritual awareness and development. Followers were encouraged to embrace what they found appealing and helpful, and to regard God as manifesting throughout creation. Just as there are over 250 different Christian faiths, an abundance of New Thought churches spans the globe.

Before meeting Reverend DeGrace, I did not know radically different churches, which may harmonize with my beliefs, had emerged from Christianity more than a century before I was born. I remained for several more years ignorant of the Universalist Church of America, established in 1793; the American Unitarian Association, established in 1825; the establishment of Unitarian Universalism in 1961; and the Spiritualist Movement that inspired Spiritualist churches in both the United States and Great Britain. Less influenced by conservative Christianity and skeptics of "paranormal" phenomena, people in Great Britain are more inclined to believe that science can and should explore the capabilities of consciousness beyond the bounds of matter. Among the subjects taught at London's College of Psychic Studies, which was founded in 1884, are mediumship, working with your guides and angels, inspirational and automatic writing, shamanism, tarot, remote viewing, and college-accredited healing. The Spiritualists' National Union (SNU) administers Arthur Findlay College. Fees for spiritualism and psychic science courses at Arthur Findlay College include room and board. If I had been introduced to liberal theologies in my youth, I would not be writing this book because I would not have prayed to be led to a contemporary, Jesus-like person.

Our beliefs and understandings emerge from inevitably limited experiences and obliviousness to the significance and magnitude of our ignorance. My initial awareness of only mainstream versions of Christianity reveals to me that what we do not know is at least as significant as what we think we know. This book is about what most people are oblivious to, and what Christianity, science, and academia ignore.

The Church of Religious Science was established in 1927 by Ernest Holmes. He initially wrote *The Science of Mind* as a textbook of New Thought philosophy to be used as a college-level course. The book was so well-received that it inspired another New Thought faith. As I read the church's pamphlets, I thought about experiencing a church service for the first time since I was in the eighth grade; but it took another six years before my curiosity overcame my reticence to risk reexperiencing being at odds with a minister's sermon and congregation.

THE PARAPSYCHOLOGY
ASSOCIATION OF RIVERSIDE (PAR)

The rapid succession of "paranormal" experiences—the clairvoyant experience with the letter, the mysterious puddles on my desk, Reverend DeGrace introducing me to metaphysics, and my positive experiences with astrology—motivated me to join the Parapsychology Association of Riverside (PAR). These experiences happened soon after I responded with skepticism to Gail's description of her past-life regression experiences and her praise of PAR's monthly meetings.

Ecclesiastes 3:1 says that "There is a time for everything, and a season for every activity under the heavens." In 1976, my sense of the range of possible human experiences was greatly expanded. Reverend DeGrace played a significant role in helping me to realize the diversity of religious sects, and the availability of books about "paranormal" phenomena. PAR enabled me to realize the existence of an occult or "wizarding world" within the "muggle" culture of my birth. It was not long before I felt as if I was passing in and out of two radically different cultures. Then, as now, most people identified with the nonmagical, muggle population and were oblivious to the interests of PAR's over seven hundred members in 1976, when interest in occult phenomena and PAR's membership peaked.

PAR emerged with the 1970s New Age Movement's interest in spiritualism, New Thought, Theosophy, channeling, and speculation about the coming Age of Aquarius. Political correctness concerns and pressure from the Christian and scientific communities' skeptical muggles resulted in the closure of parapsychology research programs in the 1980s. PAR was founded in Hazel Denning's home in 1971. The founding members were motivated "to provide research, education, and services to the community in the fields of parapsychology and metaphysics." PAR provided prescreened (by PAR's psychics) psychic referrals, eminent people in the field of parapsychology speaking at monthly meetings, psychic fairs, classes, and workshops taught by gifted and knowledgeable people living in or near Riverside. Among popular topics for classes and workshops were psychic development, astrology, channeling, tarot, healing, spirit guides, automatic writing, dream therapy, and hand and handwriting reading. PAR provided support, encouragement, and understanding for those within the community confused by their "paranormal" experiences and abilities.

Hazel Denning almost reached her ninety-ninth birthday. During the 2006 celebration of her life, while listening to people share their experiences with Hazel, I recalled the 1946 movie, *It's a Wonderful Life*. In the movie, Clarence is sent from heaven to help Peter Bailey realize the significance of his life to others. Like Peter Bailey, Hazel Denning directly and indirectly played a positive role in my life and the lives of countless others. After raising three adopted children, Hazel obtained her first of two master's degrees in psychology and became employed as her Methodist church's youth director in 1962. In prior years, Hazel served as a trustee of the church, Sunday school superintendent, president of the women's society, and drama director.

When conventional therapy was not working during her counseling sessions at the church, Hazel used her training in hypnotherapy. During a counseling session in 1962, after two unproductive sessions with a distraught and occasionally hysterical and suicidal young woman, Hazel said, "Your mind knows everything about you. Let's go into your mind and see what it has to tell you." The young woman said, "I'm Black, and I'm in a bucket brigade, and I'm trying to put the fire out. The Union soldiers set fire to my plantation, and we're trying to put it out." Then she jumped up and said, "Oh, now I know why I hate that lamp in my grandmother's house. It is just like the one here in the plantation kitchen. I'm a housemaid." Hazel realized she was hearing an experience that occurred during the Civil War. Even though Hazel believed in reincarnation, she was unaware the past-life memories of a person's soul were accessible. After the counseling session, Hazel thought, *Good Heavens! Do you mean a person can actually recall that stuff? If they can, what a fantastic tool for therapy.*[29]

During the fourteen years from 1962 to 1976, Hazel Denning did not charge clients for past-life regression therapy because she was unaware of anyone else doing it. She only used past-life regression therapy when conventional therapy was not working, and her patient was willing to explore their past lives. In addition to being the primary founding member of PAR, in 1980, Hazel Denning started the Association for Past-Life Research and Therapy with Dr. Ronald Jue. After serving for two years as both organizations' initial president,

Hazel served as both organizations' executive director for many more years. In 1981, at seventy-four years of age, Hazel became Dr. Denning by completing her doctorate in clinical psychology. After twenty-five years of past-life regression therapy, Dr. Denning wrote,

> What we think when we die is what we bring back. The curses that we make, the anger and frustration that we express, the resentments that we feel, the emotional charge that is in us at the time of our death is what we bring back and begin to express almost immediately in childhood. Therefore, what happens to us is not the important thing, but rather the way we handle it, our attitude toward it, and our motives for what we do.[30]

Dr. Denning's desire at fourteen "to prove that you don't have to grow old,"[31] and her love of learning, helping others, and figuring out the meaning of life may all have had something to do with her long and productive life. Because of the inequality of birth and life circumstances, after studying reincarnation and the world's major religions, Hazel realized reconciling a just and loving god was impossible without believing in reincarnation. In her later years, her friends encouraged Dr. Denning to write books about her experiences. She completed her first book at eighty-nine years of age and her third book when she was ninety-four. Dr. Denning's first book, *True Hauntings: Spirits with a Purpose*, recounts her "ghostbuster" experiences when homeowners asked PAR to investigate their "haunted" house. Her second book, *Life Without Guilt: Healing through Past Life Regression*, shares her insights from decades of being a past-life regression therapist. Dr. Denning's third book, *Intuition and Synchronicity*, recounts experiences that imply that "when **intuition** is at work, synchronicity follows, filling life with meaningful guideposts that those not in touch with their intuition might otherwise call coincidences." Dr. Denning wrote numerous articles for professional journals and was a guest on many radio and television shows, including those of Oprah Winfrey, Joan Rivers, and Tom Snyder.

If past-life and between-lives memories were merely imagined, the clients of past-life regression therapists would be unlikely to harmoniously provide the following information about reincarnation. To achieve spiritual growth concerns, past-life regression therapy reveals that souls reincarnate into all possible life circumstances. What we despise or mistreat may be our reality in our next life. Souls are never born, never die, and never suffer; they witness and hopefully learn from the experiences of their physical hosts. What is also worth noting is how perfectly past-life regression clients, who are Christians and do not believe in reincarnation, reveal the influence on their lives of what ancient Hindu scriptures call Karma. The accumulation of cause and effect, good as well as bad, consequences to our actions in this and previous lives is called Karma. Reincarnation, Karma, and liberation, which are understood in the East, can be confusing and easily misunderstood in the West.

For two decades, PAR's activities and the insights and abilities of its members harmonized with my curiosity about occult phenomena. Because the speakers always added to my knowledge of our phenomenal reality, I rarely missed PAR's monthly meetings, and I attended many of PAR's classes and workshops taught by uniquely talented and knowledgeable instructors. PAR enabled me to experience mediums conversing with spirit guides, trance channeling of nonphysical entities, and psychics reading tarot cards as if they were able to read my mind. My first PAR class was hatha yoga taught by a man who had studied yoga while living in India. He discovered, while in high school, books about "paranormal" phenomena. Determined to read everything possible related to metaphysics, he went to a bookstore that contained several rooms filled with thousands of books and asked to be directed to the metaphysics section. The surprised salesclerk said, "All our books deal with metaphysics!" Instantly, he realized metaphysics contained more books than he could read in several lifetimes.

Among the books in PAR's metaphysics library and those loaned to me by Reverend DeGrace were books by and about people with "paranormal" abilities. First published in 1975, in addition to the book about Arigo, were The Link: Matthew Manning's Own Story of His Extraordinary Psychic Gifts and Uri Geller: My Story. Both Manning and Geller, despite being among the world's most extraordinary and studied psychics, revealed in their first books that they were as mystified by their abilities as the scientists who studied them. Manning's book, published when he was only nineteen years old, describes unbelievable poltergeist phenomena that occurred in his home and boarding school. The book contains examples of automatic writing and drawing executed through Manning by discarnate spirits. Distinctly different drawing styles, like those of famous deceased artists, and even languages other than English persuasively suggest that Manning's hand was guided by consciousnesses other than his own.

Uri Geller is famous for his apparent ability to bend keys and spoons with an unknown force or power. The first occurrence of his unusual ability to bend metal occurred when he was five years old, and his spoon curled up and broke during a meal. By googling "Secret CIA psychic lab experiments with Uri Geller at Stanford University," you can see the experiments conducted in 1973 at Stanford Research Institute (SRI). Skeptics will claim that Geller was simply a magician, or criticize the procedures followed during the experiments. Mastering performing optical illusions can require years of practice. In these films, you can see Geller accomplish on his first attempts unexplainable—from a materialistic perspective—feats conjured up and supervised by SRI's physicists. These videos are a small fraction of the evidence habitually ignored by the skeptics who control Western science's paradigms. Instead of persisting in categorizing extrasensory perception, telekinesis, ghosts, life after death, reincarnation, faith healing, human auras, and the like as "paranormal" and "unscientific," Western science should establish an esoteric or occult branch of science.

EDGAR CAYCE

Among PAR's library books were books about Edgar Cayce, who is called "the sleeping prophet," "the father of holistic medicine," and "the most documented psychic of the twentieth century." Apparently psychic since his birth on a Kentucky farm in 1877, Cayce played with spirit friends and talked to his late grandfather's spirit during his early childhood. In his early twenties, he developed a severe case of laryngitis that lasted for several months. After hearing about Cayce's inability to speak above a whisper, a traveling stage-show hypnotist claimed that he could cure Cayce's laryngitis with a posthypnotic suggestion. Despite being able to speak normally while hypnotized, several posthypnotic suggestions failed to cure Cayce's laryngitis. Aware of hypnosis's ability to increase clairvoyance, a New York specialist suggested Cayce diagnose his own condition. Al Layne, a local student of osteopathy familiar with hypnotism, asked hypnotized Cayce about his laryngitis. During the 1901 hypnosis session, Cayce said his laryngitis was caused by the partial paralysis of his vocal cords due to stress.

To help his parents with their financial problems, Cayce became a school dropout after only one year of high school. His stress was caused by his subsequent difficulty earning enough money to marry his fiancée. While hypnotized, Cayce told Layne to instruct him to normalize the flow of blood in his body to the areas responsible for his laryngitis, and to maintain normal blood circulation after the hypnosis session.

When Cayce woke up from the hypnosis session, he was able to speak normally for the first time in almost a year.

Impressed by Cayce's ability to diagnose and treat his own health problem, and bothered by chronic stomach problems, Layne asked Cayce to give what became known as "readings" on his stomach problem. By lying on a couch with his hands folded over his stomach while closing his eyes, Cayce entered a self-induced sleep state. From this trance state, Cayce described Layne's symptoms exactly and prescribed herbal medicines, foods, and exercises. Layne's symptoms improved significantly within a week of following Cayce's recommendations.

Initially, Cayce's "readings" were for Layne's patients, but after Cayce's fame spread and it became apparent that "readings" merely required a person's name and location, a stenographer recorded and maintained copies of the readings as well as the correspondence received from those who received readings. While in a trancelike state, Edgar Cayce's readings began with "We have the body." "We" instead of "I" signifies Cayce's role as a transmitter of information from a higher, or transcendent, level of consciousness lying outside the usual limits of time and space. When "the sleeping prophet" was asked about the source of his information, "we" said the information came from the subconscious mind or soul of the person receiving the reading and from accessing the information and wisdom available from the Akashic records.

The Akashic records, or the "Book of Life," as it is referred to in the Bible, signifies God's data storage and retrieval system or supercomputer containing the interconnected memories of every soul since their initial creation. For centuries, seers, saints, and highly evolved souls have claimed access to the wisdom contained in the Akashic records. The concept of God having or being like a computer is traceable back to the ancient Semitic-speaking civilizations: Assyrians, Phoenicians, Babylonians, and Hebrews. The first reference in the Bible to God's book is

Exodus 32:32–33. In Psalm 139:16, King David said to God, "In your book they were all written, the days that were ordained for me, when as yet there were none of them." The apostle Paul in Philippians 4:3 pleads for "my fellow workers, whose names are in the book of life." A description of life reviews, which even atheists report experiencing during near-death experiences, is recorded in Revelation 20:12: "Another book was opened, which is the book of life. The dead were judged out of the things which were written in the books, according to their works." Without some basis in fact and experience by ancient and contemporary psychics and mystics, what are the odds for ancient civilizations and "the sleeping prophet" conceptualizing a transcendent computer with information-gathering, storage, and retrieval capabilities comparable to today's internet?

With religious devotion and self-discipline, Edgar Cayce went to church every Sunday, taught Sunday school, and reputedly read the entire Bible every year of his adult life. For forty-three years, the responses to his readings motivated Edgar Cayce to provide over fourteen thousand readings for the over six thousand people who requested them. Because the readings prevented him from being able to support his family, Cayce reluctantly charged for the readings. During his readings, Edgar Cayce identified and recommended seldom-used treatments and medicines while responding knowledgeably in twenty-five different languages to thousands of questions and topics.

Edgar Cayce's first two decades of readings were usually "physical readings" dealing with medical problems. In 1923, he initiated a new topic, "past-life readings," when he responded to a question about horoscopes by saying, "He was once a monk." Edgar Cayce's discomfort with the unchristian concept of reincarnation faded as people responded positively to "past-life readings" that related previous incarnations to the reading requestor's unmentioned marriage and other difficulties. During these past-life readings, Cayce used the words "the entity" to refer to the person's immortal soul as it incarnated from one lifetime to another. Subsequent readings for the same person coincided exactly with earlier readings while agreeing with historical facts. Despite the complexity and unique nature of each person's life, Western science ignores the profound implications and potential significance of documented evidence of Edgar Cayce's ability to describe, diagnose, and treat distant strangers.

The Association for Research and Enlightenment (ARE), a nonprofit organization founded by Edgar Cayce in 1931, provides online access to all of Cayce's 14,306 readings and follow-up reports, as well as access to ARE's physical library and visitors' center in Virginia Beach, Virginia. Cayce's collected readings are the world's largest collection of psychic information obtained from a single source. ARE contains evidence of Edgar Cayce's remarkable psychic ability, and evidence that his treatments—the patient's role in preventing and treating disease, and the importance of diet and exercise— were decades ahead of his time.

CHANNELING AND *A COURSE IN MIRACLES*

Channeling refers to transmitting or conveying thoughts or words from the discarnate or spirit world while in a trance or meditative state. Self-described discarnate intelligences that spoke to or through a medium, like Edgar Cayce, were popular sources for books in the 1950s through the 1970s and a frequent topic during PAR's classes and monthly meetings. The existence of allegedly channeled material, including whole books, extends from ancient spiritual texts to recently published books. The vast number of channeled books and their content imply that consciousness functions without any difficulty on "the other side" without bodies and brains. Channeled material implies the ability of human consciousness to receive information from discarnate sources as well as the existence of a nonmaterial, "spiritual" reality.

The unusual and well-documented story behind the creation of *A Course in Miracles*, abbreviated *ACIM*, provides more than antidotal evidence that it was channeled. *ACIM*'s standard three volume set consists of a 622-page *Text*, a 478-page *Workbook for Students* which has a lesson for each day of the year, and an 88-page *Manual for Teachers*. Translated into twenty-five languages, *ACIM* has been purchased without paid advertising by over three million people. Originally published in 1976 by a nonprofit foundation, *ACIM* is a self-study course in spiritual discernment reluctantly channeled by Helen Schucman during the years 1965 to 1972. Ironically, even though Schucman described and thought of herself as an atheist, she channeled what has been described as "the most important spiritual document of our age."

Helen Schucman (1909–1981) returned to college in her early forties, earned a PhD in 1957, and the following year, William Thetford (full professor of medical psychology at Columbia University College of Physicians and Surgeons in New York and director of the clinical psychology department at Presbyterian/Columbia University Medical Center) hired her as a research psychologist and assistant. Even though Helen Schucman was fourteen years older than Professor Thetford, they became good friends in a competitive academic setting. Prior to a meeting they were about to attend in the summer of 1965, the stress related to their work environment motivated Thetford to say to Schucman, "There must be another way. Our attitudes are so negative that we can't work anything out." After Thetford expressed his determination to find a better way of adapting to competitive and stressful circumstances, Schucman expressed her desire to help him.[32] Trained in rational scientific principles, and agnostic to atheistic in belief, neither Thetford nor Schucman could have anticipated how a better way of thinking, acting, and being in this world would be revealed to them.

Shortly after this conversation, Schucman began to have unusually vivid dreams, psychic visions or premonitions, and hear an "**inner voice**" in her head. Afraid she was losing her mind, she told Thetford about her experiences. He reassured her and encouraged her to write descriptions of her experiences, and to talk to him if the problem continued. One evening in October, the inner voice began repeating, "This is a course in miracles. Please take notes." In a state of panic, Schucman called Thetford. He told her to use her proficiency with shorthand to take notes, which they could read and discuss in the morning. He also told her that creative people like playwrights, poets, and even Einstein claimed to have received inspiration in mystical ways. "I'm not a mystical poet," Schucman protested, but she took his advice and brought what would become the introduction for *A Course in Miracles* to work the next day. After Schucman read her shorthand notes, Thetford said, "Sounds rather interesting to me, Helen. How do the words come?" She replied, "There's no actual sound, and the words come mentally but very clearly. It's kind of an inner dictation, you might say."[33]

For seven years, at favorable moments, Schucman reluctantly took dictation that picked up from her last entry. Despite their busy lives, she continued dictating the previous day's shorthand notes as Thetford typed them. Their initial desire to find a better way of coping with discord motivated their cooperation with the voice. They would have assumed that anyone, other than themselves, doing what they were doing must be delusional.

Because of the conservative academic atmosphere in which they worked, when Thetford and Schucman completed the voice's unedited manuscript, they were reluctant to reveal or discuss it with anyone. Then, as now, "paranormal" phenomena like channeling were not viewed favorably by Western science and academia. Until they could figure out what to do with the manuscript, they hid it in a drawer. Hoping to discover what to do with the manuscript, they reluctantly made copies to share with a few friends. In late 1972, one of those friends—a Roman Catholic priest and previous graduate-level psychology student of Thetford and Schucman—introduced psychologist Kenneth Wapnick to them because of Wapnick's interest in mystical religious experiences. Wapnick initially declined their offers to look at the manuscript, but reoccurring dreams during the months after his refusals motivated him to ask Schucman for permission to review the manuscript.

Ken Wapnick's doctoral dissertation was on the sixteenth-century Spanish mystic, Saint Teresa of Avila, and he was contemplating becoming a Trappist monk.[34] The manuscript's content and poetic language motivated Wapnick to make *ACIM* his life's work. After pointing out to Schucman and Thetford the manuscript's need for editing before it could be published, Wapnick volunteered to do the editing with their guidance. He completed the editing process in early 1975 and devoted the last four decades of his life to promoting and teaching *ACIM*, which he described as the most important spiritual document of our age. If Wapnick had not experienced those reoccurring dreams, *ACIM* may have never been published. Ken Wapnick and Helen Schucman (who did not want her association with *ACIM* revealed until after her death) became good friends. He wrote her only biography, *Absence from Felicity: The Story of Helen Schucman and Her Scribing of A Course in Miracles*.

Even though *ACIM* uses Christian themes and terminology, its Eastern and New Age spiritual concepts—channeling Jesus?—make *ACIM* difficult for Christians to embrace. Apparently aware of the marketing challenges for *ACIM*, the voice told Schucman, "A woman would come along who would know what to do with it."

Mystical and psychic experiences during Judith (Judy) Sketch's childhood and her daughter's telepathic, clairvoyant, and precognitive psychic abilities motivated Judith Sketch to study parapsychology and become actively involved with several parapsychology researchers and organizations. In addition to radio and TV appearances to increase the public's interest in "paranormal" phenomena, Sketch was a faculty member at New York University, where she taught a course in experimental parapsychology and alternative methods of healing.

While attending a 1975 New York Academy of Medicine research seminar to encourage a more holistic approach to health care, Sketch met Professor Thetford, who realized that she matched the description of the woman the voice wanted to assume control of the manuscript. Thetford invited Sketch and Schucman to lunch. After lunch, they took Sketch to their private offices to reveal their secret manuscript. What they regarded as too weird to discuss without fear of embarrassment was Sketch's favorite topic of conversation.

When Sketch met Thetford and Schucman, she was frustrated by the inability of scientific (both regular and parapsychology) research to provide answers to her spiritual questions. Mystical experiences provided her with the awareness of a spiritual reality without providing spiritual understanding or guidance. She did not have to read far into the manuscript before she realized it contained the spiritual guidance she hoped to find. Like Ken Wapnick, she almost immediately imagined the manuscript becoming her life's work.

They jointly studied and in 1976 decided to publish the manuscript. *ACIM* focuses upon abstract themes common to other channeled works, the New Thought Movement, and the spiritual themes of most religions. The course claims, "A universal theology is impossible, but a universal experience is not only possible but necessary."[35] In contrast to Christianity's assertion that it is the best or only valid theology, the voice validated any theology that stimulates mystical, "universal," spiritual experiences that arise from the spiritual or love dimension underlying our phenomenal reality.

Intensely aware of their underlying spiritual reality, Wapnick and Sketch readily related to and appreciated the manuscript's themes. Thetford, while typing the manuscript, realized the voice's ideas harmonized with Eastern religious themes and his desire to find "another way" of living in a stressful and competitive environment. But Schucman was never able to relate to *ACIM*'s abstract themes, and for seven long years, she required Thetford's encouragement to continue taking the voice's dictation.

Do you remember when my desire for a *Lone Ranger* gun and holster set led to the realization that my egoic sense of myself is no more substantial than thoughts? The exercises in *ACIM* are designed to promote similar insights, or *"miracles"* as *ACIM* calls them. Students of the course are encouraged to replace their conditioned, ego-bound personalities' perspective with an experience-based awareness of an underlying, all-knowing, and loving source of guidance that enables life to flow with less stress and effort. Using Christian terminology, the course teaches the primary spiritual themes of both Jesus and the world's major religions. I doubt that history has anyone more motivated than Jesus to dictate to a medium proficient at shorthand.

Serving on the board of directors of the Institute of Noetic Sciences—which, like this book, exists because of Western science's attitude toward "paranormal" phenomena—was one of the many ways Judith Sketch promoted *ACIM* along with psi and consciousness research. Serving on the board with Sketch was Willis Harman, PhD in electrical engineering, who served as the institute's president from 1975 until his death in 1997. When Sketch and Harman first met, she kept him "spellbound" for two hours telling him about *ACIM*.

Six months after Willis Harman began reading *ACIM*, he was amazed by the book's apparent ability to connect him with an underlying source of guidance that enabled his life to flow with less stress and effort. He described its effect on his experiences as follows:

> One day I would realize that a situation which once would have aroused fear or hostility no longer did so – and yet I would have had no conscious awareness of the deep-seated changes taking place. I would find that my trust in a deep intuition, an all-knowing and an all-forgiving part of myself, had strengthened noticeably, again without my direct conscious knowledge of the change taking place in the unconscious part of my mind. Stress and pain disappeared. My life was more active than at any previous period, and yet it happened more effortlessly than I would have been able to believe possible in earlier years. Aspects of my life fell into place in ways that were nothing short of mysterious. What impressed me the most about the transformation I felt was the utter simplicity of the new way. A deeper part of myself, an "Inner Teacher," guided action and removed obstacles, and the conscious mind – that rational, analytical ego-mind which once seemed my best precarious hold on some semblances of security – became naturally and comfortably the servant of the deeper mind. It will likely sound like a gross over-simplification, but my deeply felt conclusion came to be that all the problems we experience in our lives are illusory. There is only one problem, namely our resistance to seeing the wholeness as it is.[36]

Willis Harman's quote reveals that the spirit world's author of *ACIM* unmistakably prescribed "another way" for us to live

139

in this world. Harman's description of being surrendered to and immersed within God's plan reveals that we require many lifetimes to achieve what monarch butterflies experience as their birthright. The New Testament's Gospel of Matthew contains Jesus's original prescription, the Lord's Prayer, for achieving the same *miracle* Willis Harman achieved by studying *ACIM*. By preceding the Lord's Prayer, "[God's] kingdom come, [God's] will be done, on earth as it is in heaven," with "your Father knows what you need before you ask him," Jesus made it abundantly clear two thousand years ago that, because God knows our needs before and better than we do, it behooves us to surrender our will to God's divine will. *ACIM* contains do-it-yourself (DIY) instruction for surrendering our ego's will to God's will. In Matthew 6:26, Jesus said, "Look at the birds of the air, they do not sow or reap or store away in barns, and yet your heavenly Father feeds them. Are you not much more valuable than they?" Willis Harman's quote reveals his experience of our "heavenly Father" playing a positive role in his life. Besides enabling a person to experience the divine within oneself, *ACIM* promotes and develops a person's ability to experience "equanimity to all circumstances, inner peace, and freedom from all fears and anxieties."[37]

I quoted Willis Harman's description of his experiences after six months of studying *ACIM* because his quote provides anecdotal evidence of the course's ability to foster "universal experiences," which can lead to replacing one's self-concept or ego with the Oneself in the heart of everyone. "What is the ego? Nothingness, but in a form that seems like something."[38]

In the Gospel of John 14:10–12, Jesus provided a description of his profoundly advanced level of self-realization with these words:

> Don't you believe that I am in the Father, and the
> Father in me? The words that I tell you, I speak not from

myself, but the Father who lives in me does his works. Believe me that I am in the Father, and the Father in me; or else believe me for the very works' sake. Most certainly I tell you, he who believes in me, the works that I do, he will do also; and he will do greater works than these, because I am going to the Father.

These and other misunderstood and ignored statements in the Bible contain insights into the nature of the "universal experience" and self-realization. When Jesus said, "I am in the Father, and the Father in me," he not only described his experience of self-realization but also proclaimed the point I am trying to make by writing this book: my experiences and the abundance of "paranormal" phenomena would be impossibly improbable without "the Father" manifesting within creation itself. Can it be just a coincidence that Jesus's instruction for how to pray and his advanced level of self-realization harmonize with the voice's instructions for how to achieve miracles? The Bible and the words of Jesus contain the same understanding of reincarnation and self-realization as proclaimed in India centuries before Jesus's birth. Self-realization is believed to confer liberation from accumulated Karma and the cycle of rebirths.

ACIM provides the reader with a guru-disciple relationship with, quite possibly, Jesus. We cannot wrap our minds around our souls' fundamental unity with God any more than we can wrap our minds around light simultaneously being a particle and a wave, which is why the voice's lessons focus on creating *miracles* or "universal experiences" that reveal that our sense of separation from everyone and everything, including God, is an illusion. Instead of being concerned with creating a new theology or religion, the voice is concerned with inspiring mystical experiences of the inexplicable. Mystical experiences lead to what philosopher and metaphysician Frithjof Schuon

(1907–1998) called **esoteric believers**. Schuon observed that mystical spiritual experiences inspire within the experiencer, despite the variety of possible previous beliefs, the same inner awareness of their soul's unity with God and creation. The lessons in *A Course in Miracles* focus on fostering an experience of the oneness that connects us all within what Jesus called the kingdom of heaven, and that quantum physics may be describing in its unified field theory.

Frithjof Schuon referred to most religious believers, who have a dualistic understanding of God and creation, as **exoteric believers**. Because they have not experienced or embraced humanity's oneness with God, exoteric believers imagine God as a transcendent, super being. Schuon made the profound observation that the beliefs of the world's religions are more compatible than the beliefs within the same religion of esoteric and exoteric believers.

While getting to know Helen Schucman, Willis Harman observed that she lacked the attitudes and beliefs of successful students of *ACIM*. After replacing her childhood fear of eternal suffering in hell with a materialistic understanding of reality, Schucman closed her mind to religious concepts. For skeptics like her, Willis Harman wanted to document the course's provenance. After getting to know Schucman, Thetford, and Wapnick, as well as Sketch—the people responsible for the existence and marketing success of *ACIM*— Willis felt that Sketch's husband, Bob Sketch, with his writing experience, should document the unusual story of *ACIM*. Bob wrote *Journey without Distance: The Story behind A Course in Miracles*, and asked Willis Harman to write the foreword. My sources for the last few pages have been Bob's book and the websites for the Foundation for Inner Peace (https://acim.org/) and the Foundation for *A Course in Miracles* (https://facim.org/) where you can learn more about and purchase *ACIM*.

Chapter 6
NONDUALITY

One God and Father of all, who is over all
and through all, and in us all.
—*Ephesians 4:6*

In a 1999 polling of 130 of the world's leading physicists, Caltech Nobel laureate Richard Feynman was ranked as one of the 10 greatest physicists of all time. Because of the mysterious nature of the subatomic realm, Professor Feynman described quantum mechanics as too inexplicable to be understood by anyone. The difficulty of understanding phenomena like wave-particle duality and quantum entanglement did not prevent physicists from studying matter at its most mysterious and fundamental level. Despite the "paranormal" behavior of matter's elemental constituents, today's technological achievements were made possible because scientists combined quantum mechanics research with their knowledge of chemistry and physics to develop the semiconductor transistor and today's computers, LEDs, lasers, solar cells, digital cameras, and atomic clocks that make global positioning systems (GPS) possible.

Consciousness and the mystery alluded to by the word God can be added to Richard Feynman's contention about quantum mechanics: no one understands them. Experiencing things indirectly with our physical senses does not provide much assistance relating to those who are able to experience things directly with their spiritual eyes, ears, and soul. Because we all experience consciousness, but most of us do not use our spiritual eyes and ears, Western science acknowledges consciousness but not "paranormal" phenomena, even though neither can be explained from a reductionistic and materialistic perspective. Mystics, mediums, and psychics receive information directly with their spiritual eyes and ears in the same way we all experience consciousness. Near-death experiences are one of this book's many examples of phenomena that suggest we have spiritual eyes and ears. Psychic mediums use their spiritual eyes and ears to experience the spiritual dimension but are unable to adequately share or explain their experiences to dualistic and materialistic, exoteric, believers. Someday, today's scientists are going to look ridiculous explaining the other side of life from their dualistic and materialistic perspective. Objective, verifiable, and indisputable evidence of spiritual phenomena may not be possible. But, just as quantum mechanics does not have to make sense to yield its secrets, this book's first chapter provides examples of the other side of life yielding its secrets to competent scientific research. To understand consciousness (our fundamental reality, or God) Western science needs to free itself from its atheistic paradigms.

You know you have or are consciousness, and that without it you could not consciously exist. But consciousness, like quantum mechanics, is not easy to understand. The point I am trying to make is that you do not have to understand consciousness to know it exists. An esoteric believer does not have to understand their or God's fundamental reality to know that they are a spiritual being immersed in God because, like their experience of being conscious, they experience it directly.

Because we often do not have the energy or take the time to understand what we are hearing and seeing, I want to devote this chapter to the counterintuitive concept of nonduality. My hope is that, after this chapter, I will be able to simply share my experiences, and you will understand them better than I did while I was experiencing them. Because many of the experiences that motivated the writing of this book suggest to me the possibility of God literally being in me as me, I want to stimulate curiosity about the concept of nonduality.

The subjective or mystical experience of nonduality, the fundamental unity or oneness of God and creation, distinguishes mystics and esoteric believers from those who have difficulty integrating the divine with the material world. Like particles and waves in quantum physics, God and the world are not the same thing, but neither are they different or two separate things. The apostle Paul, in his letter to the Ephesians, provided a clear, concise definition of nonduality: *One God and Father of all, who is over all and through all, and in us all.* Because most believers are exoteric believers, I focused in the first chapter on empirical evidence for a nonphysical, spiritual component to reality. The contents of the first chapter provide a portion of the abundant evidence for reincarnation and human consciousness' existence before the birth and after the death of bodies and brains. The contents of the first chapter cannot be explained without assuming we are spiritual beings or souls who have formed a temporary association with a body and its brain. If Western science and academia approached near-death experiences, the past-life memories of children and hypnotized adults, and the abilities of psychic mediums with the same tolerance for the inexplicable applied to the subatomic realm, knowledge of our spiritual reality would enable a quantum leap in human understanding and behavior comparable to the technological achievements of the twentieth century. To my knowledge, the evidence for our spiritual reality is the only topic systematically ignored and disparaged by Western science and academia. Western science's most consequential and least desirable achievement in the last century may be ignoring "paranormal" phenomena.

Mystics, prophets, and avatars have for millennia been providing remarkably consistent insights into a nonmaterial, spiritual realm. Relating to what they have been telling us

145

revolves around the concept of nonduality, which makes as much sense from our worldly perspective as wave-particle duality. Would it be reasonable to expect the spiritual realm to be less mysterious than the subatomic realm? Because you are unlikely to respond favorably to ideas that conflict with your experiences and beliefs, before exploring nonduality further, I want to review and clarify previously addressed topics.

"UNIVERSAL" EXPERIENCES, AND ESOTERIC AND EXOTERIC BELIEVERS

Until I went to India and learned a few Sanskrit (the ancient language of India and Hinduism) words for concepts that do not exist in the West, I was unappreciative of our dependence upon the concepts contained within and conveyed by words. Because everything in this book relates to "universal" experiences, esoteric believers, and exoteric believers, I want you to understand these three concepts, and I want them to influence your thoughts.

The title of this book, *Encounters with God*, serendipitously means the same thing as "universal" experiences, which transform exoteric believers into esoteric believers. Miracles in *A Course in Miracles* allude to the desirability of "universal" experiences that reveal our oneness with God. The primary concern of this book is the same as *ACIM*: transforming nonbelievers and exoteric believers into esoteric believers. When your culture's economy runs on promoting worldly desires, and its educational system assumes matter is the only reality, "universal" experiences are few and far between. For those who live in the West, it really does take a *miracle* to experience so much as a glimmer of being other than flesh and blood.

My "universal" experience of samadhi, the direct experience of God's omnipresence and love, instantly made me an esoteric believer. Listening to an exoteric belief–inspired sermon when I was thirteen made me acutely aware that few people realize they are imbued with or immersed within God's light and love. Until I was in my forties, the esoteric wisdom of Jesus, history's most influential mystic, and Rotary's service-minded members provided my only experiences that harmonized with the experience of samadhi.

Did you notice the voice's use of the word "universal" (available everywhere by everyone) to describe experiencing God's love and grace? The concept of a "universal" God conflicts with those who describe and promote themselves as God's chosen people. The concept of a preferential relationship with God did not originate with the Abrahamic religions, but they perfected using the concept to subjugate adherents. The New Testament portrays Jesus's Jewish apostles claiming that salvation is "through faith"[39] in "our Lord and Savior, Jesus Christ."[40] Promoting belief in the inherent superiority of one's ethnic group, culture, and/or religion is not in harmony with Ephesians 4:6: "One God and Father of all." Belief in racial and cultural superiority appeals to human egos, white supremacist sects, and prison gangs such as the Aryan Brotherhood (which is a neo-Nazi organized crime syndicate). It was not until I went to India in 1986 that I realized the followers of Eastern religions do not automatically assume their religion is superior. They are inclined to assume the obvious: God would regard aspects of His creation with impartiality. The voice's characterization of experiencing God's presence and grace as "universal experiences" suggests to me that two thousand years of Christianity getting his life and ministry wrong motivated Jesus's discarnate soul to spend seven years dictating *ACIM*.

When Judith Sketch was a child, she experienced mystical experiences as well as psychic experiences. Like me, she probably assumed that people with psychic experiences and abilities would have the esoteric spiritual perspective of those who have had mystical spiritual experiences. But her years of

147

involvement with psi or ESP research and promotion did not provide the spiritual insights and understandings she hoped to find. When she read *ACIM*, she realized it provided the spiritual guidance she was looking for.

Like Judith Sketch, during my many years as a member of the Parapsychology Association of Riverside (PAR), I was surprised that psi talents and experiences did not inspire esoteric beliefs. Only those PAR members who, like Judith Sketch, had experienced "universal" mystical experiences as well as psi experiences were esoteric believers. The explanation for the uniquely different effects of "universal" experiences and psi experiences upon beliefs relates to our receiver/transmitter or radio-like capabilities. Our seven chakra centers provide us with seven different receiving stations. In contrast to those who do not even get static on their "radio," one of PAR's psychic mediums claimed that chain-smoking enabled her to live a more normal life because smoking "grounded" her from the thoughts and sight of discarnate beings.

Psi abilities like clairvoyance, clairaudience, and clear feeling or sensing, as well as "universal" experiences, are mediated by different chakra centers. Thousands of years ago, Hinduism's Rig Veda described chakras as seven wheels of energy. Because of the persistent influence of the eighteenth century's Enlightenment, which glorified human reason at the expense of spiritual concerns, information about chakras is more readily and reliably available from occult sources than contemporary science. Despite Western science and academia's skepticism, when I lie on my back and pass a pendulum above my midline from the base of my spine to the top of my head, the pendulum hangs motionless except when it orbits in eight-inch diameter circles precisely above the location of my seven "wheels of energy."

Assuming our reality has two components (worldly and spiritual), human experience can be unexplainable or misunderstood when the most significant component of our reality is ignored. Difficulty replicating phenomena, like my demonstration of chakras, combined with ignoring the possibility of a spiritual dimension leads to classifying phenomena as "paranormal." When I became a self-employed optometrist, I knew nothing about reincarnation and the progression of self-absorbed young souls into loving, caring "old souls." It never occurred to me that those whose deplorable deeds caused my depression incarnated with souls which lacked the life lessons and wisdom of the souls incarnated in service-minded Rotarians. A new age of tolerance, understanding, and peace is likely when Western academia and science acknowledge the evidence for reincarnation and our underlying spiritual reality. "Paranormal" phenomena are too abundant to be forever regarded and classified as inconsequential abnormalities. In view of the persistent influence of the eighteenth century's Enlightenment on science's paradigms, until Western science becomes enlightened, I propose the establishment of an esoteric branch of science to investigate "paranormal" and "supernormal" phenomena.

NONDUALITY

When calling "heads or tails," we are aware of a coin's two distinctly different sides, but a coin is normally simply a coin. This is the *nonduality* understanding of mystics and those who have achieved self-realization: the kingdom of God and the physical world of people, places, and things are inseparable aspects of a single, interconnected reality, oneness, or "coin." When I experienced samadhi, I experienced the oneness of God and creation.

My grandparents' Christmas present when I was eleven years old was a King James Bible with my name engraved on the cover. The words of Jesus, printed in red, harmonized with my experience of samadhi, but Jesus's level of consciousness was much more than a brief mystical experience. Jesus served as the vehicle through which God performed miracles and revealed the oneness or nonduality of the material world and the kingdom of heaven. Unfortunately, even though we deal with complex and nuanced issues, human social psychology research reveals that we evolved with minds that overly simplify and see issues in black-and-white terms. Instead of seeing the unity in the diversity of creation, our minds experience and process information in terms of binary pairs of opposites such as matter/spirit, self/other, here/there, life/ death, good/evil, and true/false. The belief that spirit and matter exist separate and apart from each other is called duality or dualism. Dualism is the understanding of reality embraced by exoteric believers and mainstream versions of most religions.

The esoteric branches of most religions encourage seeing the oneness in the diversity of creation. The words of Jesus appear in this book because they express the nonduality perspective of samadhi and Eastern religions. When reading Jesus's instructions for how to pray in Matthew 6:6–13, consider a monarch butterfly's need for guidance, and notice how the interplay between "Our Father in heaven" and "us" suggests that we are not separate from God. These are Jesus's instructions for how to pray: "Pray like this: Our Father in heaven, may your name be kept holy. Let your kingdom come. Let your will be done on earth as it is in heaven. Give us today our daily bread. …" Are we (us) separate from God, or is the sense of separation an illusion?

"Universal" experiences occur when we surrender our little will to the Will of God. The only way I can explain the migration of monarch butterflies is by assuming that what is difficult for people to accomplish—surrendering their little will to God's Will—is the birthright of monarch butterflies.

How else would you explain insects migrating thousands of miles to precise locations without God's GPS assistance? Carl Sagan famously wrote, "Extraordinary claims require extraordinary evidence." The extraordinary life cycle of monarch butterflies is extraordinary evidence that supports the Old Testament's (Job 12:7–10) claim,

> But ask the animals, now, and they will teach you; the birds in the sky, and they will tell you. Or speak to the earth, and it will teach you. The fish of the sea will declare to you. Who doesn't know that in all these, Yahweh's [God's] hand has done this, in whose hand is the life of every living thing, and the breath of all mankind?

The concept of nonduality, also called nondualism, comprehends the dualistic perspective of self/other and the experience of being the doer as illusions to be "transcended." The concept of transcending the perspective of one's ego is an essential element of Islamic Sufism, Christian mysticism, Jewish Kabbalah, Hinduism's Advaita Vedanta, and most Buddhist traditions. These esoteric, nonduality religions were inspired by and frequently maintained by people who were either born with or achieved advanced levels of spiritual consciousness. Many religious traditions, paths, or yogas exist that can be pursued to attain enlightenment, which is also referred to as self-realization and liberation. Even though there are many paths, there is little variation in the apparent understanding and experience of enlightenment other than the level of consciousness achieved. Automobiles and the internet—relative to past centuries—make it easy to locate and experience people purported to have transcended the perspective of their ego. The awareness of just one Jesus-like person, with divinely inspired wisdom, would have satisfied my high school prayers. Fortunately, there are many wise, old souls to choose from.

"I AM THAT I AM"

Before resuming my experiences, which reveal to me that God is alive and well, I want to "prove" that the world's religions emerged from a common source by looking at them from an esoteric perspective. The existence of similar counterintuitive, mystical understandings of reality within religions that emerged within different cultures and geographical locations provide support for the concept of revealed religions. Because mainstream Western religions typically ignore the concept of nonduality, I want to point out Old Testament scripture that expresses the same nonduality understanding of reality as Hindu scripture. The Abrahamic religions—Judaism, Christianity, and Islam—recognize the prophet Abraham as a common forefather and are regarded as "sister" religions. All three religions emerged from what is now called the Middle East, and their adherents span the globe, comprising over half of the world's population.

I assume most religions arose from a common source of inspiration, but I have been dissatisfied with several attempts to link the histories of Hinduism and Judaism. Most of the world's inhabitants are followers of these quintessential— divinely revealed along with their revealed doctrines— religions and their offshoots. Hopefully, a Bible quote on a bookmark (which I found yesterday in a book that belonged to my mother-in-law) will provide fortuitous assistance suggesting that, because of their many similarities, Hinduism and Judaism must have arisen from a common source of inspiration. The Old Testament quote is Joshua 1:9: "Be strong and courageous. Don't be afraid. Don't be dismayed, for Yahweh your **God is with you wherever you go**." Over a thousand years before Jesus proclaimed that God's power manifested in and through him by saying: "My Father and I are one," Joshua expressed God's oneness within everyone by stating that God is always with us.

During the second millennium BC, Joshua, like Moses, was born a slave in Egypt. After Moses's death, Joshua led the Israelite tribes in their conquest of Canaan. On the Indian subcontinent over three thousand miles away from where Joshua proclaimed God's omnipresence with everyone, the promulgators of Hinduism taught the concept of the unity or oneness of the Creator with creation. The Bhagavad Gita, Hinduism's most popular Hindu text, contains the avatar (an incarnation of God) Krishna's counsel to Arjuna. In verses 34–35 of the fourth chapter, Krishna explains Joshua's above statement about God being with us by saying,

> Just try to learn the truth by appreciating a spiritual master. Inquire from him submissively and render service unto him. The self-realized soul can impart knowledge unto you because he has seen the truth. And when you have thus learned the truth, you will know that all living beings are but parts of Me – and that they are in Me and are Mine.[41]

Both the Jewish and Hindu cultures began prior to the second millennium BC. For centuries prior to their development of an alphabet, oral traditions enabled both cultures to verbally transmit knowledge from one generation to the next. During the second millennium BC, the Jewish and Hindu cultures began writing their orally preserved histories, philosophies, and *encounters with God*. Along with the documents they preserved, both the Hebrew language and the Sanskrit language were regarded as holy or sacred. The cultural histories and ideas recorded in their sacred texts profoundly influenced Jewish and Hindu history and culture while providing Jews and Hindus with spiritual, moral, and practical guidance.

God's revelation to humanity came from Abraham, Moses, Joshua, and many other Old Testament prophets. God's prophets played a hero's role, like that of Rama and Krishna in Hinduism's two major Sanskrit epics, the Ramayana and the Mahabharata, which is three times the length of the Bible and contains the Bhagavad Gita. The Old Testament prophets, the New Testament's Jesus, Islam's Muhammad, and Hinduism's Rama and Krishna provide role models and encouragement to rise above human impulses and become ideal human beings. What would be the history of humanity without the improbably preserved cultural histories of prophets and avatars providing spiritual wisdom and inspiration?

Because of the fortuitous discovery of a bookmark, I will not fail to include one of the many *encounters with God* described in the Bible. In Exodus, the second book of the Bible, Egypt's Hebrew slaves prayed to be freed from Egypt's pharaoh and his mighty army. God responded to their prayers with a long series of miracles, which began with God, in the form of a brightly burning bush, asking Moses to return to Egypt and free the Hebrew slaves. While terrified by the thought of attempting such a ridiculously impossible task, Moses asked God how to tell Egypt's slaves who told him to return to Egypt and rescue them. "God said to Moses, "I AM THAT I AM," and he said, "You shall tell the children of Israel this: "I AM has sent me to you."[42] Because of Moses's lack of faith in their combined ability to free Egypt's slaves, God, in the form of a burning bush, said: "Now therefore go, and I will be with your mouth, and teach you what you shall speak."[43] How would you know if God was in you, as you, thinking, speaking, and acting? Have you ever wondered, as Ahab did in Herman Melville's *Moby Dick*, "Is Ahab, Ahab? Is it I, God, or who that lifts his arm?" Let's explore the idea that consciousness, your "*I am*" sense of self-awareness, arises from spirit or God instead of matter. After all, science's inability to explain consciousness may be because consciousness arises from a nonmaterial source, God, instead of brains.

What did God imply by using "I AM" for self-description? As previously pointed out, Jesus provided his nonduality experience of God manifesting in and through him with the words, "I and the Father are one." Jesus's statement implies that his "I am" or sense of self-awareness comes from God. In 1 Corinthians 6:19, the apostle Paul's doctrine of the divine, indwelling Holy Spirit clearly expresses the concept of nonduality with these words: "or don't you know that your body is a temple of the Holy Spirit who is in you, whom you have from God?"

At the end of chapter 3, I wrote about the appeal of the philosophical notions of René Descartes, which helped the Scientific Revolution confer upon human intellect the status previously reserved for saints, prophets, and God. Despite the mind's inability to distinguish between true and false statements—which is why we have scam artists, deceptive advertising, and dishonest propaganda networks and politicians—Descartes imagined his reasoning mind capable of manufacturing knowledge. What he experienced as an unequivocally true statement—"I think therefore *I am*"— became the first principle of his philosophy, his best-known philosophical statement, and contains the same words, *I am*, that God used for self-identification. The concept of God, the absolute experienced through the veil of illusion as *I am*, is in harmony with Hinduism's nondualism philosophy of Advaita Vedanta, or the unity of matter and energy, time and space, God and soul.

Nonduality is so contrary to our usual experience of duality that people have difficulty discerning the concept, even when it is clearly expressed in the Bible. Despite the doctrine of the divine indwelling, Christian tradition does not embrace nonduality's esoteric understanding of "reality." In view of the counterintuitive nature of nonduality and the separation of ancient Hindu and Jewish cultures by over three thousand miles, the concept's early appearance in both cultures supports the hypothesis that revealed religions are inspired by a common source: God. Can you think of another explanation for the appearance and preservation, within distant ancient cultures, of the counterintuitive concept of nonduality?

An esoteric understanding of nonduality enables the reader to relate to what Jesus meant by saying, "My Father and I are one," and what God meant by using "I AM" for self-identification. For those who experience God's power manifesting in and through them, the how and why of consciousness is self-evident: God. Since the Scientific Revolution, when the reasoning mind replaced mystics, prophets, and God, Western science has reflected both humanity's low level of spiritual consciousness and the best of humanity's intellectual ability. Simply being aware of the vast variation in levels of spiritual consciousness as well as intellect might encourage science to recognize and appreciate the wisdom and insights of those with "paranormal" and "supernormal" abilities.

PERENNIAL PHILOSOPHY, PERENNIAL OR AGELESS WISDOM, AND PERENNIALISM

I did not realize while writing the previous pages on nonduality and "I am that I am" that countless mystics, religious and historical scholars, and philosophers throughout history have made similar observations and arguments that are embraced under the umbrella of the perennial philosophy. Under the perennial philosophy's umbrella are Universalism, which appreciates the truths reflected by all religions, transcendentalism, which emphasizes mystical experience, and the Traditionalist School, which focuses on the ancient wisdom traditions. Aldous Huxley wrote *The Perennial Philosophy*, which was first published in 1945. On the first page of his introduction, Aldous Huxley wrote,

> Rudiments of the Perennial Philosophy may be found among the traditionary lore of primitive peoples in every region of the world, and in the fully developed forms it has a place in every one of the higher religions. A version of this Highest Common Factor in all preceding and subsequent theologies was first committed to writing more than twenty-five centuries ago, and since that time the inexhaustible theme has been treated again and again, from the standpoint of every religious tradition and in all the principal languages of Asia and Europe.[44]

SRI NISARGADATTA MAHARAJ

Those who have achieved self-realization, like Sri Nisargadatta Maharaj, provide insights into the perennial philosophy's nonduality understanding of reality. Despite being raised in poverty without a formal education in Bombay, where he died in 1981 at the age of eighty-four, Sri Nisargadatta is revered as one of India's greatest teachers and revealers of self-realization. He experienced what has been called cosmic consciousness after following his guru's guidance and meditating on the source of his sense of "I am." Spiritual seekers from around the world traveled to Sri Nisargadatta's home in Bombay to obtain his insights and guidance. Sri Nisargadatta's tape-recorded and translated answers to their questions are preserved in the book, *I Am That*.

The similarity of Sri Nisargadatta's self-description ("I am that") to Moses's quote of God's self-description ("I am that

I am") in Exodus is not a coincidence. Utterances that mean "that" are commonly used to allude to cosmic consciousness and God. Sacred words or chants with spiritual significance, when slowly and repetitively turned over in the mind, are called mantras. The English translation of So-ham, my favorite mantra, is "I am that." "So," which means "that" in Sanskrit, is silently chanted with each in breath; and "ham," meaning "I" or "me," is silently chanted with each exhalation. Alluding to cosmic consciousness and God with the word "that" is not limited to ancient Hebrew and Sanskrit. The major theme of history's most translated and popular poet, Rumi, is nonduality or the oneness of being. The thirteenth-century Persian Islamic scholar and Sufi mystical poet wrote, "There is nothing outside of yourself. Look within, everything you want is there. You are That." Like colors, the absolute can be experienced but not described any better than red, blue, or that. Sri Nisargadatta's responses to his followers' questions reduce the mystery of our "I am" sense of self. In contrast to Descartes's egocentric "I think, therefore I am," Sri Nisargadatta said,

> All I can say truly is: "I am," all else is inference. But the inference has become a habit. Destroy all habits of thinking and seeing. The sense of "I am" is the manifestation of a deeper cause, which you may call self, God, Reality, or by any other name. The "I am" is in the world, but it is the key which can open the door out of the world.[45] ... You imagine me as separate, ... There is no "myself" and "his self." There is the Self, the only Self of all. Mislead by the diversity of names and shapes, minds and bodies; you imagine multiple selves. We both are the Self, but you seem to be unconvinced. This talk of personal self and universal self is the learner's stage, go beyond, don't

be stuck in duality.[46] ... The same power that makes the fire burn and the water flow, the seeds sprout, and the trees grow makes me answer your questions. A person is a set pattern of desires and thoughts and resulting actions. There is no such pattern in my case. I am pure Consciousness itself, unbroken awareness of all that is. As long as the body lasts, it has its needs like any other, but my mental process has come to an end.[47]

In the Western world, neither science nor Christianity acknowledge the existence of Sri Nisargadatta Maharaj or any other living example of a Jesus-like person. To maintain the Western world's spiritual ignorance, taboos encompass more than living revealers of cosmic consciousness. Did you notice that near-death experiences, past-life regression, and afterlife communication with mediums reveal that the "I am" passes sans body but otherwise unmodified into the afterlife? The powerful grip on our consciousness of our egoic sense of ourselves is revealed in Dr. Ian Stevenson's research findings. Those children who remembered verifiable previous lives provided one level of evidence for reincarnation, but an even more unequivocal level of evidence was provided by those children born with the "I am" sense of self or the consciousness of a person who died a relatively recent traumatic death. Near-death experiences, past-life regression, afterlife communication, and children who remember previous lives are distinctly different phenomena whose harmonious agreement provide overwhelming empirical evidence that our consciousness arises from souls, which incarnate from lifetime to lifetime.

In the West, it is easy to live a long life and never hear of the concepts of nonduality and self-realization. Even though our planet has become a "global village," materialistic understandings of reality isolate minds from alternative perspectives as effectively as the mountains and oceans of centuries past. Reading *I Am That* in 1997 increased my motivation to learn about those who have achieved self-realization.

MEDITATION

The first step in the pursuit of achieving self-realization and the ability of a medium is obtaining appropriate spiritual guidance. You probably have no idea, unless you were raised in the East or attended a Spiritualist church, where to find a "guru" or someone who teaches mediumship; but meditation will be the primary "tool" to develop your spiritual eyes and ears. To make up for any cultural disadvantages you may have in appreciating the transformative potential of meditation, I highly recommend reading *Autobiography of a Yogi* by Paramahansa Yogananda and *Spirit Lights a Path to Mediumship* by Pat Chalfant.

For thousands of years, meditation techniques enabled members of religious communities to alter the mind's usual programing to experience the unity behind our phenomenal reality. Despite being referred to twenty-three times in the Bible, meditation's role in the Judeo-Christian tradition is not as significant as in Eastern religions and philosophy. Hinduism's Upanishads describe meditation as the union of the meditator's mind with universal divine consciousness, or Brahman. The Upanishads, in harmony with the burning bush identifying God as "I am," describe God, Brahman, as the source of everyone's sense of "I."

Instead of the Western world's focus upon loving, accepting, and finding one's "true self," Eastern philosophers like Confucius, Xunzi, and Laozi—like Jesus—encouraged people to discover and correct their own undesirable tendencies and behaviors. Jesus's statements "Do not judge" and "Why do you look at the speck of sawdust in your brother's eye and pay no attention to the plank in your own eye" suggest Christianity's seven virtues and deadly sins are meant to be applied to ourselves and not others. When we point a finger in judgment of others, Eastern religions and philosophers advise us to focus on the three fingers pointing back at ourselves. Reincarnation philosophy teaches that we are born to become aware of and correct our own faults and to wisely choose the company we keep. Meditation provides a tool to replace egocentric tendencies with the realization of the unity within creation's diversity.

In India, gurus or spiritual teachers like Sri Nisargadatta Maharaj "certify" the level of spiritual consciousness achieved by their followers or students. Spiritual wisdom is acquired through personal experience, and not by reading books. Because our aptitudes and abilities are different, Hinduism has four paths, or yogas, to realize the unity—"I and the Father are One"—in the diversity of creation. The easiest path for most people is loving devotion, Bhakti Yoga, to God, one's guru, and others. By emphasizing love, Jesus's ministry and Christianity harmonizes with Hinduism's Bhakti Yoga. Karma Yoga, which includes the goal of being unaffected by praise or blame, may be the most difficult for most Americans. Jnana Yoga, wisdom or knowledge, is considered the most intellectually difficult. Raja Yoga, the mind investigating itself, is the path taught in *A Course in Miracles* and most closely relates to and involves meditation.

Ralph Waldo Emerson was among the first and most influential in the United States to embrace India's Hindu religion. In contrast to the mindless conformity in New England during his lifetime, Emerson—transcendentalism's primary proponent—asked in the first paragraph of his 1836 book, *Nature*, "Why should we not have a poetry and philosophy of insight and not of tradition, and a religion by revelation to us, and not the history of theirs?" Emerson shared his thoughts in books, essays, and hundreds of public lectures. Mystical spiritual experiences inspired his philosophy and identification with Hinduism, which he revealed by copying passages from Hindu texts in his poems and essays. In *Nature*, he described experiencing samadhi with these words: "I became a transparent eyeball. I am nothing, I see all; The currents of the universal being circulated through me."

The followers of many of the world's religions attended the 1893 World's Parliament of Religions in Chicago. When systematic racism was more apparent than today, India's Vivekananda addressed his audience as "brothers and sisters of America." Well over a century after Vivekananda's speech, the Black Lives Matter Movement is justifiably impatient with Western religion and education's progress reducing prejudice and discrimination by teaching children to treat everyone, with no exceptions, as they would want to be treated.

Wouldn't a god capable of manifesting over time our physical circumstances and reality also be capable of and motivated to advance our level of spiritual consciousness? Ancient Sanskrit and Hebrew texts proclaim that God periodically sends advanced souls like the Old Testament's profits, Jesus, and Hinduism's avatars to raise humanity's spiritual consciousness. In the Western world, unfortunately, God's efforts to raise spiritual consciousness levels are undermined by science's atheism, Christianity's adherence to tradition, and Western education's avoidance of teaching children "how to live."

Paramhansa Yogananda was the first Indian monk or guru to significantly influence thousands of people in the United States. After his arrival in Boston, he went on speaking tours, purchased properties for his followers, and created a worldwide spiritual organization—the Self-Realization Fellowship, abbreviated SRF—which today has over five hundred temples, retreats, ashrams, and meditation centers around the world. California has seven temples and the SRF's headquarters building. SRF maintains and makes available Yogananda's writings, teachings, and the teaching of Kriya Yoga.

If you read books by and about Yogananda, you will find that he, like Jesus, had "supernormal" powers and abilities. Years before his arrival in Boston in 1920, Yogananda's spiritual eyes saw images of the California SRF buildings, which he knew related to God's plan for his life. Before they met, Yogananda's guru also knew of God's plan for Yogananda and his role as Yogananda's guru. When Yogananda made his unannounced initial approach to Swami Sri Yukteswar Giri's hermitage, the swami psychically knew when Yogananda was close to his hermitage and sent a disciple to greet Yogananda. After his arrival in Boston, Yogananda lived in near poverty. Despite his humble circumstances, Yogananda confidently told potential followers about the spiritual communities and buildings God would manifest through their efforts. Skeptics of God's behind-the-scenes role have the problem of accounting for the odds against Yogananda's mystical premonitions becoming a reality. The response to Jesus's brief life and ministry, Christianity, is even more incredible and improbable.

No discussion of Yogananda, whose Sunday sermons combined Jesus's spiritual teachings with those of Hinduism, would be complete without an explanation of his and his guru's decision to leave their bodies and enter Mahasamadhi. The first chapter's research findings and reincarnation philosophy suggest that souls maintain their accumulated Karma and are subject to rebirth until self-realization is achieved. Growth in the spiritual consciousness of incarnating souls primarily takes place in flesh-and-blood bodies, which is why prophets and avatars for millennia have been providing us with spiritual guidance. Because Yogananda and his guru probably achieved self-realization before they were born, they were not bound by Karma and the cycle of rebirths; they were free to enter Mahasamadhi and join other liberated souls at a higher stage of spiritual development.

With his disciples assembled about him, Swami Sri Yukteswar Giri went into a meditative state after telling his disciples that it was time for him to leave this world. His soul left his body, and from our perspective, he died a normal death. But, prior to entering Mahasamadhi and leaving this world, a yogi's consciousness is wholly absorbed in God and not worldly concerns. After telling his disciples it was his time to leave this world, Yogananda decided to enter Mahasamadhi on March 7, 1952, at the conclusion of a banquet at the Los Angeles Biltmore Hotel honoring India's ambassador to the United States. Yogananda concluded his speech with his poem, "My India," looked up toward his third-eye chakra, entered Mahasamadhi, and his body fell to the floor. The official cause of death was heart failure, but his followers knew better.

During the 1960s and 1970s, several of India's swamis (gurus, or spiritual teachers) came to the United States. Among the swamis who wrote philosophical and spiritual books during this period were Satchidananda Saraswati and Muktananda. Swami Vivekananda's books, from decades earlier, also provide the insights and wisdom of a Hindu monk and Hinduism. Maharishi Mahesh Yogi popularized a mantra method of meditation, transcendental meditation (or TM), which he described as easy to learn. For decades prior to the influence of transcendental meditation, the medical and scientific communities regarded meditation as occult nonsense because of its association with Eastern religions and esoteric, "paranormal" beliefs. Fortunately, Harvard Medical School professor and medical researcher Herbert

Benson, MD, became aware of and studied the claim of TM's meditators that meditation lowered their blood pressure. His studies in the 1960s and 1970s found that meditation reduces the body's response to stress, which plays a significant role in many health conditions. In 1975, Dr. Benson's book, *The Relaxation Response*, demystified meditation and provided the Western world with its own name for meditation: the relaxation response. In the decades since the publication of *The Relaxation Response*, subsequent research and defining meditation as a health promoting exercise instead of a spiritual practice has transformed meditation into a multibillion-dollar wellness industry. The National Center for Health Statistics reported an increase in meditation in the United States from 4 percent in 2012 to 14 percent in 2017. Because of significant clinically proven health benefits, doctors increasingly use meditation as a treatment or complementary therapy for an amazingly long list of health problems. Besides stress management and reducing the risks of heart disease, meditation's benefits include reducing chronic pain; relieving migraines; slowing age-related atrophy of the brain and bones (osteoporosis); and reducing symptoms of MS, IBS, and fibromyalgia. Stress management's benefits include increasing positive (joyful) emotions while reducing negative emotions, reducing arterial-damaging inflammation, decreasing levels of the stress hormone cortisol, increasing the body's energy levels, and increasing the ability to appropriately modify one's own thoughts and responses.

Besides making the meditator's life more joyful and healthy, meditation addresses the spiritual goals of those who want to raise their level of spiritual consciousness. Harvard scientists found that meditation increases the gray-matter density and activity in the regions of the brain involved with learning, memory, decision-making, planning, abstract thinking, and regulating emotions; but meditation decreases gray-matter density in the region of the brain associated with anxiety and stress. After years of meditation, meditators experience a decrease in egocentrism coupled with an increase in compassion and spirituality, which makes their goals less materialistic and more focused on the needs of others as they spend less time living in their heads, their "monkey mind," and more time living in the present moment.

Another Western word for meditation is mindfulness. Instead of living in one's head and experiencing the random thoughts associated with anxiety, stress, and depression, mindfulness training directs our awareness to the thoughts, feelings, sensations, and everyone and everything surrounding us as they are experienced in the present moment. The concept and practice of mindfulness can be applied to just about everything. While eating, driving, and walking, it is desirable to be fully present with what we are doing and experiencing. Even though we seem to be programmed to seldom pay attention to the present moment, our peak experiences and best performances require our full attention. Paradoxically, instead of being aware of and appreciating each moment as it arises, our minds usually wander in a remembered past or an imagined future. The only time in our lives that is real and not imagined is each moment as it arises.

If you are not already a meditator and want to get started meditating, finding a style of yoga or meditation that appeals to you can be a complex task because of the many forms of meditation and providers of instruction. An internet search for online instruction or local meditation groups and instructors may be a good way to get started. If you have never meditated, before you read the next paragraph, I want you to experience a few minutes of being fully present with each moment as it arises. Sit with a straight back, without using the backrest of a chair. Place your feet flat on the floor, with your hands on your lap. Breathe slowly through your nose while concentrating on the air flowing in and out of your nostrils. Be aware of your belly going in and out with each breath. Focus on your breathing to help stay connected with the present moment as it arises. Simply notice everything you hear (and see, if your eyes are open). When thoughts arise, notice them but do not follow them. Refocus upon your breathing when thoughts pull you out of the world of here and now.

Did you notice that, while your "I am" or sense of self is focusing on something in the world of here and now, unanticipated thoughts pulled you into the world of your mind? Thoughts that did not emanate from your meditating "I am" sense of self caused you to no longer be aware of each moment as it arose. Thoughts can be so compelling, and meditation can at first be so boring that our attention switches from the present moment to incoming thoughts. When this happens, instead of meditating, we experience ourselves as the thinker and source of thoughts that do not come from our "I am" sense of self. Meditation reveals that you have two identities. In presence, you experience the real you, your soul, experienced as the observer of your thoughts. While experiencing random thoughts associated with stress and anxiety, you are experiencing your "monkey mind's" illusory sense of "reality." Eastern religions refer to the sense of "reality" that emanates from our head as "maya," or illusion. It may be natural or normal to allow the mind to monopolize our attention, but Western science and medicine discovered meditation's health benefits, and the prophets and avatars informed us of the spiritual benefits of spending time immersed in the omnipresent oneness of "I AM." Because God's _Revelation_ to humanity promoted meditation thousands of years before Western science and medicine even noticed meditation's profound effects on human health and brains; during their so-called Enlightenment, scientists should have discarded their inflated egos instead of God.

167

MY SECOND CHURCH SERMON

Six years after Reverend Madalyn DeGrace and I shared a "paranormal" experience, and she introduced me to books about them, I finally overcame my reticence to risk reexperiencing an exoteric belief–inspired church sermon. Reverend Warren Chester was the minister when I finally showed up at Riverside's Church of Religious Science. Reverend Warren's esoteric belief–inspired sermon filled me with the joy of hearing for the first time beliefs that harmonized with my own, and regret that I had not come sooner. My eyes filled with tears when Reverend Warren proclaimed, "God is in all, above all, and through all; there is not a spot where God is not." After Reverend Warren's clear expression of samadhi's insight—God manifests throughout creation—I assumed the beliefs of the congregation harmonized with my own. When the service was over, I struck up a conversation with the people around me, but to my surprise, they seemed to be oblivious to God's omnipresence and the sermon's esoteric content.

ADDING FACTS TO FAITH

Unable to fulfill his early 1984 commitment to be the Parapsychology Association of Riverside's monthly speaker, the 1934 founder of the Philosophical Research Society, Manly Palmer Hall, asked his good friend Franklin Loehr to fulfill his commitment. I wish I had experienced one of Manly Hall's over eight thousand lectures, but I am glad he gave me the opportunity to learn about Franklin Loehr and Helen Roberts. Other than Franklin Loehr's book, *The Power of Prayer on Plants*, I knew nothing about him or Helen Roberts.

Because of his love for science's systematic and logical approach to discovering how things work, Franklin Loehr majored in chemistry. Despite graduating at the top of his class and receiving a four-year chemistry teaching fellowship at Columbia University, he wanted to be a minister like his father. While pursuing his Doctor of Divinity degree, he wished theology, like chemistry, was validated with "proven facts" instead of tradition and authority. After again graduating with honors, Loehr's ministerial career included serving as chaplain for the 471st Heavy Bomber Group during World War II. After the war, while pastoring in Massachusetts, he joined a small group of ministers who studied things like meditation, psi phenomena, other religions, philosophy, and even hypnosis and past-life regression. Their open-minded research included Everett, Massachusetts's, gifted psychic and medium Reverend Ruth Mathias. While demonstrating her abilities as a trance channel, a few of the young men who died serving in the 471st bomber group and a few of his deceased chemistry professors spoke to Reverend Loehr. Reverend Mathias could not possibly know about or mimic these prior acquaintances of Reverend Loehr. Reverend Mathias provided Reverend Loehr with proof of the survival of consciousness in an afterlife. As a minister, Franklin Loehr wished he could provide the members of his congregation with equally convincing proof.

Reverend Loehr called these unorthodox (for Christian ministers) investigations R&D for research and development. With the motto *Adding Facts to Faith*, in 1951, he established the Religious Research Foundation. Confident that scientific inquiry applied to the spiritual realm will add facts to faith and bridge the gap between faith-based and scientific communities, Franklin Loehr became a full-time seeker of facts to support faith.

Using the scientific method to verify or falsify the question, "Is prayer effective," Reverend Loehr directed a carefully controlled laboratory study on the power of prayer to influence plant growth. For three years, 156 volunteers conducted over 700 experiments requiring thousands of measurements. The conditions for germination and plant growth were identical for seeds that differed only in whether they were ignored, received positive prayers, or received negative prayers. In 1959, after all the experimental results were recorded, photographed, and analyzed, Franklin Loehr published a full report in *The Power of Prayer on Plants*. Besides providing evidence of the power of prayer and the scientific method's applicability to the concerns of religion, the book was a bestseller. McGill University was among those motivated by the book to conduct their own experiments with plants. They found a dramatic difference between plants watered by a healer and those watered by a depressed psychotic. Franklin Loehr's book stimulated many scientific experiments with plants that provide evidence for a nonmaterial, spiritual connection between people and plants. The ability of plants to respond to love and prayer seems more plausible from the "nothing is solid, and everything is energy" perspective of quantum physics than from materialist science's perspective which seems unable to grasp the obvious: the significance to human beings of their temporary physical existence pales in comparison to the significance of their underlying spiritual reality.

During the Religious Research Foundation's first few years, Franklin Loehr's curious mind investigated many things other than the power of prayer. What turned out to be the foundation's primary focus began in 1951, when Reverend Loehr was still a full-time minister, and Grace Whittenberger scheduled a counseling appointment. More than a decade before Hazel Denning accidentally discovered past-life regression while counseling in a Methodist church, Reverend Loehr was using past-life regression to uncover the causes of mental and physical symptoms. While hypnotizing Grace Whittenberger to see if her symptoms related to a subconscious past-life memory, Reverend Loehr found that Whittenberger was quickly and deeply hypnotized. Aware of the possibility of a disincarnate spirit capable of revealing the cause of her physical symptoms, Reverend Loehr asked, "Is there anyone present who wishes to speak?" A spirit entity, who identified himself as Dr. John Christopher Daniels, used Whittenberger's vocal cords to reply, "I am here." In subsequent contacts, Dr. Daniels described himself as "the unearthly one" who spent the last four thousand years studying the Akashic records to provide humanity with insight into the nature and purpose of reincarnation.

Prior to Franklin Loehr's death in 1988, Dr. Daniels provided, for thirty-six years, spiritual teachings and insights into what it means to be a spiritual being by speaking through Grace Whittenberger or Franklin Loehr while they were in a hypnotic trance. Dr. Daniels answered questions about the spiritual realm and provided over five thousand Loehr-Daniels life readings that included shared past-life experiences with an average of eight significant people in the requestor's current life. Each requestor's soul histories contain specifics about male or female, where and when in history, life circumstances, and relationships. When those who are mentioned in previous readings request their own reading, it becomes possible to determine if their reading is factually consistent with previous readings. Horton W. Amidon (Professor Emeritus, State University of New York at Farmingdale) found 163 instances of "cross-correspondence" while searching through the world's largest body of past-life readings. In only one of those coinciding matches did he find any inconsistencies. Professor Amidon documented his verification of the Loehr-Daniels life readings in his book *Cross-Correspondence Among the Loehr-Daniels Life Readings*. For those who are willing to look, the Loehr-Daniels life readings provide proof of the existence of reincarnation and the Akashic records. Reincarnation became the Religious Research Foundation's primary focus because evidence for reincarnation is also evidence for souls—the fundamental premise and concern of all religions.

Experimentation during the initial life readings revealed the necessity of a "conductor" to ask Dr. Daniels the questions of the person requesting a reading and questions that clarify and expand upon Dr. Daniels's answers. The conductor's questions and Dr. Daniels's responses were recorded for later transcription. As the primary conductor during the 1980s, Helen Roberts was uniquely qualified to write books about our spiritual reality from a transcendent (Dr. Daniels's) level of spiritual knowledge. A small portion of the information in Helen Roberts's books inspired the following paragraphs. Her books, as well as books by Franklin Loehr and other members of the Religious Research Foundation, are available from the Religious Research Foundation's website.

God's greatest commandments, Matthew 22:37–39, are to love "God with all your heart," and "your neighbor as yourself." Why would God expect us to love our neighbor, others, as ourselves? Is there something that everyone has in common that warrants everyone's love? By explaining the origin of souls, everyone's underlying reality, Dr. Daniels revealed what we all have in common—even with our enemies—which warrants our continuous awareness and love. Everyone's soul comes from the same source: God. We are all God's children.

Remember my childhood experience of discovering fossils inside rocks after experiencing the omnipresent love of God, samadhi? The two experiences combined to provide a profound sense of God and creation's unimaginably long coexistence. Before the beginning of human civilization, and long before people progressed from elementary school to advanced college degrees, divine sparks (or portions of God capable of developing latent powers and abilities) began progressing through God's educational program. Human beings are not unique or special because we have souls. What makes us unique, according to Dr. Daniels, is our enrollment in God's curriculum designed to transform souls into God's compatible companions.

The primitive beginning, incarnational stage of development is merely a portion of God's mostly spiritual realms of conscious existence. Over the course of several stages of development, the individuated portions, or children of God, are expected to discover, develop, and realize latent godlike qualities and capabilities. As Jesus proclaimed, "In my Father's house are many homes,"[48] or cosmic schools in which God cares for and educates His children.

Earth School emphasizes "doingness" to learn by experience those ways of thinking, acting, and being that are in harmony with God's will. To graduate from the Earth's incarnational stage of development, Dr. Daniels said souls usually require sixty to one hundred significant incarnations. To help Earth School achieve each incarnation's intended learning and soul development goals, a well-organized spiritual realm uses spirit guides and teachers working with cause and effect (Karma) to guide each soul's progress. Dr. Daniels said the average spacing of incarnations is about one century, but can be several centuries; and, as in the case of children who remember previous lives, souls can fail to take advantage of the between-lives assistance available to process their prior-life's experiences and to plan their next incarnation. The souls of those who requested readings received their "grade" in Earth School from Dr. Daniels. He broke soul development into five stages: just started, well started, middle souls, well along, and near the end. Because, according to Dr. Daniels, the spiritual content of souls that fail to develop desirable character traits in a timely manner are returned to God (recycled), reincarnation is the most important subject for everyone to understand and appreciate.

As spiritual beings, what could be more important than liberation, or graduating from Earth School and avoiding being recycled? Being recycled sounds a lot better than an eternity in hell, but everyone should want to graduate from Earth School. Dr. Daniels spent four thousand years studying the Akashic records so you can understand your life from a larger perspective than was previously possible. In addition to looking back in time thousands of years, Dr. Daniels knows what comes after liberation. From the "many homes" perspective of God's educational program, liberation is no more significant than graduating from elementary school. We are oblivious to our soul's potential to develop godlike qualities and capabilities.

Middle school, like all spiritual realms other than Earth School, takes place in a spiritual, nonmaterial realm called the realm of Cohesion, which emphasizes the development of "beingness." High school, the Elohim level of spiritual instruction, stresses responsibility and discerning God's will. Advanced spiritual beings occasionally incarnate from the Elohim and higher realms of spiritual consciousness. Dr. Daniels said Ralph Waldo Emerson, Manley Palmer Hall, and Franklin Loehr incarnated from the Elohim realm. Those who achieve college-level capability requirements, like Dr. Daniels, graduate to the Mini-Creator realm; and those who make it to graduate school become Co-Ccreators with God. From these higher levels of spiritual consciousness, God provided us with prophets, like Jesus, and avatars to inspire and influence the development of the world's religions. Over many lifetimes, discrimination combined with free will enables just-started souls to eventually graduate from Earth School. Those whose actions flow from a desire to be truthful, fair, beneficial, and loving progress in their spiritual journeys; while those who fail to regret and learn from the pain that they inflict on others are recycled. The Western world's *taboo against knowing who you are*, and science's atheistic paradigms must add to the difficulty of graduating from Earth School.

Because the opportunity to have Loehr-Daniels life readings ended with Franklin Loehr's death, past-life regression is the primary (if not the only) way to obtain information about your past lives. You merely need to be hypnotized. The ease with which Grace Whittenberger became a trance channel facilitated Dr. Daniel's initial appearance. If Virginia Tighe did not easily and deeply become hypnotized, *The Search for Bridey Murphy* would not exist. In my case, when I went to past-life regression therapists, they were unable to hypnotize me; and I failed to hypnotize myself when guided by a book on self-hypnosis. My subconscious mind's resistance to being hypnotized motivated my decision during Franklin Loehr and Helen Roberts's presentation to request my own Loehr-Daniels life reading.

I asked Dr. Daniels, along with other questions, if my mother's soul and my soul knew each other during previous incarnations. While thinking of questions to ask Dr. Daniels about my mother, who at only forty-nine years of age unexpectedly died in 1966, feelings of melancholy prompted me to write, "Hi Mom, I love you." When the conductor, Helen Roberts, read what I wrote, Dr. Daniels said, "Well, that is fine. I'll see to it that that statement of his is put on a postcard and posted on some bulletin board where it will get to her." Dr. Daniels also said that in the afterlife my mom "had a continuing interest in the family she left behind, but she was shown how they have their own guides and teachers, and she has more learning to do. After the initial period of adjustment following her death, she has found her place, her grade in school with her associates for growing. She is not constantly with them, of course, but she is aware of them."

I included this portion of my Loehr-Daniels life reading because two years later, in 1986, an unexpected event reminded me what Dr. Daniels had said about my mom's "continuing interest in the family she left behind."

"Religions are many, but God is One."
—*Sathya Sai Baba*

Chapter 7
1986

It is the heart which perceives God and not the reason.

—Blaise Pascal, Pesées

The experiences that motivated me to join the Parapsychology Association of Riverside (PAR) cannot be explained by ordinary physical causes, and they suggest that we are puppets controlled by hidden strings. Mysterious puddles of liquid on my receptionist's desk while Reverend DeGrace held my first metaphysics book, Gail's past-life regression experiences at Hazel Denning's home, coincidences with astrology, and my clairvoyant experience with a letter floating in a pink cloud are phenomena that would not exist if Western science's materialistic paradigms contained the full truth of our reality. Prior to these experiences, PAR did not interest me because I was skeptical of psi phenomena and did not believe in astrology or reincarnation.

The divinely choreographed experiences, which motivated my curiosity about PAR and "paranormal" phenomena, revolved around my Fox Theater optometry practice; and the experiences that led to the answers to my high school prayers revolved around my involvement with PAR. In 1986, I was in my forties, and my high school pleadings or prayers to be led to someone like Jesus were a distant memory. The intense desire for spiritual truth or wisdom, which motivated my high school prayers, disappeared after I turned the problem over to God and focused upon worldly concerns. Before I get into the events of 1986, which also suggest that we are puppets controlled by hidden strings, I want to share a few PAR memories before they no longer have any relevance to what I am writing about.

In 1984, Hazel Denning asked me to become a member of PAR's board of directors. She said my qualifications were that I was a man (somewhat of a rarity in PAR), and that the "Dr." before my name lent credibility to a poorly perceived and understood organization. Serving on PAR's board allowed me to interact with interesting, service-minded people, and I had the honor of serving as PAR's president during 1988. As president, I was asked to write a two-hundred-word "President's Column" each month for the newsletter. When I sat down to write the column, one clairvoyant experience did not keep me from feeling miscast as PAR's president, but the words usually flowed out as if from a wiser and more fluent voice than my own. On one occasion, while driving hundreds of miles from home, I suddenly realized PAR's newsletter editor expected my column the next morning. Immediately after thinking "What am I going to write," a voice in my head dictated what to write. When I got home, I grabbed a pen and paper and thought, "Tell me again what to write." The voice immediately repeated what I remembered hearing while driving home. During PAR's next monthly meeting, two members told me that "what I wrote" applied to and helped with their personal concerns. I believe PAR's service to the community reflected the efforts of both disincarnate and incarnate souls.

One of PAR's annual events, August Dialogues, was made possible by the members who volunteered to host classes and discussions on topics of interest to PAR's members. August Dialogues dealt with what Dr. Daniels might describe as discovering, developing, and realizing our "latent godlike qualities and capabilities." PAR's members liked to discuss and experience magical beliefs, practices, and phenomena like divination that tap into the infinite energy field that surrounds us. Eastern religions think of soul and God as one reality and attribute "paranormal" abilities to an underlying spiritual reality; but, in the West, soul and God are thought of as separate, independent things, which is why Westerners attribute "their" paranormal abilities to "their higher consciousness."

DIVINATION

The variety of topics and the number of volunteering hosts made it possible to go to an August Dialogue almost every day in August. Occult methods of divination were popular August Dialogue topics. Divination refers to methods for obtaining insight into a question or situation by "paranormal" or "supernormal" means. From a materialistic perspective, most forms of divination appear ridiculously impossible because, from a materialistic perspective, they are impossible! Reality will never seem the same after experiencing consistently accurate insights from divination. Diviners may attribute their ability to worldly things, but the inadequacy of materialistic explanations suggest God's omnipresent availability to answer the questions of those with "the gift" or the diviners blessed with God's grace.

Astrology, which was discussed previously, is one of many forms of divination. Besides traits and tendencies, astrology is used to reveal insight into a person's future from astrological charts. A well-documented example of the use of astrology to foretell and guide future activities occurred during the last seven years of Ronald Reagan's presidency. After an astrologer warned Nancy Reagan about "an incident" that would occur on March 30, 1981—the day President Reagan was shot during an assassination attempt—she contacted Joan Quigley, San Francisco's Vassar-educated astrologer, to guide and coordinate President Regan's political activities with the insights provided by his horoscope.

During the portion of a PAR class dealing with how to read tarot cards, everyone received detailed written instructions that included descriptions of the images, symbolism, and significance of each of the seventy-eight tarot cards. Because of her psychic ability and interest, I gave the instructions to Jill Mix a decade or more before we were married. After buying a deck of tarot cards, Jill very quickly became, as Harry Potter might say, a real wizard with tarot cards. By alternately reading tarot cards with similarly gifted friends, Jill developed confidence with the cards. On several occasions before completing her college education, she attracted additional business for friends who owned restaurants while getting paid to read tarot cards.

A person requesting a tarot reading is asked to shuffle the cards face down while thinking about the question they want the cards to answer. When they feel the cards are sufficiently shuffled, Jill has them cut the cards and indicate which half goes on top. Jill picks up the cards and lays them down face up in a specific pattern called a spread. The reading is inspired by the concepts symbolized on each card and its location in the spread. Jill does not want to know the question she and the cards are expected to answer. Even though the question may be about relationships, health concerns, money, or any other concern, somehow the specific cards that apply to the question inexplicably and appropriately appear in the spread. Even though the cards have a range of meanings and interpretations, Jill's intuitive ability tunes into the appropriate response to the concern of the person receiving the reading. Often, when the question is about health concerns, Jill experiences in her body the discomfort that prompted the reading. When Jill describes the person's unmentioned physical symptoms, they look as if they are having a religious experience.

The large variety and number of methods of divination and fortune-telling suggest they emerged over the centuries within many cultures. Besides astrology and tarot, commonly known methods are crystal ball and tea leaf readings, I Ching, numerology, palmistry, and runes. Like the migration of monarch butterflies, they all defy explanation and acceptance from a materialistic perspective. Despite being perplexed by and uncomfortable with divination, I fortunately attended an August Dialogue that featured a method of divination that required a minimal amount of interest and effort on my part. An aptitude or God's grace may be required, but the magic and power behind divination must be experienced to be appreciated. The method taught at this August Dialogue was divination with a pendulum. After a pendulum—a crystal, glass, or metal weight suspended on a six-inch chain—was given to everyone, they were told to ask their pendulum to show them their starting position. When I held the end of the chain between the tips of my thumb and pointer (index) finger and asked the dangling metal weight to "show me our starting position," the pendulum magically began orbiting in a large counterclockwise circle. We were then asked to put the pendulum into its starting position and ask the pendulum to reveal its yes response. Hanging motionlessly would be the starting position for a pendulum that did not move when asked to reveal its starting position. After making the pendulum spin in a counterclockwise orbit and asking it to "show me a yes response," the pendulum immediately bobbed toward and away from me to indicate a yes response. When asked to show its no response, the pendulum switched from its counterclockwise orbit to swinging from side to side, or a left-right swing. Because not all questions can or will be answered by the pendulum, the third and last response to get from the pendulum is its "I'm not going to answer that question" response. When I put the pendulum into a counterclockwise orbit and said, "Show me our not today, ask another question response," it swung away from me on my left and toward my right side. To confirm our pendulum's responses, we were instructed to ask the pendulum questions we knew the answers to, like "Is the sky blue?" Because the pendulum tends to respond literally to questions, this would not be a good question to ask on an overcast day or during evening hours.

My pendulum has been answering my questions for over forty years. Whatever answers my questions is always immediately accessible and answers the questions before I finish silently asking them in my mind. To change its answer, the pendulum goes into an energetic counterclockwise orbit, as if to erase its previous answer, and energetically gives the alternative response. I wanted to know how to address the source of the answers to my questions. I experimented with "my higher consciousness" and other possibilities before I finally obtained a yes response to "divine consciousness." The pendulum seems to delight in answering questions about ethics and morality, and the writing of this book. It will not help or assist me to "time the market" or benefit financially from its answers.

Often, my pendulum's answers provide me with proof of the divine, otherworldly nature of the answers. Curious to see if I could use a pendulum for water dowsing while staying with my dad, I asked my pendulum if we could find the best place to locate water on Dad's seven steeply sloped acres. After the pendulum said yes, from several locations on Dad's property, where he built his retirement home, I asked the pendulum to indicate which direction led to the best place to find water. I expected the pendulum to point in the direction of Dad's well, but wherever I stood, the pendulum always led me to a small, white stake. The next day, I told my dad that if he ever needed more water, I may have found a better place to locate a well than his well's current location. He told me that when his property was dowsed, the dowser put a white stake in the ground where he said three underground streams crossed, but because that location was down the slope from where Dad wanted to locate his house, a higher location for the well was selected. Finding the same spot on seven acres as a professional dowser proved to me the divine, otherworldly nature of my pendulum's responses and the wisdom of hiring a dowser. One of my patients, who built a house outside Moreno Valley's city limits, told me that his dowser correctly predicted his well's flow rate and depth. Because Dad's nearest neighbor did not believe in "paranormal" phenomena like dowsing for water, his three wells only provided a few gallons of water per day. Dad's neighbor's other nearest neighbor, my uncle Oscar, built a small pond and two large hydroponic greenhouses because his dowser found an underground spring.

On another occasion, a pendulum may have saved my life. I retired to a city that is adjacent to a second-growth Douglas fir forest with fifty-five miles of narrow walking trails that crisscross through the dense forest. On a map of the trails, I noticed a trail that went in the direction of a lake I wanted to see. Without the map, telling anyone where I was going, my cell phone, or a compass, I foolishly headed down a trail I assumed led to a lake. At the end of the trail, another trail ran to the left and to the right. Despite exploring on both sides of the trail, I did not find access to or see a lake. For the next three hours, I tried without success to locate the trail leading back to my car. The overcast sky made it impossible to have a sense of direction; it was getting dark, and I began to realize I was in danger of dying without my body being found for a long time. While thinking that what would be remembered about me, if my body was ever found, would be how stupidly I had taken off without a cell phone or telling anyone where I was going, I remembered my pendulum. With my handkerchief and keys, I made a pendulum that told me it would lead me back to my car. After asking the pendulum left, right, or straight ahead at three or four intersecting trails, and another hour of walking, I walked onto the only road going through the forest. My car was a mile or two down the road. Thanks to a pendulum, I was no longer lost.

When I read David R. Hawkins's book, *Power versus Force: The Hidden Determinants of Human Behavior*, I learned about a medical science-based method of divination. Dr. Hawkins describes experiencing samadhi on page ten, self-realization on page twelve, and pages 68–69 have a "map of consciousness" levels obtained from "indicator muscles" that answer yes or no questions without the brain's involvement by becoming stronger or weaker. The kinesiology research findings of Dr. George Goodheart combined with Dr. John Diamond's discovery that indicator muscles respond to thoughts and emotions led to science's discovery of a method of divination. Indicator muscles answer yes or no questions as readily as my pendulum. Dr. Hawkins described the power that answers questions by making muscles stronger or weaker as the "basis of all consciousness – which has traditionally been called divinity."[49] Dr. Hawkins's research with indicator muscles found that reliable and consistent findings were not obtained unless the consciousness levels of those doing muscle testing were above a certain level.

The dictionary defines self-confidence as confidence, which may be inflated or realistic, in one's own capabilities. Divination inspires Self-confidence, with a capital S, in the ability and availability of an unseen, godlike power to answer questions. Jill does not foolishly and egotistically believe she possesses a "paranormal" ability to arrange unseen tarot cards and to know things that are outside the range of her five senses. She developed confidence in the willingness of an invisible, omnipresent power to appropriately organize the tarot cards as they are shuffled. She also developed confidence that she would receive otherworldly, divine guidance when reading the cards. When I hold a pendulum, it is not self-confidence that anticipates the pendulum's response. It is Self-confidence in the ability of the omnipresent divine power of God to respond to and answer the question.

ANITA BURNS AND CORONA LIGHT

My interest in occult or "paranormal" phenomena frequently led me to the classes and speakers at Riverside's Corona Light, as well as the Parapsychology Association of Riverside. PAR owed its existence to a group of women who were aware of the desirability of showcasing people with occult abilities and knowledge. Corona Light showcased the extraordinary "paranormal" abilities of Anita Burns. Before she was old enough to go to school, Anita's spiritual eyes and ears enabled her to see and talk with discarnate beings, astral travel, and reveal both psychic and healing abilities. Because our underlying reality as spiritual beings with usually dormant spiritual eyes and ears is not embraced or taught by Christianity or Western science and education, parents are seldom appreciative or encouraging of the "paranormal" abilities of children. Psychically gifted children are encouraged to be and act more "normal." New members of the Parapsychology Association of Riverside were often pleasantly surprised to find people who embraced and encouraged their unusual abilities. Anita Burns' psychic gifts were not lost because her mother, who was initiated into the practice of Kriya Yoga as a devotee of Yogananda, appreciated and encouraged her daughter's unusual talents.

During a weekly Corona Light event, Anita Burns told the attendees sitting before her about their spirit guides and teachers. Other than ideas that I am inclined to attribute to them, I am oblivious to having spirit guides and teachers, and I am inclined to be skeptical of statements made by psychic mediums. But Anita Burns and other mediums always told me the same thing: "Your spirit guides can get messages through to you." During my Loehr-Daniels life reading, Dr. Daniels responded to my request to be told "something about my soul's guides and teachers" by saying, "Well, they are not with him every minute. They have other things to do as well. It is the nature of God, what He has established [...] the great guidelines, and the protection of His beingness. Aside from that, they are capable. They know various aspects of his life's purpose [...]. Things can be brought to him, as he knows from his own experience." My experiences and what Dr. Daniels said harmonized with what Anita Burns told me about my spirit guides.

Early in 1986, a man spoke at Corona Light about his experiences at Sathya Sai Baba's ashram in Puttaparthi, India. Sathya Sai Baba is purported to be an avatar. *Avatar* was a new word and concept for me, but I attended because his trip to India reminded me of my high school fantasy of finding a Jesus-like person in India. Unlike the god of the Abrahamic religions sending His "only begotten son," prophets, and messengers, Hinduism's god responds to declines in human conduct and values by taking birth in human form to serve as a role model and teacher of ideal human behavior. Rama, the seventh incarnation of Vishnu (God), and Krishna, Vishnu's eighth incarnation, are Hinduism's most notable avatars. Instead of having just one sacred text like Christianity's Bible, Hinduism has five primary sacred texts: *Vedic Verses*, *Upanishads*, *Laws of Manu*, *Ramayana*, and the *Mahabharata*. The last two are extremely long epic poems about government, kings, wars, and avatars in Ancient India.

Shirdi Sai Baba (1838–1918) is revered by many Hindus as a recent avatar. A few of my patients, who immigrated from India, seemed to revere Shirdi Sai Baba in the same way Christians revere Jesus. Prior to his death in 1918, Shirdi Sai Baba said he would reincarnate in eight years. Eight years later, in 1926, Sathya Raju was born in a small rural community that was isolated by language and culture from Shirdi Sai Baba's life and prophecy. Fourteen years later, in 1940, fourteen-year-old

Sathya Raju announced that henceforth, as the reincarnation of Shirdi Sai Baba, his name would be Sathya Sai Baba, whose mission was to bring about the world's spiritual transformation. The five core "human values" which he emphasized are truth, right conduct (**dharma**), peace, love, and nonviolence. Like Jesus, avatars perform miracles to attract devotees and to provide evidence of the divine nature of their incarnation.

I do not remember what Corona Light's speaker said about Sathya Sai Baba, but I remember projected on the screen beside him were photographs taken during his trip to Sathya Sai Baba's ashram and place of birth in Puttaparthi, India. In 1940, Puttaparthi was a small village that rapidly grew along with Sathya Sai Baba's ashram to accommodate devotees from around the world. The only thing I recall with certainty was a picture taken at the ashram with four rainbows. I have seen a double rainbow, but I reacted to four rainbows captured on one 35-millimeter color slide in the same way I reacted to puddles of liquid on my receptionist's desk. The speaker's description of Sathya Sai Baba harmonized with my high school fantasy of finding a Jesus-like person in India, but I was no longer inclined to drop everything and travel to India. The salaries of three employees and other office overhead expenses made me too absorbed in worldly concerns to contemplate going to India.

For a few months in early 1986, I attended weekly Rainbow Bridge Guided Meditation sessions. At one of the sessions, the leader and organizer of the group covered her dining room table with books about Sathya Sai Baba and requested that we select a book to read and keep. I selected *Sai Baba: The Ultimate Experience* by Phyllis Krystal.

PHYLLIS KRYSTAL

I owe a debt of gratitude to the remarkable women, like Phyllis Krystal, who have informed and inspired my spiritual journey. Born in 1914, Phyllis Krystal's search for life's meaning and purpose began before I was born. Relative to men, women tend to be more aware of their intuitive abilities, to think of themselves as spiritual beings, and women are less likely to be religiously unaffiliated or "nones." Science's atheistic paradigms probably play a significant role in the rapid increase in America's nones. If most scientists were women, science's paradigms would accommodate those with an interest in investigating "paranormal" phenomena.

In the late 1950s, Mrs. Krystal and another college graduate, housewife, and mother became aware that they were waking up aware of dreams that were relevant to and contained solutions to the previous day's concerns. They met regularly to find out how to access and use their minds' unconscious knowledge and "superconscious" abilities. Their efforts seemed to be assisted by an inner source of guidance that inspired visualization techniques for "cutting the ties" to life's traumatic experiences—especially during childhood—that influence our habits of thinking, acting, and being. Meditation techniques enabled them to tap into an inner source of security and wisdom. Applying what they learned enabled Mrs. Krystal to teach clients how to replace unreliable and undesirable emotional responses like grief, anger, and jealousy with what she described as "the indwelling God or High Self."

In 1972, Phyllis Krystal heard about Sathya Sai Baba; and, in 1973, she and her husband, Sidney, made their first of many annual trips from California to Sai Baba's ashrams in India. Sai Baba's main ashram in Puttaparthi is called Prasanthi Nilayam, which means "abode of supreme peace." His summer home, Brindavan Ashram in Whitefield, is a thirty-minute drive from Bangalore, whose name was changed to Bengaluru. To escape the summer heat, Sai Baba also met with devotees in Kodaikanal, India. Prior to the 1980s, few spiritual seekers in the United States were aware of Sai Baba, who claimed that it was his will that brought people to him at appropriate times in their lives. Prior to hearing about Sai Baba, Phyllis and Sidney traveled the world seeking a spiritual guide or teacher capable of helping them to achieve "liberation from attachment to the material world and eventual enlightenment."[50] The hope that Sai Baba was the spiritual teacher they'd traveled the world to find brought them to Sai Baba's ashrams.

Despite all the devotees from around the world competing for Sai Baba's attention, Phyllis and Sidney received a great deal of Sai Baba's time and attention. Phyllis quickly became in awe of his detailed knowledge of her prior incarnations as well as her current life. Sai Baba told Phyllis she needed to and was going to write books. Prior to Sai Baba's insistence that everyone needed to know how to cut *the ties that bind* them to this material world, Phyllis did not realize the desirability of writing a book. She began writing her first "cutting the ties" book at the ashram. While writing, she was amazed to realize that the "guidance from within" which she'd received since the late 1950s came from Sathya Sai Baba. "But perhaps what amazed [Phyllis] most was his apparent awareness of literally everything and everyone, which gave the impression that he was constantly tuned into the whole world and everyone in it."[51]

Sai Baba said he gave people what they wanted— wristwatches, rings that mysteriously fit, and other wearable symbols of his love—to encourage people to want what he incarnated to give: liberation from worldly desires. Sai Baba said the keepsakes can be used to alert him of the wearers' need for assistance. While at Brindavan Ashram in 1973, Phyllis and Sidney witnessed two couples barge into the interview room to thank Sai Baba for saving their lives the previous evening. While riding in a taxicab from the ashram to their hotel in Bangalore, their taxicab driver recklessly attempted to pass a bus without regard for oncoming traffic. Instead of an unavoidable head-on collision, the car that was in front of them appeared to pass through and behind them. Sai Baba said he had prevented the accident even though no one had thought to call for his assistance. When Arabs armed with machine guns and dynamite hijacked Phyllis and Sidney's flight from Bombay to London, Phyllis remembered Sathya Sai Baba's ability to remotely provide assistance, and used the ring Sai Baba gave her to obtain his assistance.

Phyllis and Sidney also witnessed parapsychologists Karlis Osis, PhD, and Erlendur Haraldsson, PhD, (Their research on deathbed visions is discussed in the first chapter.) attempt to investigate Sai Baba's "supernormal" abilities. They asked Sai Baba if he could provide them with a scientific explanation for his ability to manifest the keepsakes that he gives his devotees and other "miracles" attributed to him by his devotees. Sai Baba did not cooperate with these two parapsychologists or the efforts of other investigators to validate and explain the phenomena attributed to him. Such requests miss the point of why, throughout history, the great spiritual teachers manifested miracles and provided spiritual instruction. They did not incarnate to reveal their greatness. They incarnated to teach us about our underlying spiritual reality or soul. Sai Baba told the parapsychologists that "if we develop our mental power and purify our hearts, we can also do it, provided we love the entire creation as he does."[52]

Coincidentally, Phyllis, the author of my first Sai Baba book, and Sidney were close friends with Henry Puharich, MD who wrote the afterword for *Arigo: Surgeon of the Rusty Knife*, which was my first book about "paranormal" phenomena. Reverend Madalyn DeGrace had loaned the borrowed book to me while we were examining puddles on a desk's glass surface. Without the still unexplained mystery of blobs of liquid on the receptionist's desk, it would have been unlikely that Reverend DeGrace would loan (and insist on continuing to loan) books to me.

Because medical specialists and modern medicine failed to reduce the severity and frequency of her headaches, before Phyllis knew about Sai Baba, Dr. Puharich talked her into seeing Arigo about her headaches. A Brazilian friend of Dr. Puharich agreed to be Phyllis and Sidney's guide and interpreter. When Phyllis and Sidney reached the small village where Arigo lived, they learned he was in prison for performing surgery without a medical license. By pretending to be Arigo's relatives, Phyllis and their interpreter were able to see Arigo during family visiting hours. Guided by his spirit guide, Fritz, Arigo typed instructions for taking nine different drugs for several weeks. Because the drugs made her feel worse instead of better, Phyllis quit taking them before completing the full course of treatment.

Several years later, when Phyllis and Sidney were making annual trips to Sai Baba's ashrams, Sai Baba told Phyllis that the drugs that had caused her early onset of menopause contributed to her current headache problem. Unaware that menopause had begun earlier for her than normal, and completely forgetting her trip to Brazil, Phyllis exclaimed, "Oh Baba, I never take drugs, as I am allergic to so many of them."[53] From a worldly, materialistic perspective, Sai Baba should have no way of knowing what Phyllis did not know or remember, yet he insisted that he was correct. A few days later, Phyllis woke up realizing how young she was when the symptoms of menopause began, and she remembered her trip to Brazil and all the drugs prescribed by Arigo.

ARMAND MARCOTTE

In October of 1986, Armand Marcotte (1929–1999) was PAR's monthly speaker. His extraordinary clairvoyant ability inspired authors to write books for and about him. Anatol Brunton wrote Marcotte's first-person singular "autobiography," *Tomorrow Knocks*, which was published in

1982. Ann Druffel wrote *The Psychic and the Detective*, which examines eight crimes that Marcotte's psychic ability helped to solve; and *Past Lives, Future Growth*, which focuses on Marcotte's insights as a psychic counselor into his clients' past and current lives.

Instead of initially talking about or demonstrating his remarkable psychic ability, Marcotte talked about his March trip to India to see Sathya Sai Baba. Reminiscent of my clairvoyant experience with a letter floating in a pink cloud, Marcotte's initial experience with Sai Baba revealed Sai Baba's ability to know the content of letters without opening them. Marcotte and his traveling companion brought letters to give to Sai Baba during **darshan**. Darshan refers to seeing or "breathing the same air as" a great person. Sai Baba's devotees might say, "I received Baba's darshan," or "I attended darshan." Because of the large number of people attending darshan by the 1980s, devotees sat closely spaced on the ground several long rows deep. Darshan provided devotees with two opportunities each day to see Sai Baba, to potentially be invited to Sai Baba's interview room, and to pass letters to the front row to be given to Sai Baba. Both Marcotte, whose letter contained only one request, and his friend attempted to get their letters passed to Sai Baba. When Sai Baba saw their letters coming toward him, he pointed at Marcotte's friend's letter and said, "Pass it back to him. He has requested the fulfillment of eleven desires. When his desires are reduced to one, I will take his letter." Marcotte's friend shouted, "But they are not all for me." After saying that the interview room was already full, Sai Baba asked Marcotte when they were leaving and said he wanted to talk to him before they left.

Despite attending both daily darshan sessions, Marcotte was not selected to go to the interview room. Before beginning their trip home, from outside the wall surrounding the darshan area, Marcotte took "Sathya Sai Baba's radiant hands picture" which is on the cover of this book. When prints were made from his film, Marcotte's picture of Sai Baba contained physical evidence of Sai Baba's extraordinary powers and abilities. Sathya Sai Baba must have enabled the image to contain a white, ghostlike image standing to his right, and light radiating from his hands as if they were light bulbs and he was the power source. Marcotte assumed that Sai Baba blessed him with the "radiant hands" picture to take the place of the anticipated interview. Marcotte brought enough four-by-six-inch prints of the "radiant hands" picture to give one to everyone. A framed eleven-by-fourteen-inch enlargement of my print (which I lost) hangs in my home. The highly magnified, poor-quality image of Sai Baba's radiant hands provides physical evidence of Sathya Sai Baba's supernatural ability. Because the physical body of an avatar is supposed to be like any other person's body, I assume the photograph, like his materialization of rings that fit, is a keepsake manifested by Sathya Sai Baba. Several devotees of Sathya Sai Baba have experienced and written about Sai Baba's apparent ability to influence or alter the film in their camera when they attempted to take his picture.

Marcotte also passed out Sai Baba's recommended daily prayers. As I read the following prayers, I noticed their similarity to Jesus's instructions for how to pray in Matthew 6:6–13. The words in Sathya Sai Baba's morning prayer— "Make my thoughts, words, and deeds sacred and pure" and "Direct me, guide me"—convey the same understanding of God's relationship with us as the Lord's Prayer: "Let your will be done on earth as it is in heaven. Give us today our daily bread. ... Bring us not into temptation ..." Both prayers imply God's ability to act within us as us while elevating the understanding of our reality from physical to spiritual beings. Think about the Lord's Prayer as you read Sathya Sai Baba's suggested morning and evening prayers.

Do not fritter away the time alloted to you; offer it to the Triune Lord, who is the embodiment of time. Know that waking from sleep is but birth and going into sleep is death. On walking, pray every morning of your life: "O Lord, I am born now from the womb of sleep. I am determined to carry out all tasks of this day as offering to You, with You ever present before my mind's eye. Make my thoughts, words, and deeds scared and pure. Let me not inflict pain on anyone; let no one inflict pain on me. Direct me, guide me, this day."

And when you enter the portals of sleep at night, pray: "O Lord, the tasks of this day, the burden of which I placed on You this morning, are over. It was You who made me walk, and talk, and think, and act. I therefore place at Your Feet all my thoughts, words, and deeds. My task is done. Receive me, I am coming back to You."

Adopt these as your daily prayers.

As a child, I experienced the Lord's Prayer as wishful thinking about an imagined future, but Sai Baba's prayers are unmistakable present-tense understandings of God's relationship with us. When Jesus compared, in Matthew 6:26–34, our "of little faith" understanding of God's relationship with us to

God's relationship with birds and lilies, Jesus clearly expressed the same nonduality understanding of our relationship with God as that expressed by Sathya Sai Baba.

I memorized Sai Baba's prayers before going to bed that evening and have faithfully continued reciting them morning and evening because they gradually ring truer and truer as my circumstances, thoughts, and actions increasingly appear to be divinely guided. Without assuming God's grace, I am as mystified by the sequence of experiences described in this chapter as the life cycle of monarch butterflies, whose mantra must be "Direct me, guide me, this day."

Along with the unusual photograph of Sai Baba's radiant hands and Sai Baba's recommended prayers, Marcotte passed out his business card. At the conclusion of his presentation, he asked if anyone wanted a brief psychic reading. Almost everyone raised their hand. After requesting their month and day of birth, he told them something they already knew and something that was supposed to happen in their future. What an amazing demonstration of psychic ability, if what Marcotte said and predicted were true statements.

The next week, at PAR's monthly board meeting, the board members wanted to talk about Marcotte's presentation. Bill Nichols said Marcotte described his front yard's naturally occurring boulders as if he was looking at them and correctly predicted that he was about to receive a great deal of unexpected money. During the few days since Marcotte's prediction, Bill Nichols said he received almost$10,000 from the sale of a bankrupt company's assets. When the company declared bankruptcy, Bill did not anticipate a partial return of his investment. Hazel Denning told us about a small group of PAR's members who went to India to see Sai Baba in the early 1970s. When they returned from India and Sai Baba's ashram, a member of the group, who claimed to see auras, said Sai Baba's aura extended to the horizon. Claiming that he would prove that Sai Baba was a fraud, a skeptical husband left the group after they arrived at the ashram and asked where he could find Sai Baba. As he approached the entrance to the indicated building, he saw a rainbow floating above the entrance. Intimidated by the rainbow, he rejoined his traveling companions without telling them about the rainbow. The next morning, Sai Baba walked by the group during darshan and asked the skeptic, "How did you like the rainbow?" Despite being unaware of avatars and Sathya Sai Baba prior to 1986, in a matter of months, I saw, read, and heard about three different Sai Baba–related manifestations of rainbows.

TRUDY PHILPOT KIESCHNICK

A few days after PAR's board meeting, Trudy, my office manager, told me that her oncologist did not expect chemotherapy to cure her usually fatal form of cancer and did not expect her to live more than six months. In the hope of receiving an optimistic prognosis, Trudy said she had gone to a psychic. Because Trudy was taught as a child to associate occult phenomena with the devil, if she had not told me about consulting a psychic, I would not have given her Armand Marcotte's business card with the words, "This psychic seems to be pretty good. You might want to see him for a third opinion."

Later that week, while leaving Colton Piano and Organ, Trudy found Armand Marcotte's business card while looking in her purse for her car keys. After noticing that Marcotte's office was on the same street as Colton Piano and Organ, Trudy drove the short distance to his office, entered, and said, "I do not have an appointment." Marcotte said, "That's OK. I just had a cancellation." Trudy told Marcotte about her cancer situation and her hope that she had more than six months to live. He dismissed Trudy's concerns with, "You'll be fine," and by telling Trudy she was going to marry an older, spiritual man, whom she already knew, with a daughter and three sons. He upset Trudy by bizarrely appearing more interested in me than her concern about her doctor's prognosis. He told Trudy that her boss was supposed to go with him to India in less than a month and needed to call him as soon as possible.

Trudy left Marcotte's office without receiving relief from the stress of having only six months to live. She could not figure out who this "older, spiritual man that she already knew" could be, and she dismissed Marcotte's prediction as improbable nonsense. Six years later, in 1992, when Trudy married her minister, Reverend O. J. (Bill) Philpot, she realized that Reverend Philpot had a daughter and three sons. That realization reminded Trudy of Marcotte's dismissed but remarkably accurate prediction. I learned about Marcotte's prediction for the first time when I asked Trudy to help me write about the experiences that brought me to India. Born twenty years before Trudy, Reverend Philpot was a charter and honorary member of the Moreno Valley Rotary Club. As I write, it is thirty-five years since Armand Marcotte casually dismissed Trudy's concern about having only six months to live, and Trudy is enjoying life and helping me to accurately share her experiences.

Trudy was visibly angry when she saw me after her session with Marcotte. He gave her the impression of being more concerned with me than her life-and-death situation. Instead of telling me about his marriage prediction, Trudy merely said that Marcotte seemed more interested in me than her and wanted me to call him.

Marcotte did not know me. I was merely a member of the audience when he spoke at PAR. Despite my recent experiences that suggested that Sai Baba could be the Jesus-like person I wanted to find when I was in high school, keeping up with office overhead expenses concerned me much more than spiritual concerns. But Trudy's anger regarding Marcotte's apparent lack of empathy for her situation and the bazaar nature of his interest in me motivated me to call him. When I called, Marcotte said he was leaving in the middle of December and returning in the middle of January. Christmastime, Marcotte said, was the best time for me to take time out of the office because fewer appointments are made in December. As he was talking, *I thought, Why and how can he be arguing against my unmentioned reasons for not wanting to go with him to India?* When I called Marcotte's travel agent, the part of me that wanted to go won out over the part that was concerned with office overhead expenses.

Within a week of talking to Marcotte's travel agent, I was able to attend a presentation by Phyllis Krystal at Corona Light. She gave me good advice about desirable vaccinations before going to India and what to bring, but she did not reduce my fear of returning from India without having determined if Sai Baba really is a Jesus-like spiritual teacher. The rainbows and other remarkable things that I read and heard about Sai Baba did not inspire the sense of belief provided by personal experience. The experience of samadhi had convinced me of God's omnipresence, and Jesus's Sermon on the Mount convinced me that God spoke through Jesus. I did not want to return from India without knowing if God spoke through Sathya Sai Baba.

KATHRYN LEEMAN

It occurred to me that clairvoyant ability might assist me in determining if Sathya Sai Baba really was a Jesus-like spiritual teacher. Because comments made by PAR's board members suggested that Kathryn Leeman was PAR's most respected and talented psychic, I made an appointment to see her. When I opened her office door for my appointment, Kathryn was sitting behind a desk in the narrow room's back-right corner. As I sat in the chair in front of Kathryn's desk, I noticed in the room's back-left corner an empty, straight-backed chair.

Kathryn began by telling me the session would be recorded, clicking on a cassette recorder, and asking if my mother was deceased. After I said "Yes," Kathryn pointed at the straight-backed chair and said, "She is sitting right here." As Kathryn described my mother's "continuing interest in the family she left behind" with what sounded to me like the same words used by Dr. Daniels, it occurred to me that the cassette recording of what Kathryn was saying, when combined with the transcript of what Dr. Daniels had said, provided evidence of life after death. But when I got home and played the cassette, there were no intelligible sounds, only static. Another psychic counselor told me that recordings made in the presence of discarnate spirits often contain static or random sounds. The intentional and unintentional recording of sounds assumed to be made by discarnate spirits are called electronic voice phenomena, or EVP. EVP enables those whose spiritual eyes and ears are not open to experience at least something in a haunted house.

Kathryn told me what motivated Hazel Denning to ask me to join PAR's board of directors. Kathryn said she told Hazel, while they were standing behind me at a monthly PAR meeting, that my aura was purple, and I was an old soul. On two occasions, when I turned around in a crowded room, the person standing behind me asked if I knew that my aura was purple and that I was an old soul. Because no one else has said anything about my aura, it seems unlikely that three people said the same thing by coincidence. It seems more likely that we are radiant spiritual beings, and our auras are seen similarly by those blessed with the uncommon clairvoyant ability to see auras. This speculation would be common knowledge within occult communities, but not among paradigm-compliant scientists. If significant psychic ability was common, Western science would not dismiss most of the content of this book as wishful, magical, and unscientific thinking. It only takes one truly psychic or spiritual experience to know, without doubt, that human consciousness extends well beyond the limits of matter and brains. If even a small percentage of scientists learned how to open their spiritual eyes and ears, science's paradigms would embrace our spiritual reality. A scientific discipline should be created with scientists whose spiritual eyes and ears are open.

Apparently guided by my spirit guides, Kathryn told me that instead of continuing to primarily be an observer of life, I was supposed to spend the next ten years improving my communication ability. If I experienced success as a clairvoyant, Kathryn said, I would be distracted from focusing on improving my communication skills. When I returned home from India, I knew that I had a book to write, but not the time or communication skills to write it. For twenty years, which began my first week home from India, the members of the Dawn Busters Toastmasters Club provided feedback and encouragement to my attempts to explain "abstract concepts." It is now thirty-seven years since I realized I needed to figure out how to reveal insights that conflict with Western science and culture's understanding of reality.

Kathryn told me to keep a notebook under my bed, to pick it up when I wake up, and to write what comes to me. The next morning when I woke up, I wrote,

> When the beautiful, profound thoughts pass through me in perfect prose, if I am quick enough, I can write them down as if they are mine. But, if I delay, the words no longer flow with beauty or ease. I cannot be the source of these thoughts if they just pass through me, but the recipient joined in oneness with God.

A significant portion of this book's content comes from the thoughts that flow into my mind when I wake up. Kathryn also told me to anticipate and record a dream. I am seldom aware of dreaming and usually remember only bits and pieces that are quickly forgotten. But I fully remembered that night's weird dream. Our apparent ability to influence our dreams surprised me.

INDIA AND SATHYA SAI BABA

My Singapore Airlines flight left Los Angeles and landed at Seattle-Tacoma Airport in Washington to pick up passengers for its polar route flight to Singapore. Two ladies boarded the plane and sat next to me. As we talked, I realized they, like me, had signed up with Armand Marcotte's travel agent to see Sai Baba. Besides Marcotte, who I learned was our tour guide, and the two ladies, the seven-member group included a couple in their late twenties and a man from San Diego. One of the ladies sitting with me was younger, and the other was older than me. The young lady said that no one comes to see Sai Baba unless, according to Sai Baba, it is his will. She believed that Sai Baba's will enabled her house to sell in time to pay for this trip with her friend. I did not know Sai Baba claimed to control who sees him, but as I recalled the improbable sequence of events that had led to that moment in my life, God in the form of Sathya Sai Baba answering my high school prayers seemed like a plausible explanation. If Trudy had not told me she'd gone to a psychic, or if she had not found Marcotte's business card while looking for her car keys, and if Marcotte had not bizarrely said that I was supposed to accompany him, I would not have been on that flight sitting with those two ladies.

Like Marcotte, this was the older lady's second trip to see Sathya Sai Baba. She showed me a ring and said Sai Baba gave it to her in his interview room. After giving Sai Baba her recently diseased husband's wedding ring, her wedding ring, and her engagement ring, she said, "I want to give you these three rings in exchange for one ring from you." Sai Baba grasped the three rings in his hand, blew on his hand, and opened his hand to reveal what her jeweler guessed was a seven-carat diamond ring. Without taking the diamond out of its setting, her jeweler said he could not accurately determine the number of carats. Because Sai Baba's gifts, which are not valued as keepsakes, are rumored to suddenly disappear, she did not let her jeweler examine the ring more closely. Sai Baba's ability to manifest valuable rings is not as inexplicable to me as his ability to manifest rings that fit.

Because I did not think to ask questions, I assumed we were going as directly as possible to Sai Baba's ashram. Instead of only seeing airports, Armand Marcotte's travel agent arranged for us to spend a few days sightseeing between flights. I am thankful for what I saw and experienced in Singapore, Madras (which is now called Chennai), and Bangalore (which is now called Bengaluru). Names have been changed in India to reduce the legacy of British colonialism. The names used in this book are contemporary with the events described. Bangalore was our destination's nearest city with a commercial aviation airport.

After a couple days in Bangalore, we boarded taxicabs for the three-hour drive to Sai Baba's ashram in Puttaparthi. Other than a small village or two and flat, barren ground, there was nothing to see between Bangalore and Sai Baba's main ashram: Prasanthi Nilayam. The difficulty of getting to Prasanthi Nilayam surprised me. I wondered how Sai Baba attracted thousands of devotees from around the world to such a remote and difficult-to-reach location.

As we approached Sai Baba's Prasanthi Nilayam Ashram, we drove by large buildings that looked out of place in such a rural setting. Sri Sathya Sai University was the first university in India to have a planetarium. The colorfully painted planetarium, with a seating capacity of two hundred, was near other surprisingly large buildings. The number and size of the buildings have increased significantly since I was there. The best way for you to have a sense of Sai Baba's influence upon the small, rural community of his birth is to do an online search of Puttaparthi and Prasanthi Nilayam Ashram. Only a few small (less than a thousand square feet) buildings existed in Puttaparthi when I was there.

Despite Sai Baba's death in 2011, the ashram continues to attract devotees, and the various institutions created by Sai Baba continue under the guidance of organizations and trusts created by Sai Baba. Without Sai Baba's "supernormal" abilities, this economically poor and isolated rural community would not be a showplace for how humanity should educate its youth, care for those in need of medical assistance, and understand the world's religious heritage.

When our taxicabs dropped us off at Prasanthi Nilayam's main gate, we went straight to accommodations to obtain meal tickets for the period of our stay and a place to sleep and put our belongings. Because we were told that Sai Baba was about to give his annual Christmas discourse in the Poornachandra Auditorium, we quickly placed our belongings in our assigned quarters and rushed to the Poornachandra Auditorium, which was built in 1973 to provide sitting space on a concrete floor for fifteen thousand devotees.

When we arrived, the auditorium was full, but the building's open sides enabled latecomers to fan out along the sides. A few seconds after we sat cross-legged on the edge of the overflowing crowd, Sai Baba appeared at the back of the stage, walked to the far side of the stage, and down the steps into the sea of devotees. From our vantage point, Sai Baba appeared to float into the sea of devotees and back toward the stage while slowly moving in our direction. His gaze darted here and there above everyone's head, as if he was looking for someone and receiving guidance from invisible beings. Apparently without stepping on anyone, Sai Baba got within twenty feet of where I was sitting, lowered his gaze, and stared straight into my eyes. The energy of love, which I'd experienced during samadhi, immediately began flowing into my chest or heart. My chest felt like it was going to explode with the energy of divine love. I have no idea how long Sai Baba looked into my eyes, but it was probably only a few seconds. After staring into my eyes, Sai Baba headed back to the stage and began his Christmas discourse.

Wow! What a blessing! Sathya Sai Baba's transmission of divine love left no doubt that he was a Jesus-like divine incarnation or avatar. I did not know what would eliminate my hesitancy to accept Sai Baba as the answer to my high school prayers, but Sai Baba knew how to eliminate any doubts. Nothing that Sai Baba could have done would have been as appropriate or convincing as filling my heart with samadhi's divine love. Was it Sai Baba that spoke to me during that sermon when I was in the eighth grade? Did Sai Baba hear and respond to my high school prayers that were motivated by envy of those who experienced Jesus two thousand years ago? Did Sai Baba orchestrate the sequence of events that brought me to his ashram?

My personal confirmation of Sathya Sai Baba's extraordinary "supernormal" powers and abilities enabled me to know, without doubt, that I had access to spiritual knowledge that has not been filtered through worldly perspectives and agendas. Transcripts of Sai Baba's discourses are available in books, and Sathya Sai Baba even wrote books or *vahinis*.

Chapter 8
Experiences As A Devotee
of Sathya Sai Baba

"The more human values are cherished,
the better will be the growth of society,
the nation, and the world."
—*Sathya Sai Baba*

One of the many blessings of going to India was spending time with Armand Marcotte. He told me that he had been a monk in a prior life, and his spiritual eyes and ears enabled three prior-life monk buddies to communicate with him. He received their thoughts but only saw three brown hoods instead of faces. They told Marcotte that they had achieved self-realization during that previous lifetime and are part of his inner experience to help him achieve self-realization so that he can join them at a higher level of consciousness. He told me that his friends from that prior life informed him about and motivated him to see Sathya Sai Baba.

Marcotte also told me about a near-death experience, his own, which harmonizes with my interest in finding evidence which validates "paranormal" phenomena. A year after enlisting in the US Navy when he was eighteen, Marcotte became deathly ill aboard a destroyer. Unaware of the seriousness of his illness, he suddenly realized he was on the ceiling looking at himself lying in his bunk. This out-of-body experience was followed by seeing a bright light in which the blessed Virgin Mary said, "It is not your time yet. You have a lot of work to do." A few of Marcotte's friends and relatives were there to see him. His spirit or soul saw and exchanged thoughts with his grandfather and a neighbor. Because they both died before

Marcotte entered the Navy, Marcotte's soul was not surprised to see them in the afterlife but was surprised to see a cousin, who described his recent accidental death. Because Marcotte still had "a lot of work to do," his soul returned to his body, which was surrounded by the destroyer's rescue squad and a Catholic priest administering a dying Catholic's last rites. He surprised the priest by not only regaining consciousness but by recalling his near-death experience. While Marcotte shared his near-death experience, the priest held a yellow telegram informing Marcotte of his cousin's death. The priest said that, without the telegram, he would have assumed Marcotte was hallucinating. You can read a more detailed description of his near-death experience on pages 12–15 in *Tomorrow Knocks* by Anatol Brunton.

A few years after my trip to India, a minister who provided pastoral care at Riverside General Hospital spoke at the Moreno Valley Rotary Club. The minister talked about the need in hospitals for spiritual support, bereavement care, and visitation services. While he was speaking, I remembered how Marcotte's yellow telegram provided evidence that "paranormal" spiritual experiences are not necessarily imagined, as assumed by Western science. Because the minister did not allow time for questions, I followed him to his car and asked if he recalled an experience that contained evidence for a spiritual reality. He told me about a couple whose first child, a boy, died during his preschool years. After their first child's death, the couple had another child, also a boy, who during his preschool years had a near-death experience at Riverside General Hospital. The second son described meeting, during his near-death experience, a boy with the same name as his deceased brother. When his parents showed him pictures of his brother, he identified the boy in the pictures as the boy in his near-death experience. Prior to his near-death experience, his parents said that they had never told their second son about the brother he met in heaven.

Before transitioning away from Marcotte and psychic phenomena, I want to make some observations and speculations about his "psychic" ability. Marcotte's ability to accurately predict the future was dependent upon what the monks revealed to his spiritual eyes and ears. He said that seeing and hearing his clients' past lives and future experiences was like watching television. Once, when I was walking with him at Prasanthi Nilayam, he introduced himself to a woman he did not know and told her what his "inner television" was revealing. On another occasion, a woman ran toward him and said, "Armand, what you told me would happen happened exactly as you said it would." I did not eavesdrop as she told Marcotte about the accuracy of his predictions when they met during Marcotte's March trip to the ashram.

Feeling left out of his insights into everyone's futures, I asked Marcotte what he saw in my future. He told me that "his psychic ability" works best with complete strangers. In my experience, his psychic ability was not so miraculous with people he knew or wanted to impress. I believe his ability to channel information from the three monks was misunderstood as clairvoyant or "psychic" ability. I wonder what percentage of "paranormal," psychic ability involves mediumship or channeling information from invisible beings.

Accurate predictions—like SRI's research findings and Trudy marrying an older, spiritual man with a daughter and three sons—suggest that our lives are preplanned. Reincarnation philosophy and between-lives regression suggest that our lives are planned to address Karma and spiritual growth concerns. The ability of invisible spiritual beings to tune in to our planned or intended futures and relay that information to "psychics" supports belief in reincarnation, Karma, and our enrollment in Earth School. Predictable futures suggest that our lives, like the physical reality that made human existence possible, are governed by influences that are not compatible with a materialistic understandings of reality.

Because we have free will, we are free to go off script. While reading the lines on my hands, Linda Martin (PAR's remarkably knowledgeable hand-reading authority) said the nondominant hand reveals what was planned for us, while the dominant hand reveals what we have done. Helen Roberts (who facilitated and transcribed the Loehr-Daniels life readings) told me that Dr. Daniels often scolded the recipients of his Akashic records readings for going off script and risking being recycled. The Gospels reveal Jesus's interest in the thoughts and actions that reveal a person's character. If you study Sai Baba's speeches and books, you will discover that he, like Dr. Daniels and Jesus, emphasized the development of desirable character traits.

Toward the end of our stay at the ashram, one of my traveling companions and I watched darshan form outside the wall surrounding the darshan area. We were tall enough to look over the wall and see Sai Baba beyond the rows of devotees staring at him. A boy, who was not tall enough to see over the wall, asked us to lift him so he could also observe darshan. When we returned the boy to the ground, he said his father, a wealthy business owner in India, had a dream in which Sai Baba told him to fly with his family to Bangalore where a limousine would be waiting to bring them to his ashram. Because of the unusual nature of the dream, he flew with his family to Bangalore where there was a limousine waiting for them. The boy said his family had a private session with Sai Baba the previous evening and early that morning. The "dream" experienced by the boy's dad revealed how it was possible in a remote location to attract followers from around the world while also obtaining funding for ambitious and expensive service and building projects.

BACK HOME AFTER RECEIVING
SAI BABA'S DARSHAN

Prior to going to India, I went to bed at ten in the evening, read myself to sleep, and woke up at seven in the morning. After returning home from India, I woke up wide awake at three in the morning. At first, I tried to go back to sleep. When I realized I was fully rested and did not require more sleep, I spent the extra hours reading the books I had purchased at Sai Baba's ashram. After a few days, I remembered passing a letter to Sai Baba during darshan that requested that my life's spiritual journey benefit from traveling to his ashram. When I read in my Sai Baba books that the best time to meditate, according to Sai Baba, is at three in the morning, I used the extra hours for meditation as well as reading. After three or four months, I abruptly returned to waking up at seven. When I asked my pendulum the explanation for my temporarily reduced need for sleep, it said no to the energy received from Sai Baba's darshan and coincidence, but yes to Sai Baba's response to my letter.

When I returned home, like Jesus's disciples, I wanted to share the "good news" that we are living contemporaneously with an avatar: God in the physical form of Sathya Sai Baba. Sai Baba's teachings harmonize with the good-news teachings in the Old Testament and Jesus's public ministry "preaching the Good News of God's kingdom."[54] Sai Baba said that his underlying reality was that of Hinduism's previous avatars and the God of the Old and New Testaments. After Jesus's death and Christ's Resurrection, "good news" referred to salvation through Jesus Christ as Jesus's disciples "went out, and preached everywhere, the Lord working with them, and confirming the word by the signs that followed."[55] Without "the Lord working with them" could Jesus Christ's disciples transform the life and death of a crucified (like a common criminal) Jewish minister into the world's largest religion: *Christianity?*

A few days after I returned home from India, a Temecula parapsychology association asked me to speak about Sathya Sai Baba at their monthly meeting. For a few years during August Dialogues, I provided free Sai Baba books and pendulums while talking about Sai Baba and divination with a pendulum. I assumed people would want to learn about a contemporary Jesus-like person. To my surprise, no one seemed interested in avatars. The "Lord" was not "working with" me. I obtained a sense of the spiritual dimension's influence upon human behavior when I learned that God incarnated as Sathya Sai Baba to enable people to dive deeper into their own religion and not to start another religion.

Not long after returning home from India, I learned that Sai Baba's devotees were organized around the world into regional and local community groups. For three days in May 1987, I attended a regional Sathya Sai Baba Conference. The annual Southern California retreat enabled me to learn about the Sathya Sai Center Bookstore, monthly first Sunday meetings at the Ebell Theater in Santa Ana, and the locations of weekly Sathya Sai Baba Center meetings that took place in the homes of devotees. For over twenty years, I looked forward to spending Tuesday evenings at my nearest Sathya Sai Baba Center.

The speakers at annual conferences and first Sunday meetings shared amazing firsthand experiences with Sathya Sai Baba, and they often played significant roles within the Sai Organization. From over fifty cassette recordings of hourlong or longer talks, I want to share a few of the miraculous powers and abilities witnessed by Sai Baba's devotees. Despite not putting himself in a test tube for scientists and skeptics, Sai Baba often revealed "supernormal" abilities to his devotees. Divine spiritual teachers, like Jesus and Sai Baba, perform miracles more frequently at the beginning of their ministry to attract devotees. *Sai Baba: Man of Miracles* by Howard Murphet is an excellent book on the amazing capabilities of an avatar witnessed during

Sathya Sai Baba's youth and the beginning of his ministry. Sai Baba may not have performed miracles as frequently as he got older, but his inner circle of devotees continued to experience Sathya Sai Baba's "supernormal" powers and abilities.

Dr. Michael Goldstein, who served for decades as a leader within the Sai Organization, and a newly appointed member of Sai Baba's World Council, James Sinclair, were among the speakers at the May 22–25, 1987, regional conference at Camp Colby in the Angeles National Forest. They both experienced Sai Baba's "supernormal" ability to communicate with current and prospective devotees who lived thousands of miles from India. Whether or not Jesus walked on water is a matter of faith, but while people like Dr. Goldstein and James Sinclair are alive, evidence of Sathya Sai Baba's "supernormal" ability or miracles can be documented.

Because commercial airlines regarded hijackings as an unavoidable cost of doing business, over a hundred hijackings of commercial airline flights took place prior to the use of passenger-filled airplanes as weapons on September 11, 2001. Before I realized how many hijackings took place, I thought it was an improbable coincidence for Dr. Goldstein and his wife to experience, like Phyllis and Sidney Krystal, the terror of being on a hijacked flight.

The following transcripts are edited to reduce their length. Because Sai Baba referred to speeches which are read as "It was just a written thing," Sai Baba's devotees seldom used notes and usually prayed, prior to speaking, for Sai Baba to speak through them. Before I begin Dr. Goldstein's presentation at the 1987 regional conference, I want to share what happened after Sai Baba offered to perform the marriage ceremony for Dr. and Mrs. Goldstein's son.

During the marriage ceremony, Sai Baba manifested a necklace made with gold and diamonds called a *mangalsutra*, which is Southern India's equivalent of a wedding ring.

211

During a subsequent trip to India, after thieves stole the mangalsutra from the young couple's home in New York, Sai Baba remanifested the mangalsutra while saying that the thieves in New York were frantically looking for it.

CONDENSED TRANSCRIPT OF TALK
BY DR. MICHAEL GOLDSTEIN

Who is Swami? When humankind loses sight of its divine heritage, the Lord in His boundless compassion assumes the form of man to restore dharma in the world. Bhagavan Sri Sathya Sai Baba has come to us for that purpose. What is a Sai devotee? As Sai devotees, we believe our true self is one with God and can be realized in this lifetime. What is the purpose of the Sai Organization? Officers and trustees are appointed or approved by Swami to promote faith in God and godliness.

My wife and I just returned from India. We traveled with Swami from Bangalore to Ooty to Kodaikanal, where Swami held many small, intimate meetings. While talking about dreams, Swami said dreams are of two types: subconscious dreams, which consist of a phantasmagoria of shifting scenes with no relevance, coherence, or significance; and dreams of pure consciousness, which are lucid, relevant, and should be heeded. During my thirteen years of devotion to Swami, I experienced several seemingly meaningless dreams in which Swami appeared. I did not interpret or act upon these dreams. Swami also appeared without background content in a few vivid dreams in which he gave me a clear, relevant-to-external-events message, which I took seriously and acted upon.

I experienced one of these dreams last year when I was scheduled to meet Swami in Ooty. About a week before my departure, Swami instructed me in a dream to change my travel plans and meet him at a different time. When I met Swami in Ooty, as instructed in the dream, Swami greeted me in a delightful manner. I did not discuss the dream with Swami.

A week prior to departing on my last trip, I experienced a vivid, lucid dream in which Swami told a prominent Sai officer about the medication his wife needed for a specific health problem. When I woke up, I called the man to tell him about the dream and to encourage him to tell his wife to see her doctor.

Please return with me to that house in Kodaikanal in which Swami talked about two types of dreams. During his discussion, Swami looked at me and said, "Goldstein, tell them about the dream I gave you last year in which I changed when I wanted to meet you in Ooty." I was astonished because I had not discussed this dream with Swami or anyone. After I described the dream, Swami said, "Now, tell everyone about your recent dream concerning your friend's wife's illness." After I related this second dream, Swami said, "These are real dreams. You must pay attention to them." If you think about what I have told you, you will see that Swami has demonstrated that he knows what you are dreaming, and that he can indeed communicate with you in your dreams. Most of the dreams experienced by Westerners, according to Swami, are the unconsciousness type and have no significance. You must use your ability to discriminate between the two types of dreams.

In addition to restoring righteousness in the world, the mission of an avatar includes protecting devotees. On at least two occasions, Swami miraculously saved my wife and me. The last time Swami saved us began as we approached Kodaikanal after an eight-hour trip from Ooty in Swami's car. Swami asked, "Goldstein, where are you staying?" I replied, "Swami, I have made reservations at the Carlton Hotel." Swami emphatically said, "No, you will not stay in the Carlton Hotel." Swami then instructed my wife and I to stay in the home of devotees. That night, the Carlton Hotel burned down. When I told Swami about the fire, he simply said, "I know."

In Kodaikanal, Swami asked me to tell the assembled devotees about the events of last September, when Swami had tried to get me to change my plans. Instead of avoiding staying in a hotel that was about to burn down, Swami tried to get me to avoid a plane flight that was going to be hijacked. I began by telling the devotees about several significant events that had occurred prior to our departure from India. Three days before we left, Swami said the following to me: "The mind is the key. The heart is the lock. If you turn the key outward toward the world, there is endless chaos and desires. If you turn the key inward toward God, there is detachment and serenity. God gives bad experiences and good experiences for whatever purpose. You must maintain your equanimity in good and bad experiences." Two days before our departure, Swami ominously materialized some Vibhuti for me and said, "Keep this Vibhuti with you always." One day prior to our departure, Swami told us to delay our departure by one day. On the morning of our departure, Swami took me with him in his car from the mandir to the university. I was very happy as Swami talked to his driver in Telugu. Suddenly, Swami looked at me and said in a most ominous and frightening voice, "Goldstein, this is your last chance!" I was frightened and said, "Baba, you're breaking my heart. I am scheduled to come back in November for your birthday." Swami was silent before saying, "Yes, don't worry; you'll come in November." When I took leave of Swami, he was extraordinarily affectionate, and I was very happy.

I initially obeyed Swami by delaying our departure from Puttaparthi by one day but condensed my Bombay meetings to enable departing India on our previously scheduled Pan Am flight. When we arrived in Karachi, I was sleeping when two terrorists grabbed a stewardess around the neck while pointing a pistol at her head. Another hijacker pointed a machine gun at my wife. When I woke up, he pointed the machine gun at me and said, "Hands up. Move back." All the first-class passengers moved to the middle of the plane. The hijacking lasted about sixteen hours. Two terrorists had machine guns, one had a pistol, and another had two hand grenades. One of the terrorists with a machine gun wore a belt of plastic explosives.

The stewardesses courageously hid American passports. This meant a lot to me because I felt like, and may have been, the only Jewish man on a plane hijacked by Muslim terrorists. The passengers were very calm and did not become hysterical, even when chaos broke out. During these sixteen hours, I repeatedly remembered what Swami had said about turning the mind inward toward God instead of outward toward endless chaos and desire. After sixteen hours, the plane's generator apparently ran out of fuel, the lights and air conditioning went off, and the temperature began to rise. Suddenly, the terrorists opened fire into men, women, and children. Hand grenades exploding on the plane's floor caused the plane to fill with smoke. Light from an open door motivated those standing in the aisle to press toward the open door. Finally, my wife and I came to the door and went down the escape chute.

When I returned to India in November, Swami asked me, "Do you remember in the car when I said this is your last chance?" I said, "Yes, Swami, but I am trying to forget it." Then Swami said, "When I said this is your last chance, I saw them shooting you on the plane. Then I made a complete change." This is an example of the avatar manipulating maya to suit his own purpose. My wife and I are very grateful for Swami's mercy.

CONDENSED TRANSCRIPT OF TALK BY JAMES SINCLAIR

I want to share experiences that I do not intellectually understand but that I feel because I have experienced them since 1969. An entrepreneur since I was twelve years old, my life has been very much involved with worldly activities. I

215

have been a member of every financial exchange in the United States and some in Europe. I had an investment firm in New York that employed over two hundred people, and at any one time, as many as seven hundred people have called me boss. I have built cable TV systems in forty-three cities in the United States and Puerto Rico. I have had a very full business career and been graced by Swami with a wonderful life.

But, in 1969, my life was not so wonderful. Business was miserable. The IRS was looking for me. My health was not good. It was the darkest of dark times. It was so bad that I went down into my cellar, sat at a desk, and said, "I don't know where You are. I don't have the slightest idea who You are. I don't know what You are. About the only thing I know is that You are. So, I have a great idea. Why don't You run it, because I can't. If You don't, I'm not leaving my cellar." And there I sat with my great prayer. If thought packed with emotion has added significance, that was the beginning. The darkest night of the soul must yield the greatest prayer because, prior to that night, no matter how hard I tried, it wouldn't happen. My life since that point has been the most magnificent, exciting adventure it could possibly be, because Swami has been in my life. Not in a subjective way, but objectively. In the first deep meditation that I ever had, Swami's appearance in the middle of a flame in my mind's eye scared the life out of me. I'm not talking about something that might have looked like Swami. I saw his absolute personage long before I had any idea who he was, or where he was. It was the beginning of experiences that not until 1985 did I realize was Swami in my presence whispering to me, and finally yelling until my attention came alive. There were multiple times and ways Swami's form entered my life and my wife's life. These experiences are not a topic of conversation; they are not what you talk to your friends and neighbors about. Meditations became deeper as meditation became something that happened to me and not something that I did.

I'm new to this. Last year, I was on a business trip in London when I became so overcome with the desire to see Sai Baba after seeing his picture in a bookstore window, that I went to Puttaparthi with a blue blazer, pink shirt, wing tips, and wool pants. I got a good bawling out when I had the privilege of an interview by Swami. Swami looked at me and said, "I gave you a lot, but you have never been happy one moment." He told me things about myself that I forgot. He asked me what I wanted. I couldn't talk. He knew what I wanted. He made it happen. He looked at me and said, "What makes you think there is any problem so large I can't solve it?" Then he addressed my worst fears and told me how foolish I was. Toward the end of the interview, Swami said, "Would you like to do something for me?" As I nodded my head, Swami asked, "Will you be happy?"

When I last saw Swami, he looked at me and said, "You think you're sick." I said, "Yes." He said, "You're not sick." I said, "I am sick." He said, "When you go home, you will feel the need for lots of doctors, but they're going to find nothing wrong with you." I had them all, and as Swami predicted, they didn't find anything wrong with me.

When I was a youngster, and I thank my rosary beads and my Catholicism for having brought me to Swami, I had hoped I would have had the chance to meet Jesus Christ, and I felt, *What a bummer; here I am, two thousand years too late.* Instead of meeting Jesus Christ, I met the man who had sent him. I met all the avatars and forms of the divine that have ever existed. What a blessing to have been allowed the tiniest little look at the magnificence of the divine.

I selected the previous two speakers and the following talk by Isaac Tigrett because their experiences provide tangible (at least for them) evidence of Sathya Sai Baba's

(God's) omnipresence and "supernormal" powers. From our human perspective, "supernormal" powers are impossible, and therefore, not believable. Skeptics may become less skeptical by realizing that the miracles described in this book are a small fraction of those experienced by all of Sai Baba's devotees, and by thinking about the following statements by Sathya Sai Baba.

- Science must confine its inquiries only to things belonging to the physical senses, while spiritualism transcends the senses. If you want to understand the nature of spiritual power, you can do so only through the path of spirituality, and not science. What science has been able to uncover is only a fraction of the cosmic phenomena.
- The Atma is not subject to worldly limitations or laws.
- I am not this body. I am the all-pervading reality, all names and all forms in every atom and cell.

In his introduction, James Sinclair said, "I want to share experiences which I do not intellectually understand but which I feel." Sai Baba said that God can do anything except cause a person's heart to open to God. He also said, "Take one step toward me, I shall take a hundred toward you." One of the reasons Sai Baba gave Dr. Goldstein leadership positions in the Sai Organization and rescued James Sinclair from his financial difficulties would be their love for God. Until a person loves God, they must examine the experiences of believers to realize God's omnipresent reality. Skeptics make a categorical mistake when they use materialistic assumptions to refute "paranormal" phenomena. Materialistic assumptions do not logically apply to the investigation of the source of consciousness itself: God.

ISAAC TIGRETT: "MY STORY"

From the many talks by Sai Baba's devotees that I have heard since the 1987 regional conference, I want to share one more: Isaac Tigrett's February 2, 1992, talk at the Ebell Theater in Santa Ana sponsored by the Sathya Sai Baba Society and its Southern California centers. The Isaac Tigrett Official Website reveals that Tigrett is the cofounder of both the Hard Rock Cafe and the House of Blues. Please scroll down the website to see a panoramic picture of the Sri Sathya Sai Institute of Higher Medical Sciences. This hospital was built near the Prasanthi Nilayam Ashram with Isaac Tigrett's money and supervision of its design and construction. The website provides insight into Tigrett's life and accomplishments.

The following is a third-person version of a transcript of Isaac Tigrett's 1992 Ebell Theater presentation. He grew up in a small town near Memphis, Tennessee. Witnessing his younger brother's accidental death brought an abrupt end to thirteen-year-old Isaac Tigrett's "beautiful childhood." His younger brother's death led to his parents' marital difficulties and his older brother's insanity and suicide. Two years after witnessing his younger brother's death, fifteen-year-old Isaac Tigrett moved with his dad to London, England. Like Harry Potter, Tigrett was "the boy who lived." Instead of a visible scar on his forehead, the tragedy and death experienced by Tigrett, when he was a teenager, left invisible, emotional scars that influenced his thoughts and actions for many years. When he asked Sathya Sai Baba, "Why was I born into a family with so much insanity, death, and destruction?" Sai Baba replied, "To soften your heart." Suddenly, Tigrett realized that his "horrible upbringing" had made him "sensitive to everyone and everything in the world." To cut "the ties that bind," Sai Baba encouraged Tigrett to see Phyllis Krystal in California and to learn her meditation techniques.

In 1973, a couple years after starting the first Hard Rock Cafe—the world's first multinational chain of theme restaurants—in London, Tigrett read in *Time* magazine about a new book titled *The Secret Life of Plants*. Mystical and psychic experiences, which he experienced since childhood, motivated him to buy the book's movie rights. After obtaining the movie rights, Tigrett went to psychics and the parapsychology departments of several universities to obtain an explanation for "paranormal" phenomena. No one could explain the phenomena he wanted to make a movie about. They suggested that Eastern mystics and religions may have an explanation. He heard about Sathya Sai Baba during his first trip to the East, and while sitting in a hotel lobby in Northern India, a voice in his mind said, "You've come at last, come and see me." The next day, he went to Sai Baba's ashram in Whitefield near Bangalore. One of India's many religious festivals filled the ashram with thousands of people. Like my first darshan, thousands of people did not prevent Sai Baba from acknowledging Isaac Tigrett's arrival. Ignoring everyone else, Sai Baba walked straight at Tigrett and greeted him with a circular motion of his hand that manifested sacred ash, Vibhuti, which Sai Baba placed in Tigrett's hand. The devotees beside Tigrett told him to place some on his forehead and to eat the rest. For the next fifteen years, Sai Baba ignored him during his annual (and sometimes twice a year) trips to India to have Sai Baba's darshan.

Three to four months after his first darshan, while eating in Prasanthi Nilayam Ashram's men's canteen, Tigrett noticed one of Sai Baba's many short, profound spiritual teachings: "Love all, serve all," and adopted it as the perfect mission statement for the Hard Rock Cafe. Tigrett had "Love all, serve all" prominently displayed, and he promoted it along with the rapidly growing and "amazingly successful" restaurant chain. Management meetings revolved around implementing the mission statement. Because London's patrons had to wait outside when the restaurant was full, in harmony with "Love all, serve all," umbrellas were purchased for unprepared rainy-day patrons. After becoming a devotee of Sathya Sai Baba, Tigrett set up and annually funded a secret foundation with the words, "Lord, I will give you half of everything I have if you will help me with this business and guide me in my life." Fortunately, for Isaac Tigrett and his foundation, the mission of an avatar includes protecting his devotees.

After partying all night, a year or two after his first darshan, Tigrett drove a borrowed Porsche Targa to his Malibu, California, home. Shortly before sunrise, he fell asleep while driving about eight-five miles an hour without wearing a seat belt. Bouncing and spinning down a steep ravine, he woke up embraced in Sai Baba's arms as the Porsche disintegrated around him. Without a scratch on him when the Porsche reached the bottom of the ravine, Tigrett flew to India to thank Sai Baba for saving his life, but Sai Baba ignored him.

A couple years later, in a Denver, Colorado, hotel room, an epileptic fit brought on by an accidental drug overdose caused Tigrett to lose control of his muscles, fall to the floor, and die. After emerging from the top of Tigrett's head and seeing Tigrett's body on the floor, Tigrett's soul wisely called for help. You do not want to become a ghost by ignoring the evidence for your death. You want your continuing child-of-God or soul to seek assistance in the afterlife. Tigrett's assistance came in the form of Sathya Sai Baba, who placed his hands on Tigrett's chest and disappeared as Tigrett's soul returned to his body. The next day, Tigrett flew to India in another futile effort to thank Sai Baba for saving his life.

In 1988, a generous offer for his share of the Hard Rock Cafe restaurant chain provided Tigrett with "a great deal of money [...] to give in service to Sathya Sai Baba." Tigrett's wife was the only person who knew about his secret foundation. On his next trip to Prasanthi Nilayam, Sai Baba finally, after ignoring him for fifteen years, called Tigrett in for an interview. While seated in the interview room with several other devotees, Sai Baba asked Tigrett, "Where is God?" Tigrett responded, "In my heart." Sai Baba said, "No, God is everywhere! It is like a fish swimming through water. The water is above, below, and inside the fish. You are a fish swimming through God." After missing the first question, Tigrett was afraid to respond to the second question, "How do you get to God?" After others in the interview room tried and failed to answer the question, Sai Baba looked at Tigrett, smiled, and said, "Love all, serve all." Realizing for the first time that Sai Baba had been with him every step of his life's journey, Tigrett burst into tears. After taking Tigrett into his private interview room, Sai Baba told Tigrett that he wanted Tigrett to work with him. Tigrett tried to tell Sai Baba about the secret foundation that he had set up, but Sai Baba said, "I know, I know. We will use the money to build a hospital, and I want you to oversee every aspect of planning, architectural design … and I want you to do it within nine months."

Tigrett contacted England's (and possibly the world's) most appropriate architect to design a hospital to be built near the Prasanthi Nilayam Ashram. Architecture professor Keith Critchlow wrote several books inspired by his lifelong fascination with sacred numbers, symbols, art, geometry, and architecture. While meeting with Sai Baba, Professor Critchlow received Sai Baba's permission to sanctify the building site with an ancient mandala. While Tigrett accompanied Professor Critchlow to the hundred-acre building site, Professor Critchlow told Tigrett that the mandala would not work unless he could see an eagle while drawing it. When they reached the building site, five eagles were sitting or standing where Professor Critchlow drew the mandala. Instead of flying away, the eagles merely scooted a few feet away while Professor Critchlow chanted ancient sacred mantras and drew the mandala on the ground.

Sai Baba's, God's, ability to obtain the assistance of five eagles suggests to me that human beings are uniquely challenged to follow or reflect God's will. Sai Baba took the mystery out of migratory behavior when he said, "The same god is in insects, birds, and beasts, and everyone you meet." By living moment to moment, monarch butterflies respond readily to God's guidance. The "monkey mind," typical of human beings, is oblivious to each moment as it arises. Those who achieve self-realization—this chapter's concluding topic—live in the eternal present, instead of in the "reality" created within human minds.

The story of Sai Baba making it possible for anyone to obtain free, state-of-the-art medical care began in the 1950s. Because Puttaparthi was too small and isolated to have medical care, schools, or even potable water, Puttaparthi's villagers had to walk long distances to obtain health care. Sai Baba laid the cornerstone for Puttaparthi's first medical facility on his birthday in 1954. As the community and the Prasanthi Nilayam Ashram grew, so did the healthcare facilities. Isaac Tigrett's role in Sai Baba's plans took several years to blossom into "a temple of healing" with three hundred beds and a structural area of 320,000 square feet.

In less than a year, the hospital was sufficiently completed to hold its inauguration ceremony during Sai Baba's November 23, 1991, birthday celebration. During the ceremony, Sai Baba announced that free open-heart surgeries had already been successfully provided. The hospital transformed the small village of Puttaparthi into a rapidly growing town. In 2001, the inauguration ceremony for an almost identical, 330-bed hospital took place near Sai Baba's Whitefield Ashram near Bangalore. The two super-specialty hospitals are regarded as evidence of Sai Baba's love and compassion for everyone.

PROVIDING EXAMPLES OF IDEAL
HEALTH CARE AND EDUCATION

Sathya Sai Baba provided humanity with a unique approach to education called Educare and the Sathya Sai Education in Human Values (SSEHV) program. Instead of teaching inflexible rules, true education, according to Sathya Sai Baba, must "broaden the heart and expand one's love" as it "fosters the sense of oneness, draws out one's divine qualities, and promotes the blossoming of human personality."[56] Sai Baba established India's first Sri Sathya Sai Baba School in 1968. The education program, which extends from elementary school to graduate-level college degrees, expanded outside India in the early 1990s. Schools throughout the world have adopted Sai Baba's approach to education. For example, on August 26, 2022, the Federal Senate of Brazil honored the Institute of Sathya Sai Education of Brazil's twenty-two-year effort to develop values-based education in Brazil. By combining Educare with traditional curricula, students develop good character along with academic knowledge and skills.

Sathya Sai Baba provided free public education and health care in India to serve as ideal models for how society should educate its youth and provide health care. These and other service projects cost the Sathya Sai Central Trust huge amounts of money, which is provided primarily by anonymous donations. The selfless giving and service to others of Sai Baba's devotees provide examples of ideal human behavior. The recipients of compassion and generosity benefit, but those who give ultimately receive the greatest benefit. *"How much love you have shared with all of creation,"* Sathya Sai Baba said, *"is the only thing that will matter when you die."*

SATHYA SAI BOOKSTORES IN PRASANTHI
NILAYAM AND TUSTIN, CALIFORNIA

When I was at Prasanthi Nilayam, I discovered the ashram's bookstore and purchased several books. I purchased *My Baba and I* by Dr. John Hislop because I saw several devotees reading it. Like most of Sai Baba's devotees, Dr. Hislop was a spiritual seeker whose years of searching culminated in the discovery of Sathya Sai Baba. A member of the Los Angeles, California, Theosophical Society and a recipient of a PhD in education from UCLA, Dr. Hislop helped Mahesh Yogi set up a meditation academy in northern India in 1958. After his discovery of Sai Baba in 1968, Dr. Hislop, I was told, received more of Sai Baba's time and attention than anyone else from the United States. With the capabilities possessed by avatars, the God in the hearts of everyone, Sai Baba cultivated eloquent, knowledgeable devotees to spread his message, as well as devotees capable of funding his building and service projects. When I recently reread *My Baba and I*, the chapter titled "Master of Time and Space" reminded me that it was Dr. Hislop whom Phyllis Krystal witnessed thanking Sai Baba for miraculously preventing a head-on-collision the previous evening. To pass a bus on a narrow, two-lane shoulder-less road, their taxicab driver had recklessly turned onto the path of a speeding car. In the blink of an eye, the speeding car passed harmlessly behind them, even though neither time nor opportunity existed to avoid a head-on-collision.

Being saved from a head-on collision with a speeding car was one of many miracles experienced and written about by Dr. Hislop. The amazing abilities of Sai Baba experienced by his devotees suggest that Sai Baba "was constantly tuned into the whole world and everyone in it."[57] Like Jesus, Sai Baba used analogies to explain spiritual concepts. Comparing us to waves in the ocean, Sai Baba said that we are "the Atma's unconquerable, indestructible, unlimited, the Existence-Knowledge-Bliss-wave of the ocean that is God." To explain how our souls relate to his miraculous abilities, Sai Baba said, "All beings in the world of the living are aspects of my Eternal Self. [...] To recognize that the same Atma dwells in all beings is true knowledge."[58]

Besides using waves in the ocean to describe how our souls relate to God, he used electric light bulbs. A thousand-watt light bulb represented his miraculous abilities, while bulbs of varying but comparatively minuscule wattages corresponded to the waves in the ocean. Despite the differences in wattage or power, Sai Baba said that God is the power source for all. He also said that trying to get humanity to realize that God is the "I am" or self in everyone was the primary reason God incarnated as Sathya Sai Baba. Instead of worshiping Jesus, Sathya Sai Baba, or any other physical manifestation of God, Sai Baba wanted us to realize that all physical forms, unlike God, have no lasting reality. Imagine living in a world in which everyone embraced Sai Baba's teaching: **"All are one, be alike to everyone."**

I hope Sathya Sai Baba's description of his and our underlying reality helps the reader to be less skeptical of the incredible experiences of Sai Baba's devotees. Because of the infrequent occurrences of avatars in human history, Sai Baba provides science with a once-in-a-millennium opportunity to study and validate God and "supernormal" phenomena. Avatars (the ocean, "Yahweh [God], who made heaven and earth"[59] in human form) would be expected to have powers and abilities outside the perspective and understanding of scientists (waves).

I wrote the previous paragraph because Sai Baba's devotees experienced his ability to do unbelievably impossible things, like being in more than one place at a time and restoring dead people to life. In *My Baba and I*, the chapter titled "The Resurrection of Walter Cowan" tells the story of Walter Cowan's near-death (thanks to Sai Baba) experience. Walter and Elsie Cowan played a major role in creating the Sathya Sai Baba Book Center of America and an active community of Sai Baba's devotees for me to discover when I returned home from India. By being with Mrs. Cowan and Sai Baba at critical times during Walter's death and resurrection, and by talking to both Walter and Sai Baba after Walter rejoined the living, Dr. Hislop was at the right places at the right times to tell the story. The following paragraph contains interesting aspects of the story.

In December of 1971, Walter and Elsie Cowan attended the All-India Conference of Sai Organizations in Madras, India. Walter died early Christmas morning of a heart attack in Elsie's arms. Because Walter and Elsie were an elderly couple, Walter's death was accepted by everyone except Sai Baba. During his near-death experience, Walter's spirit remained near his dead body while it was taken by ambulance to a hospital, where medical doctors confirmed the hotel doctor's determination that Walter was dead. Despite being covered with a sheet in an empty room, Walter stayed with his body until Sai Baba took him, as a discarnate spiritual being, to a conference room where the Akashic records were kept. Walter's records were read in languages that Walter did not understand. After translating Walter's records for him, Sai Baba requested "that Walter be given over to Baba's care … [because] Baba had work for Walter to do."[60] When Sai Baba and Walter left the conference room, Walter reluctantly experienced descending back to the hospital and into his body. While Sai Baba was playing a prominent role in Walter's near-death experience, Dr. Hislop was with Sai Baba at the All-India Conference. After hearing Walter's description of his near-death experience and realizing that Sai Baba must have responded to Walter's death while giving speeches at the All-India Conference, Dr. Hislop asked Sai Baba if Walter had imagined his near-death experience. "Baba replied that it was not imagination. The events were real." Years later, Dr. Hislop asked Sai Baba if everyone's death experience is the same. Sai Baba said, "The corpse was common to all, but beyond that there was no common experience."[61]

SATHYA SAI BABA CENTER OF CHERRY VALLEY

When I returned home from India, in addition to a monthly speaker's program, a bookstore, and annual retreats, I discovered weekly meetings at the Sathya Sai Baba Center of Cherry Valley. The meetings were held in the home of Ray and Joy Thomas. Attendance averaged about ten devotees. Despite Sai Baba's influence in Hindu communities and Southern India, based upon the number of Baba devotees in Southern California, I estimate that less than one person in a thousand in the Western world is aware of and appreciative of avatars. Sai Baba said that his devotees have spent many lifetimes searching for God. He must have reached out to them early in his ministry, because I saw few new faces during the twenty years that I met regularly with his well-organized devotees. In John 6:44, Jesus said, "No one can come to me unless the Father who sent me draws him ..." Sathya Sai Baba said, "No one comes to me without my permission. Holy beings can only be recognized by the holy seeker."

During my first visit to the Cherry Valley Center, I learned that Sai Baba wanted the centers to have as little to do with money as possible. Soliciting donations was strictly forbidden, even from the center's members. Only anonymous and voluntary donations were permitted. Sai Baba's ashrams and bookstores provided selfless service opportunities and operated as nonprofits. Without the "supernormal" abilities of an avatar, how would Sai Baba bring under his influence appropriate people to anonymously fund the building and maintenance of ashrams, schools and universities, hospitals, service projects, and other examples of "Love all, serve all"?

Reminiscent of my high school desire to experience and learn directly from a Jesus-like spiritual teacher, the insatiable desire for Sai Baba's darshan brought five members of the Cherry Valley Center back to India year after year. I vicariously shared in their experiences, and Joy Thomas even wrote books prompted by Sai Baba's urging and guidance. He even predicted the titles of Joy's first four books. During darshan in 1986, Sai Baba stopped in front of Joy and said she would write four books whose titles would be *Life Is a Challenge, Meet It*; *Life Is Love, Share It*; *Life Is a Dream, Realize It*; and *Life Is a Game, Play It*. With little more guidance than that, all 320 pages of *Life Is a Game, Play It* were published in 1989. The front matter contains pictures of the unusual rings manifested by Sai Baba for Joy and Ray. In an interview with Sai Baba in 1984, Sai Baba asked Ray, "What do you want?" Ray said, "Let it be your choice." Few men would wear or be happy with the huge, nine-gem ring that Sai Baba gave Ray. But Ray liked showing the ring off, and he wore it proudly. I am amazed by confirmation bias's ability to enable atheists to dismiss rings that fit as a "magician's trick."

Surrounded by twenty-seven devotees in Prasanthi Nilayam Mandir's interview room on December 23, 1989, Sai Baba provided Joy with more guidance than just book titles. After Sai Baba repeated the titles of the three unwritten books, he said, "Get started on another book." He suggested writing about experiences that related to the book's theme. Sai Baba's guidance prompted Joy to write, "From contemplation of how to best play the game of life, I have reached the conclusion that beneficial moves cannot be made without spiritual awareness. For me, such awareness comes in many ways, one of which is pondering the events and occurrences of the daily dramas." In the interview room, Sai Baba spoke to Joy about "the superficiality of bookish knowledge, and the benefits to be gained from sharing our personal experiences with others."

He concluded by telling Joy, "I do not want your devotion, I want your transformation."[62]

As if motivated by "time waste is life waste," in less than five years, Joy wrote the three remaining books predicted by Sai Baba. No longer satisfied with annual trips to be near Sai Baba, Ray and Joy moved to Prasanthi Nilayam Ashram, where Joy finished writing her fifth book, *Life Is Awareness*, in 1995. After they moved to the ashram, Sai Baba showered them with attention, but that grace gradually ended. After wondering what she had done to displease Sai baba, Joy realized that their experience was not unusual. One of Joy's similarly ignored friends told Joy that Sai Baba recommended, *I Am That: Talks with Sri Nisargadatta Maharaj*, with the words, "I do not want your devotion, I want your transformation." They reluctantly realized that Sai Baba wanted them to replace their devotion to a physical manifestation of God with an inner awareness and appreciation of God. Quoting from *Sathya Sai Speaks, Volume Two*, chapter 25, Joy wrote on the back cover of *Life Is Awareness*, "What is the use of searching in the jungle of the material world for the quiet available only in the silence of inner awareness? It is like searching under the streetlamp for something you have lost in your room. Your Self you have lost. Search for it in you. That is the path of wisdom."

When I prayed to be led to a Jesus-like spiritual teacher, I knew nothing about self-realization or avatars, but Jesus's words in the Gospels harmonized enough with my experience of samadhi to know without a doubt that Jesus was a divinely inspired spiritual teacher. I was only fifteen, but I knew that what Jesus tried to convey was not understandable from a materialistic perspective. From an Eastern perspective, Jesus was a guru or spiritual teacher in tune with God. In John 16:33, Jesus tells his followers, "I have told you these things, so that you may have peace in me. Here on earth, you will have many trials and sorrows. But take heart because I have overcome the world." Overcoming the world is what self-realization is and means. Jesus's ministry, like Sathya Sai Baba's, revealed the transcendent spiritual perspective and encouraged people to achieve it. When Sai Baba told devotees, "I do not want your devotion, I want your transformation," he was talking to old souls capable of achieving self-realization.

BODY, SOUL, AND PERSON OR JIVA

Self-realization, overcoming the world, is easier to understand when we imagine that we are composed of three parts. The part that is most obvious and easiest to understand is our physical body. I am writing this book so that the reader, unlike Western science, will realize they are more than a body that was born, dies, and becomes a corpse. The second part that comes to mind is the soul, which in Sanskrit is called the Atma, the imperishable spark of God that we are blessed to have as our soul. The third part, or jiva in Sanskrit, is experienced as our sense of self, or "I am" this specific, separate from others, person. How do these two parts, jiva and soul, reveal themselves to us?

In my Loehr-Daniels life reading, Dr. Daniels said that my most recent previous incarnation took place in Indiana before Indiana became a state. My soul played the part of a farmer's wife, a mother, one of the farming community's two schoolteachers, and a Sunday school teacher. If someone could hypnotize me, past-life regression may reveal my soul's memories of that incarnation, as well as other incarnations and the periods between them. All that remains from that life is her soul, which is now experiencing being me. Souls were created—along with bodies, Earth School, and the universe—by a lonely God to eventually create compatible companions. That sounds preposterous, but it is not my idea. Thousands of years ago, Hinduism's avatars explained why God created a universe that was just right for our existence. Sai Baba said,

"What we are is God's gift to us; what we become is our gift to God." Would we live in an improbable universe, that is just right for our existence, without God? Would arguments from design appear without end in nature; would consciousness be a hard problem for atheists; could children be found with the confirmable memories and jiva of a dead person; and would past-life regression be possible if what avatars said thousands of years ago was not true?

William Shakespeare's words—"All the world's a stage, and all the men and women merely players"—insightfully describe our circumstances. In a play, the actors are real, but the roles they play reflect the playwright's imagination. If we apply the analogy of a play to the drama of human life, God is the playwright, souls are the actors, and jivas are the roles played by souls. In a play, the actor's egoic "I" is consciously aware of playing a role; but, in our worldly dream or play, jivas (each person's egoic "I's" imaginary sense of themselves) are unaware of the underlying reality that is writing, directing, and playing their roles.

My soul plays a very different jiva or person in its current incarnation than a farmer's wife. When I realized my time and place of birth gave astrologers insight into my tendencies, I wondered what existed outside my egoic sense of myself that influenced my thoughts, actions, and the life I led. Past-life and between-lives regression therapy reveals that soul development takes place through a series of incarnations planned around the qualities that our soul and the souls in our soul group need to develop. Uniquely different incarnations enable souls to accumulate and strengthen desirable qualities. The primary quality to develop is love. Jesus said, "He who doesn't love doesn't know God, for God is love."[63] Relative to those who do not experience an empathetic connection with others, those who feel the pain of others are old souls. I wrote about my first experiences with deplorable human behavior and my introduction to Rotarians because I was mystified by the extreme variation in the experience of empathy and concern for others.

Prior to waking up from their worldly dreams, souls assume they are the jiva or role played in God's play. Ghosts, near-death experiences, children born with a dead person's confirmable memories and jiva, and past-life regression reveal that the soul departs from the dying body with the same jiva as prior to death. In all these examples of the continuation of consciousness after death, the soul is experienced as the jiva after as well as before death. Liberation from a long series of incarnations takes place when the soul wakes up from its worldly dream to the realization of its (the Atma's) perspective. Karma and our soul's progress in Earth School influence a soul's ability to wake up from its worldly dream. Sai Baba's books and discourses, and books by and about people who have achieved self-realization provide guidance in reducing the number of incarnations prior to graduating from Earth School. As jivas, puppets attached to invisible strings, our journey is a mystery that Sai Baba incarnated to help us understand. During over thirty years of thinking about writing this book, I collected the following Sathya Sai Baba quotations. The quotations begin with insights and advice for older souls who realize they are spiritual beings on a spiritual journey. Sai Baba's concluding statements apply to jivas lost in their worldly dream or maya.

- Life is a divine dream. Be detached, empty mind, want inner awareness of Self [Atma].
- The goal is liberation ... the real aim of man; he who is unaware of this is ignorant, however profound his scholarship may be, if he does not know the answer to the only question that is worth asking, "Who am I?"[64]
- There is no way to know where your decisions and thoughts come from. Confusion is the beginning of wisdom.

- Your worldly intelligence cannot fathom the ways of God. He cannot be cognized by mere cleverness, which is what your intelligence mostly is. Your explanations are merely guesses, attempts to clothe your ignorance in pompous expressions. The mistake is that you give the brain more value than it deserves. God is beyond the reach of the brain. Standing on a rock, you cannot lift it. Standing in maya, you cannot discard it.
- Prayer for some benefit or gain should not be addressed to God. For it means God awaits until He is asked. Surrender to Him; He will deal with you as He feels best, and it will be the best for you.
- God will grant you what you need and deserve; there is no need to ask, no reason to grumble. Be content, be grateful for whatever happens, whenever it happens. Nothing can happen against His will.
- The best way to love God is to love all.
- How much love you have shared with all of creation is the only thing that will matter when you die. Not what you did, titles, positions, accomplishments, etcetera.
- Good conduct, good qualities, and an exemplary character are the most valuable riches one can possess.

DISCOVERING AND LEARNING FROM THOSE WHO ACHIEVED SELF-REALIZATION

When consciousness returned to my jiva after I experienced my soul's immersion in God's love (samadhi), my jiva—not realizing there are two "I's": jiva and soul—wanted to know how "I" got there and how to stay there. In the hope of providing answers to those questions, this chapter concludes with the experiences of people who realized the consciousness of their soul: achieved self-realization. The fact that they exist and can be found provides another layer of ignored evidence for souls and God. The significance of contemporary Jesus-like spiritual teachers should alter Christianity's understanding of Jesus and Western science's insistence upon giving "the brain more value than it deserves" while "standing in maya," not asking "the only question that is worth asking, 'Who am I?'"

Joy and Ray Thomas returned home to Cherry Valley in 1996. "I want your transformation" motivated Joy to form a small Advaita Vedanta or self-realization study group. Fortunately for me and this book, she asked me to join. We got together once a week to discuss books written by and about people who have achieved self-realization, and a few of Sai Baba's vahinis or books. We began by reading *I Am That: Talks with Nisargadatta Maharaj* and Sai Baba's *Geetha* (essays on the Bhagavad Gita), *Vidya* (knowledge), and *Jnana* (wisdom) *Vahinis*.

Self-realization provides a level of consciousness that is prior to the jiva's (ego's) level of awareness. But avatars like Sathya Sai Baba are God in human form. Sai Baba's interactions with devotees, and his letters, books, and discourses enable us to see ourselves from the perspective of the lonely god that created the universe and planned the play designed to turn imperishable sparks into compatible companions. Instead of being prepared in advance, Sai Baba's discourses responded to the concerns and level of spiritual sophistication of his audience. Joy Thomas told me about a devotee who arrived early for Sai Baba's discourses, thought about her question, and heard, with her spiritual ears, what no one else heard: she heard Sai Baba's answer to her specific question. Sai Baba's interactions, words, and writings range from the mundane to the insights and abilities of the source of our ability to be conscious of anything.

Because Sai Baba recommended Ramesh Balsekar, a retired banker and a disciple of Nisargadatta Maharaj, to a lady at the ashram, Joy motivated us to read several of his excellent books on self-realization. Hinduism's guru-disciple relationships provided India with generation after generation of Jesus-like spiritual teachers and provided us with the only self-realization methodology that we knew about. We wanted insight into the guidance provided by India's spiritual teachers or gurus.

Among India's most famous and interesting teachers of the nonduality perspective of self-realization, Ramana Maharshi (1879–1950) woke up without a guru's guidance from the jiva's "I am this body" perspective to the perspective of the basic unity, or Atma, upon which the material world is superimposed. The fear of death, when he was sixteen years old, motivated Ramana Maharshi to contemplate his own mortality. It must have been his destiny to realize that his underlying reality was imperishable and independent of his (jiva's) worldly perspective. No longer concerned with even the needs of his body, he left home at sixteen to become a spiritual hermit or recluse. Because spiritual seekers recognized his advanced level of spiritual consciousness (just being in his presence stimulated mystical experiences), Ramana Maharshi attracted devotees who built a relatively large ashram. During the construction of a wall to surround the ashram, Ramana Maharshi instructed his devotees to construct two parallel walls and to fill the space between them with dirt. When an unprecedented flood destroyed nearby buildings, the unusual wall protected the ashram. To facilitate achieving self-realization, Ramana Maharshi instructed his devotees to investigate and meditate upon the question, "Who am I?"

A couple living near Los Angeles, who left Prasanthi Nilayam because Sai Baba told them to look for God within themselves, told Joy Thomas that they found people living in the Los Angeles area who had achieved self-realization. Our study group wanted to learn how self-realization was described by those who were unfamiliar with Sanskrit words and Hinduism's concepts. Would self-realization be described and experienced any differently by those who had grown up in the United

States? Would their explanations be easier for us to understand? The Los Angeles couple told Joy about Byron Katie, and on December 14, 1997, we drove to Barstow to have her darshan and hopefully obtain answers to some of our questions.

The small town of Barstow, where Byron Katie grew up, is in California's high desert midway between Los Angeles and Los Vegas. We arrived at the Center for the Work prior to the start of a workshop conducted by Byron Katie. New arrivals received a folder with Byron Katie's insights into stress and unhappiness. Katie's unique method of self-inquiry harmonized with Sai Baba's insights into quieting and controlling the mind: "The mind is a thief. You must get hold of the thief and drive him out. Because of the mind you lose peace."[65]

The similarity of Byron Katie's Barstow center with Sathya Sai Baba and Ramana Maharshi's ashrams in India amazed me. For a daily $25 donation, Byron Katie's devotees received room (sleeping bag recommended) and board consisting of vegetarian meals. Before I had gone to India, Phyllis Krystal told me to bring a sleeping bag to Prasanthi Nilayam, where the meals were vegetarian. Volunteer workers at both "ashrams" received free room and board.

At the Center for the Work, I purchased the first (and at that time only) book about Byron Katie: *A Cry in the Desert: The Awakening of Byron Katie*. Christin Weber's book reveals the experiences of Byron Katie prior to, while, and after achieving self-realization. It also tells how she became a guru with an ashram in Barstow. Because jivas are not inclined to achieve self-realization while experiencing happy lives, worldly dreams that become nightmares help old souls to overcome the world. Overcoming the world, self-realization, takes place when the soul replaces a jiva's (person's) "I am" sense of self.

In 1986, forty-three-year-old Byron Katie's life was a nightmare. Her insurance company referred her to a women's counseling center to help her with anger, paranoia, anxiety, depression, and an unhappy marriage. Two weeks after her admission, Byron Katie was locked in an attic bedroom because her angry outbursts were terrifying the other women. Too ashamed of her behavior to feel deserving of a bed, Byron Katie fell asleep on the floor. When she woke up, her consciousness or awareness arose from her soul, instead of from her mind with its usual programing and memories. The first thing she noticed when she woke up was a cockroach crawling on her foot. By associating arising thoughts with her body's movements, she realized her foot, but not the cockroach, was under her control. She had to learn, like a newborn baby, how to distinguish her body from her surroundings. "When you see a light bulb burning brightly," Sathya Sai Baba said, "you think it is the bulb that gives light, but it is the electricity that provides the light. The bulb is only like a body."[66] Byron Katie woke up with the consciousness of the electricity, her soul, instead of her jiva's self-image and memories.

When her husband brought her home from the counseling center, Byron Katie's disconnect from her jiva, the light bulb, was so complete that she did not recognize her husband, children, Barstow, or her home. Her sixteen-year-old daughter "experienced her mother as having regressed to about two years of age. 'I led her around by the hand,' she remembers […] She'd lost her entire structure for perceiving reality as she had known it. The ability to communicate went with it." Because Byron Katie experienced everything "in the total present, with no past or future […] with no belief attaching itself to thought ever,"[67] Bryon Katie had to relearn how to communicate without the help of Sanskrit terms or a guru's guidance.

From her soul's (God's; remember, "My Father and I are one") perspective, stress and unhappiness often related more to the way people (jivas) think about things than actual events or circumstances. The Center for the Work and Byron Katie International evolved from discovering the benefits of self-inquiry, called "the work," into problematic attitudes and beliefs. Her first of many books written with her third husband, *Loving What Is*, was published in 2002.

I want to conclude this chapter by sharing the self-realization experiences of two more citizens of the United States. Their achievement of self-realization, like Byron Katie's, was not something they, the light bulb or jiva, intended or anticipated. Eckhart Tolle's soul woke up from a more nightmarish life than Byron Katie's soul. The following quotation comes from pages 1–2 of his first book, *The Power of Now: A Guide to Spiritual Enlightenment*.

> Until my thirtieth year, I lived in a state of almost continuous anxiety interspersed with periods of suicidal depression… One night, not long after my twenty-ninth birthday, I woke up in the early hours with a feeling of absolute dread … more intense than it had ever been before… What was the point of continuing to live with this burden of misery? … I could feel that a deep longing for annihilation, for nonexistence, was now becoming much stronger…
>
> "I cannot live with myself any longer." This was the thought which kept repeating itself in my mind. Then suddenly I became aware of what a peculiar thought it was. "Am I one or two? If I cannot live with myself, there must be two of me: the 'I' and the 'self' that 'I' cannot live with." "Maybe," I thought, "only one of them is real."
>
> I was so stunned by this strange realization that my mind stopped. I was fully consciousness, but there were no more thoughts. Then I felt drawn into what

felt like a vortex of energy. It was a slow movement at first and then accelerated. …

For the next five months, I lived in a state of uninterrupted deep peace and bliss. After that, it diminished somewhat in intensity, or perhaps it just seemed to because it became my natural state. I could still function in the world, although I realized that nothing, I ever did could possibly add anything to what I already had.

For the concluding description of the experience of self-realization, I chose someone with the educational background and vocabulary of a psychiatrist: David R. Hawkins, MD, PhD. In the previous chapter, I quoted from his book, *Power versus Force: The Hidden Determinants of Human Behavior*, and I pointed out that Dr. Hawkins describes experiencing samadhi on page 10 and self-realization on page 12. On page 11, Dr. Hawkins skims over his life leading up to becoming a "quite successful" thirty-eight-year-old psychiatrist dying from a fatal disease. He "was in a state of extreme anguish and despair" waiting for death.

> As my final moments approached, the thought flashed through my mind, *"What if there is a God?"* So, I called out in prayer, "If there is a God, I ask Him to help me now." I surrendered to whatever God there might be and went unconscious. When I awoke, a transformation of such enormity had taken place that I was struck dumb with awe.
>
> The person I had been no longer existed. There was no personal self or ego left – just an Infinite Presence of such unlimited power that it was all that was. This Presence had replaced what had been "me,"

and the body and its actions were controlled solely by the Presence's infinite will. The world was illuminated by the clarity of an infinite Oneness, which expressed itself as ... immeasurable beauty and perfection.

For nine months, this stillness persisted. I had no will of my own; unbidden, the physical entity went about its business under the direction of the infinite power, but exquisitely gentle, will of the Presence. In that state, there was no need to think about anything. All truth was self-evident, no conceptualization was necessary or even possible.

I hope these short quotations from just one of the many books written by Eckhart Tolle and Dr. David Hawkins motivate the reading of several books written by those who have achieved self-realization. When I wanted to experience people who had achieved self-realization, I had to travel to wherever they were located. Today, thanks to the internet, you can experience many people who have achieved self-realization without leaving the comfort of your home. Books and websites that I am familiar with and recommend are listed in the "For Further Study" section. If you only look at one website or one book, I recommend Leonard Jacobson's website and his book *Journey into Now*. Please investigate several Jesus-like spiritual teachers.

"Religions are many, but God is One."
—*Sathya Sai Baba*

Chapter 9
LEFT OUT ODDS AND ENDS

Politics without principles, education without character,
science without humanity, and commerce without
morality are not only useless, but positively dangerous.
—*Sathya Sai Baba*

I surmise that God's incarnations as Shirdi and Sathya Sai
Baba occurred during our planet's two world wars and the
Cold War because humanity's spiritual knowledge has not
progressed along with humanity's ability to kill and destroy.
The twentieth century's wars and conflicts were among the
worst in human history. The war to end all wars and all life
on this planet will inevitably occur in this, the twenty-first,
century if Western culture's spiritual ignorance continues.
What progress, if any, has been made teaching children
desirable character and behavior traits? The ministries
of Jesus and Sai Baba reveal little, if any, progress in the
ability of moral and spiritual concerns to influence human
behavior. Jesus's miracles, like bringing Lazarus's corpse back
to life, provided the "signs" of Jesus's divinity and helped to
motivate the writing of the Gospels. The Jewish leaders, an
elite group of rabbis called the Sanhedrin, regarded Jesus's
miracles, teachings, and influence as a threat to their power
and authority. Unable to see beyond worldly concerns, the
Sanhedrin combined Pontius Pilate's power and authority with
theirs to have Jesus crucified. Despite Jesus's teachings and the
passage of two thousand years, only a small portion of those
living in the Western world appreciate Sai Baba's "signs" and
spiritual teachings. Like the Sanhedrin, contemporary leaders
of science, academia, and Christianity are more concerned

with maintaining their power and authority than appreciating humanity's spiritual heritage. When, if ever, will Western civilization acknowledge and embrace God's efforts?

In 1961, my first year at UC Berkeley, Chancellor Clark Kerr defended communists speaking on the Berkeley campus by saying, "The University is not engaged in making ideas safe for students. It is engaged in making students safe for ideas." Today's normalization of the communication of false and deceptive information enables rich and powerful, heartless young souls to logarithmically increase the difficulty and desirability of making people, which begins with students, "safe for ideas."

A democracy relies upon well-educated, informed citizens with desirable character traits such as honesty. The willingness of almost every Republican member of the United States Congress to condone Donald Trump's obvious dishonesty does not bode well for our democratic form of government. What hope is there for a democracy whose elected leaders embrace and promote dishonesty? Our education system must teach children to expect honesty from others as well as themselves. No one can or should trust those who do not value basic and easy-to-understand concepts like honesty. Imagine the influence on human behavior if everyone was taught to believe in Karma, reincarnation, and God's omnipresent awareness and love. Instead of maintaining existing circumstances, like the Sanhedrin, science and religion would appreciate God's efforts (humanity's spiritual heritage). The taboo against knowing that reincarnation enables heartless, young souls to become bighearted, old souls enables young souls to take over school boards, become president of the United States, and Supreme Court justices. The perpetuation of Rome's version of Christianity and science's atheistic paradigms prevent people from being guided by insight into everyone's underlying reality.

Young souls have not experienced incarnating, both male and female, within as many races and cultures as older souls. Young souls oppose progressive social change because they do not experience empathy or concern for others. Bighearted old souls embrace immigration, racial integration, women's rights, and LGBTQIA+ rights as the concerns of other spiritual beings like themselves. Lifetimes spent in Earth School develop empathy, an intuitive sense of right and wrong, and a conscience. Young souls are like ships without a rudder. Putin's "leadership" in Russia, the World Wars, and the Holocaust are examples of what can happen when people are not made safe for ideas. The education system's failure to teach moral and democratic values makes it possible for the tail to wag the dog as spiritually unevolved young souls assume control of the government and its institutions.

That was more than I anticipated writing about politics. This final chapter does not have a lot to say about any one topic. Because the perspectives of avatars greatly exceed our own, I want to fill this chapter with the words of Sathya Sai Baba. Paragraphs may jump from one unrelated topic to another with little or no transition. For example, how did you react to Sai Baba's statement in the introduction to Isaac Tigrett's 1992 presentation: "What science has been able to unravel is only a fraction of the cosmic phenomena"?Do you think science has discovered so much that there cannot be much left to discover? Believe it or not, that is what physicists thought over a century ago. In 1874, when Max Planck asked the University of Munich's physics professor Phillip von Jolly about physics, Professor von Jolly expressed the prevailing view among physicists with these words: "Almost everything is already discovered, and all that remains is to fill in a few unimportant holes." Albert A. Michelson, the first American to receive the Nobel Prize in physics, summarized the beliefs of physicists at the end of the nineteenth century by saying, "Our future discoveries must be looked for at the end of the sixth decimal place." The opinions expressed by physics professors von Jolly and Michelson reveal that even physics professors can be oblivious to the magnitude of their ignorance.

SEEING DEAD PEOPLE

In addition to experiencing clairvoyance on only one occasion, I experienced seeing a "ghost" on only one occasion. I believe my life contains a variety of "paranormal" experiences because the best evidence to support beliefs is personal experience. We have judges and juries to arrive at a verdict based on available evidence, but the experiences of the person on trial enable them *to know* if they are innocent or guilty. I wonder if my prebirth life script contained the experiences that motivated the writing of this book. One of those experiences occurred nine years after Jill Mix, my wife, and Dan Knoop divorced after twenty years of marriage.

When Jill and I went to bed that night, we were unaware that Dan had died a few hours earlier from the reason Jill had left him: alcoholism. I woke up lying on my back and noticed a faint glow of light to my left where Jill was sleeping soundly on her back. To get a better look, I turned onto my side and saw floating above Jill's head a hologram-like image of Dan's head looking much younger than when I examined his eyes the previous year. Their noses almost touched. As if wondering if I could see him, Dan's head turned to stare at me. After staring at me for a few seconds, Dan went back to staring at Jill. After a minute or two, he again turned to stare at my eyes while rising to the ceiling and back toward Jill. Realizing that I could see him because of my eye movements, he rose to and through the ceiling.

When my dad died in 2007, my grandchildren, Juliette and Jacob, had similar experiences when Juliette was almost five, and Jacob was just over two years old. After learning about my dad's death in San Diego, I called my daughter, Jennifer, who lives in Florida. To my surprise, Jennifer said, "I know," when I told her about her grandfather's death. While Jennifer was driving their sedan with Juliette and Jacob sitting in child safety seats in the back, both Juliette and Jacob said that their great-grandpa's head was staring at them from above the space between the two front seats. The ability of my dad's and Dan Knoop's spirits to precisely travel wherever their thoughts took them—even thousands of miles into a moving vehicle—provides potential evidence for and insight into a nonmaterial spiritual dimension.

Young children, with the ability to see and communicate with disincarnate sprits, usually lose and forget having "paranormal" abilities. Those who keep their abilities say that the souls of those who have recently died only have enough energy to manifest a head. During the 1970s and 1980s, many of the Parapsychology Association of Riverside's members had been adults during World War II. On a few occasions, I heard them talking about the disincarnate spirits of husbands, who had died in faraway battles, appearing before their wives. The letters from the War Department confirmed what these women already knew.

THE TRUTH, THE WHOLE TRUTH, AND …

I believe the sources and quotations used in this book are honest expressions of actual human experiences. My experiences are as accurately and honestly conveyed as I am capable of writing, except for one rather significant experience: I forgot what the voice of God said while I listened to a church sermon for the first time. During the early 1970s, when I still remembered my inner sermon word for word, I saw a short description of the Baha'i faith in the newspaper's worship directory. Until I read that the Baha'is believe all religions, whether they know it or not, worship the same God, nothing that I had experienced reminded me of my inner sermon. The first of the three most important religious teachings in my inner sermon was about the oneness of God with creation. I believe the other two were about loving God and loving others, but I am not sure. When I wrote about my inner sermon, I did not want to admit that I was confident of only one of my inner sermon's three most important religious teachings or commandments.

That weekend, I went to the Baha'i faith's meeting. I was the only man in attendance. About eight women, who all appeared to be of Middle Eastern extraction, greeted me warmly and patiently explained the Baha'i faith to me. Everything they said harmonized with my inner sermon, but I was not comfortable embracing a new culture along with a new religion. Because of that experience, and the importance of religion to communities and incarnating souls, I believe children should be introduced to their family and culture's religion at an early age. I am assuming the religion and culture teach love, and not prejudice and hate.

The first commandment of my inner sermon conflicts with Christianity's claims of superiority to other religions and the uniqueness of Jesus. Christianity's claims were believable when people were illiterate and lived in isolated communities, but Christianity should acknowledge that, as Sathya Sai Baba put it, "Religions are many, but God is One," and "There is only one religion: the religion of Love." The Sarva Dharma Symbol, which Sai Baba designed for the Sri Sathya Sai International Organization, contains the symbols for six of the world's major religions. Sathya Sai Baba warned us to "Never entertain the feeling that one's religion is superior and another inferior." No wonder the first commandment of my inner sermon, which I attribute to Sathya Sai Baba, was about the oneness of God within His creation.

As I read the books in PAR's library and those loaned to me by Reverend Madalyn DeGrace, my memory of the inner sermon faded because the books, like the Baha'i faith, harmonized with my inner sermon. Samadhi and the inner sermon enabled me to be aware of an underlying spiritual reality which atheists have not experienced. Would the "paranormal" human experiences contained in this book be possible without an actual underlying spiritual reality?

LOVE

To encourage us to "develop the sense of equal mindedness and equal regard for all," Sathya Sai Baba said, "The best way to love God is to love All," and "All are One, be alike to everyone." Jesus's "commandment, that you love one another, even as I have loved you"[68] encouraged the same "sense of equal mindedness and equal regard for all." In harmony with Jesus's ministry, Sai Baba's 1995 Christmas discourse was about love from God's perspective. Sai Baba's "true and eternal" description of love reflects God's desire for compatible companions. I suspect that reincarnation and Earth School cultivate "true and eternal" love, which blossoms in older souls. Sai Baba said during his discourse,

> Love exists for love and does not expect anything in return. Love is not mercenary. It does not involve give and take like a business. Love finds joy in giving. Everything is love … The love between mother and child, between husband and wife are taken as love. They are not love. They are relationships. They are finite, with a beginning and an end. But true and eternal love has neither a beginning nor an end … Love which is true and eternal, and drenches mankind in perennial bliss is love in its truest sense … People are unable to understand this divine, ever fresh and fragrant love. They are attracted by ephemeral, transient, worldly love, and thereby they waste their

lives ... Let anyone say anything, but do not hate them. Believe that everything happens for one's own good. Do not hate anybody.

Do not accuse or criticize anyone. Do not hurt anyone. Happiness will come in the same measure as your love for God.

LOCATING AND EXPERIENCING OUR SOUL

Because we only have three parts—body, soul, and person (or jiva)—identifying and locating our soul is not as difficult as suggested by Western science's atheistic, soulless paradigms. My chest filled with love when Sai Baba stared at me because the emotions which emanate from our soul feel like they are coming from our heart. Our ability to feel empathy, love, and concern for others reveals our soul's level of spiritual development. The ability to experience empathy and concern for the needs of others characterizes old souls. The seven deadly sins and indifference to the concerns of others characterize young souls. When James Sinclair started his speech by saying, "I want to share experiences which I do not intellectually understand but which I feel," he identified the two aspects—physical thinking mind and spiritual feeling soul—which combine to create a thinking, feeling person. Sathya Sai Baba described this confusing blend of physical and spiritual by saying,

There are two "I's" in everyone: The "I" that is associated with the mind and the "I" that is associated with the Atma. The consciousness of the Atma is the real "I." When this "I" is wrongly associated with the mind, it becomes the ego. When the "I" associated with the Atma experiences Atmic bliss, it realizes the universal consciousness is One, though it may be called by different names. When you eliminate the body consciousness in you, you have the consciousness of the Universal in you.[69]

Sathya Sai Baba described our soul as our "true divine self," which, in a feeling but not in a physical sense, he located in our "heart." On March 30, 1987, in the Prasanthi Nilayam Mandir, Sai Baba related spiritual practices with where we experience our soul by saying, "Consider your heart as Atma. Soften it and make it full of compassion. That is the only spiritual exercise you need to perform. ... All practices need to be directed towards softening your heart so that it will flow with kindness and love."

The world, at least the United States, seems to have a lot of young souls whose hearts do not "flow with kindness and love." Young souls are successful politicians because of the abundance of young souls who do not know any better than to vote for them. Imagine a culture sophisticated enough to recognize and prefer the leadership of compassionate and caring old souls. After several millennia of human history, why are there so many young souls? I asked my pendulum about the timing of the sparks that became souls. To my surprise, my pendulum disagreed with my assumption that souls were created a long time ago, but it agreed with a continuous, like "sparks emanating from fire," explanation of soul creation.

The "hearts" of young souls do not readily experience compassion and concern for others like the "hearts" of old souls. The 2022 Supreme Court decision to end Roe v. Wade and a woman's right to an abortion occurred after the replacement of old souls with heartless, young souls. During the previous fifty years, the Supreme Court justices compassionately understood a pregnant woman's potential circumstances and a baby's need to be wanted and loved. Heartless, young souls, who do not feel empathy for women when their life circumstances make abortions desirable, only have their mind's attitudes and beliefs to guide them.

AN ODD, SPIRITUAL-DIMENSION
LOOK AT HISTORY

I want to share something that Hazel Denning whispered to me and two other Parapsychology Association of Riverside members prior to a monthly meeting. She whispered and I have been reluctant to share what she whispered because it sounds Antisemitic to those who do not understand and believe in reincarnation philosophy. Hazel Denning said that the souls of many of her clients, as well as those of her past-life regression therapist friends, were victims of the Holocaust during their previous incarnation. While in the spiritual dimension prior to their previous incarnation, their soul (along with an unusually large percentage of incarnating souls) needed to mitigate bad Karma—"for whatever a man sows, that he will also reap"[70]—accumulated during previous incarnations. What is worth noting about this radically different perspective on the Holocaust is the improbability of regression clients independently coming up with this explanation for the Holocaust unless past-life and between-lives regression memories are real and not imagined. What the world views as monstrous and evil may be beneficial from the perspective of a soul whose physical host's nightmarish life provides several lifetimes of bad Karma mitigation and spiritual growth. People become more sensitive to the needs of others as they experience their own pain and suffering as well as the pain and suppering of others.

BELIEVE IT OR NOT

When Joy and Ray Thomas returned home after living in India, Joy told me the most amazing thing she heard while living in Prasanthi Nilayam. I have shared many of the godlike powers and abilities that Sathya Sai Baba revealed to his devotees, but I find this extremely hard to believe. During darshan, Sathya Sai Baba invited a group of devotees from Australia into his interview room. When Sai Baba wanted to communicate something to a devotee that was too personal to discuss in the outer interview room, he invited them into a small, private room. Sai Baba invited one of the Australian group's men into the small, private room and told him that his mother was dying. Sai Baba said he could magically transport the man to his home in Australia, or he could stay with his group. If he stayed with his group, his mother would no longer be living when he returned home. After the Australians left the interview room with one less member, a lady in the group called the missing man's home in Australia. He answered and told her to have the group bring his luggage when they return home to Australia.

DHARMA

The Telugu (Sathya Sai Baba's native language) and Sanskrit words used in Sai Baba's discourses and books can be difficult for English speakers to translate and understand. The Sanskrit language conveys or assumes God's nonduality with the material world, and our status as incarnating spiritual beings instead of human—bodies with brains—beings. Sai Baba often began his discourses by addressing his audience with, "Embodiments of Divine Love." Thinking of yourself as an embodiment of divine love may be a radically different way to think about yourself, but it is a helpful way of relating to a language that, like the Bible, has been attributed to God. August 1986's *Sanathana Sarathi* (a monthly spiritual journal started by Sathya Sai Baba in 1958) contains the following definition of the Sanskrit word dharma. Sai Baba's definition reveals his insight into our ability to be guided by the inner voice as well as the thoughts and abilities of human minds and egos.

The word dharma, which is bound up with an infinite variety of meanings, is being inadequately described by one word: duty. In the modern age, Duty relates to an individual, a predicament, or a particular time or country. On the other hand, dharma is eternal, the same for everyone, everywhere. It expresses the significance of the inner voice. The birthplace of dharma is the heart. What emanates from the heart as a pure idea, translated into action, is called dharma. If you must be told in a manner that you can understand, one can say, "Do unto others as you want them to do unto you" – that is dharma. Dharma consists of avoiding actions which would hurt others. If anyone causes happiness to you then in turn you should do things that will cause happiness to others.

I wanted to share the word dharma because of the desirability of a single word that contains all the concepts related to *inner guidance* inspired exemplary human behavior. Sathya Sai Baba said, "The true sign of [exemplary human behavior] is perfect harmony and synchronization of one's thoughts, words, and deeds." Imagine the benefits to human civilization if everyone knew and understood the word dharma. From a material world perspective, dharma applies to jivas (individualized beings or persons) interacting with other jivas. But wanting to do things that make others happy and not wanting to harm others relates to and influences the spiritual journey of souls. Awareness of one's underlying spiritual reality motivates, like a carrot and stick, ideal human behavior. Dharma applies to the spiritual journeys of souls as well as the thoughts, words, and deeds of jivas.

During his November 23, 1981, birthday discourse, Sathya Sai Baba summarized what we should realize as incarnating souls.

Embodiments of Love! Sparks emanating from fire are neither different from it, nor identical with it. So, too, the jiva is neither different from human, nor identical with it. ... We should not be misled by form. The content is the important criterion, and the content is Divinity. ... Jiva and Brahman become identical only when liberation is achieved. Until the sea is reached, the river remains as a river. It has a different name and a distinct form. So too the jiva, so long as it is involved with the physical case, the senses, the mind, and the instruments of consciousness, it does not merge in God. It remains apart. The Atma is ever self-contained, self-sufficient. The material world exists on account of the Other. The Atma is the basic unity which assumes the appearance of diversity, the world, its immanence is the unifying Truth, evident as the divine in all beings. It is the duty of everyone to live in the awareness of this Truth.

WHY DO BAD THINGS HAPPEN TO GOOD PEOPLE?

Like a blacksmith shaping horseshoes with the blows of a hammer, the joys and sorrows of many lifetimes shape souls into God's compatible companions. When I am reminded of the pain and suffering continually taking place on this planet, I pray, "Lord, may all conscious beings be happy." After giving the problem to God, the discomfort associated with my empathetic response to the suffering of others leaves me. It is helpful to "have the conviction that the entire universe is filled with God," and to know that "God's joy lies in the joy of living beings."[71]

My pendulum tells me that my life experiences led to the writing of this book because God wants the world to understand and promote the spiritual growth concerns of incarnating souls. Instead of the spiritual teachings of God's prophets and avatars, the Western world teaches exoteric beliefs inspired by materialistic understandings of reality. Sathya Sai Baba said, "Good and bad, joy and sorrow are the result of our actions. Actions are responsible for your present conditions. Actions done with attachment bind man to time and the cycle of time."[72] In the same discourse, Sai Baba said,

> Actions which are selfish, egotistic, and done with expectation of the fruits lead to bondage and rebirth. If all actions are done as an offering to God, one is freed instantly. ... It is sheer ignorance to think that there are external enemies or friends. Our sins are our real enemies, and meritorious deeds are our friends. ... Among the nine types of worship, service is supreme. The hungry man must be fed first. A diseased person needs to be helped and given treatment. Encourage people to develop hope when they are forlorn. ... Good people take shelter in God and offer everything to God, pray to Him, and surrender to Him. They keep God first, and the world next, and the "I" (ego) last. Bad people keep first the "I," the world next, and lastly God. When God is last, you are lost. Whenever you give first place to God and have steady, firm faith in Him, there will be no more fear. ... Let us understand that we live not for moneymaking, not for fulfilling our wants, not for scholarly and intellectual talents, but for spiritual development.[73]

Western science and Christianity ignore the evidence that reveals the inseparable nature of spirit and matter. Because of Western culture's attitudes and beliefs, neither my parents nor my teachers were concerned with my spiritual development. The Western world, the material world of human desires, is not concerned with questions like "Who am I?" and "Why was I born?" Which is why no one informed me that I am a spiritual being needing spiritual development. Considering the evidence alluded to and contained in this book, should Western science, religion, and academia regard and treat people as spiritual beings? On July 27, 2002, Sathya Sai Baba gathered the American devotees into Prasanthi Nilayam Mandir to discuss the significance of materialism and spiritual ignorance to those living in the Western world.

> ... if you do not realize that you are Atma, what is the use of your life and all the education you acquire? You should realize the truth "I am I" – that you are with God, and you are in God, and God is in you. ... God is unity in diversity. ... That is why I frequently say, "Never consider God as separate from you." ... When you say "I," it refers to the Atma. ... If you consider that God is separate from you, God will always remain separate from you. God is in you, and you are in God.

While speaking on the theme "Who Am I?" in Prasanthi Nilayam Mandir on March 30, 1987, Sathya Sai Baba said,

> The cosmos is the manifestation of the Divine. They are foolish who, while seeing the handiwork of the Divine everywhere, think that there is no God. ... While God is omnipresent and can be cognized in the divine manifestations of Nature, the body consciousness prevents men from experiencing Oneness with the Divine.

When I pick up my pendulum and ask God a question, the pendulum moves because of God's grace and my immersion in God's kingdom. When the Pharisees asked Jesus "when the kingdom of God would come, Jesus replied, "God's kingdom doesn't come with observation; neither will they say, 'Look, here!' or 'Look, there!' for behold, God's kingdom is within you."[74]

In 1973, Sathya Sai Baba said the same thing with these words:

> God is not somewhere away from you, someone distant from you. He is in you, before you, behind you, beckoning, guarding, guiding, warning, prompting, the inner voice speaking ever with you. You need not seek Him. He is there ready to respond to the call from the heart. Call on me and I am always by your side.[75]

God is "ready to respond to the call from the heart" when bad things happen in our material world of desire and ego. God gives us opportunities to realize "the kingdom of God is within" us and to achieve the spiritual development necessary for self-realization. On March 12, 1972, Sathya Sai Baba discussed why we should be concerned with our spiritual development.

> Each human being is equipped with a return ticket at birth. Holding it in your grasp, you earn and spend, rise and fall, sing and dance, weep and laugh forgetting the end of the journey. But though you forget, the wagon of life moves toward the cemetery

which is its terminus. No glory accrues to you if you are tied helplessly to the wheel of birth and death. Your glory and greatness consist in disentangling yourself from that revolving wheel. Before death nips life and thrusts you into another birth, you must, by means of spiritual discipline, learn the mystery of the Atma.[76]

Sathya Sai Baba explained "the mystery of the Atma" in the Poornachandra Auditorium during his July 7, 1990, discourse titled "The Guru Within." While reading Sai Baba's words, imagine the influence on human behavior if science and Christianity supported these ideas.

Develop the unshakable conviction that the Divine is present in everyone. Then there will be no room for developing differences of any kind. Conflict and discord will have no place. Likes and dislikes will go …
… Dedicate your entire time to service and the discharge of your duties. Your spiritual practices must not be for selfish ends. It must promote the good of others. Giving up selfishness, cultivating selfless love for others, sanctify your lives.

History records God's efforts to reveal His reality and expectations for incarnating spiritual beings. The pages of this book contain and explain the spiritual teachings and concepts common to divinely inspired religions. Despite God's efforts, the Western world clings to Christianity's misunderstandings about Jesus and science's atheistic paradigms.

Our physical reality yields its secrets to a scientist's physical senses and logic, but our spiritual reality is not discernible with physical sense and logic. Scientists must realize that God responds to the "heart" and not the head. With a "heart" as well as a head, science could appreciate the abundant evidence in this book. Argument from design, the first chapter's scientific research findings, and those who obtain self-realization provide multiple layers of evidence for and confirmation of your underlying spiritual reality. Unfortunately, spiritually oblivious exoteric believers are in the majority, and the concepts in this book have not been appropriately applied to the task of educating reincarnating spiritual beings. When children believe in Karma and reincarnation and are taught how to live as well as how to make a living, the costs to society of undesirable human behaviors will be greatly reduced.

Despite paradigms that restrict science to studying and explaining the natural world, scientists often make the category mistake of assuming competence with nonmaterial, spiritual phenomena. The spiritually ignorant, yet arrogant, attitudes of many scientists contribute to the decline in church attendance and belief in God. God, like gravity, is omnipresent yet invisible. Despite their similarity, Western science readily acknowledges gravity's effects while ignoring those of God. Other than God, what could be the power that moves my pendulum when I ask God questions? This book is filled with phenomena that would not exist if we were not spiritual beings. In 1974, Sathya Sai Baba discussed some of the questions ignored by science.

> [Western scientists] declare that the objective world arose out of the conglomeration of desperate atoms. ... But they do not pursue the matter and explain what induced the atoms to join in particular designs and groups. How does this urge arise in the minute atom? Who planted this desire in the heart of the atom? These questions are bypassed.
>
> Most philosophers, especially in the West, ignore the problem of identifying the cause of all the effects we find every moment all around us.[77]

Besides ignoring the causes of effects, Western science is not concerned with *why* we exist. Science ignores, as if they are not important, questions about life's meaning and purpose. But what is more important than knowing the meaning or purpose of our lives? The questions that science ignores, while waging a war with religion, are life's most important questions.

Western science's atheistic paradigms have consequences for the material world besides making the Western world a spiritually ignorant place in which to be born. As belief in God and church attendance decline, polls reveal declines in community involvement, tolerance of others, and the perceived value of higher education. Religion can play an important role in teaching values and motivating desirable human behaviors. When families who do not regularly attend church are compared with those who do, those who regularly attend church are more likely to experience better physical and mental health, and happier, longer (nearly four years longer) lives. When children are raised in a religious home, they are more likely to obtain higher test scores and grades, but less likely to become depressed or engage in substance abuse or risky sexual behavior. The maxim "first do no harm" should motivate Western scientists to embrace, instead of ignoring, the evidence for God, souls, and an afterlife.

Sathya Sai Baba was concerned with correcting misunderstandings about our underlying spiritual reality and helping people to achieve liberation from future births. I am writing this book to share experiences that conflict with Western science, culture, and religion's "commonsense" understandings of reality. My hope is to stimulate greater interest in and acceptance of God's many and various communications with humanity.

I do not want to encourage people to be concerned with achieving self-realization. At a seminar that featured several speakers who had purportedly achieved self-realization, I experienced a good example of why the achievement of self-realization should be surrendered to God's will. A Buddhist speaker attributed experiencing self-realization to his daily discipline of Buddhist meditation. When he finished speaking, the Buddhist gentleman sitting next to me angrily said that he was not aware of benefiting from his identical spiritual discipline. Egoic human minds do not know if their soul has fulfilled its spiritual growth and karmic debt concerns, and worldly attachments and desires prevent achieving self-realization. Karmic debt can be thought of as the seeds of past actions that shape one's destiny as they germinate. Past and between-lives regression reveals that the periods between lives are not about punishment. They are periods of reviewing and learning from our previous lives and planning our next life to address our soul's growth and karmic debt concerns.

Saint Paul the apostle's definition of Karma in Galatians 6:7 ("whatever a man sows, that he will also reap") and Sathya Sai Baba definition ("the seeds of past actions and desires") mean the same thing. Sai Baba went on to say that, just as seeds do not sprout when covered with too much soil, good Karma—such as selfless service to others—cancels out bad Karma. In the previous chapter, I wrote about the self-realization experiences of Byron Katie, Eckhart Tolle, and Dr. David Hawkins. They were not trying to achieve self-realization. It happened when their souls fulfilled the requirements for graduation from Earth School: they reaped what they had sown over many lifetimes. I have written about self-realization because those who achieve self-realization, along with Jesus-like prophets and avatars, provide humanity with the wisdom of God instead of egoic human minds. The "For Further Study" section lists people who have achieved self-realization, so that you can confirm the nature and reality of self-realization. Instead of ignoring those who achieve self-realization, Western science and Christianity should realize that those who achieve self-realization are potential spiritual teachers, like Jesus, and evidence of everyone's underlying spiritual reality. Self-realization can be attained at various levels of consciousness. Some, like Yogananda and Jesus, have supernatural abilities. Because they all speak from and about the same kingdom of heaven, eventually, those who attain self-realization become repetitive and boring. Pretending to have achieved self-realization would not be extremely difficult. Those listed in the "For Further Study" section are not pretending.

DESTINY

Since 1986—when Sai Baba's gaze transmitted so much love that I thought my chest would explode—I knew it was my destiny to write this book. No wonder my spirit guides told psychic Kathryn Leeman that I needed to work on my communication skills. To change even one person's "commonsense," confirmation bias-maintained beliefs is nearly impossible. I assumed my mystical experiences implied God's desire that I attempt to reveal and explain to atheists the evidence for God, souls, and an afterlife. For over thirty years, I saved (without sources) Sathya Sai Baba's short but profound statements while wondering how "I" was going to do the impossible. My fear of the karmic consequences of not sharing God's grace with others eventually led to this attempt to prove that avatars and advanced spiritual beings (old souls like Jesus) are everyone's most important source of knowledge. Spiritual beings and Western civilization are poorly served by science's atheistic paradigms and Christian myths about Jesus instead of his teachings.

Imagine if Western science crawled out from under its centuries-old materialistic bias and acknowledged the existence of the phenomena contained in this book. Accepting the reality and implications of past-life and between-lives regression memories, children who remember past lives, near-death experiences, and those who achieve self-realization would enable evidence-based spiritual concepts to replace unsupportable religious dogma. Religious beliefs would embrace reincarnation philosophy, Karma, and avatars. If this happens, I believe human behavior will significantly improve as people realize they, as well as everyone else, are spiritual beings immersed in an omnipresent God of love. When religion is supported by science and based upon empirical evidence, people will fear sin instead of hell. Guided by the evidence that supports belief in reincarnation, people will want to perform actions that generate positive Karma while avoiding actions that harm others. As people accumulate more positive and less negative Karma, bad things will happen to fewer people. When people know that they are enrolled in Earth School, human behavior and graduation rates will improve. Motivating incarnating souls to be exemplary human beings benefits human civilization as well as incarnating souls. The costs to society of criminal and other undesirable behavior will decrease as people embrace humanity's spiritual heritage and understand the concepts of reincarnation and Karma. Awareness of being hopelessly tied to the wheel of Karma motivates exemplary human behavior.

How much control do you have over your destiny? Have you thought about it? In a discourse on January 14, 1964, in Prasanthi Nilayam titled "Names Do Not Matter," Sathya Sai Baba talked about the nature of everyone's destiny.

> ... there is a destiny that shapes events, irrespective of individual efforts. Well, everyone must come to that conclusion sooner or later, for there is a limit to the capacity of man to control events. Beyond that, an unseen hand takes over the wheel of events. You may call it destiny, another may call it Providence, and a

third God. Names do not matter. It is the humility that matters, the wonder, the sense of awe that matters.

WHEN THOUGHTS MARRY BELIEFS

We were born to cultivate empathy and concern for the welfare and needs of others. We were not born to cultivate beliefs. I love Byron Katie's expression, "when thoughts marry beliefs." It captures how quickly and firmly human minds turn thoughts into beliefs. Strongly held beliefs are undesirable because they close our minds to new ideas and experiences. This book is about concepts that few people understand or believe. While trying to help those who experience, as she did, troubling thoughts and beliefs, Byron Katie asked, "Who would you be without your beliefs?" When Byron Katie woke up without her troubling beliefs, she experienced being the consciousness of the spark of God that became her soul. What would Western civilization be like without taboos that prevent the widespread understanding of the phenomena contained in this book? In these last few paragraphs, I want to cover previously avoided taboo topics.

Blame your thinking monkey mind instead of your soul for recalling your past and imagining your future when you are having difficulty sleeping. To experience our true "I am," we must get out of our monkey mind's story and into the present moment. When we get out of our minds and into the present moment, our soul is experienced as "I am." Because all the sparks that become souls come from the same source or God, as Sathya Sai Baba said, "The same God is in insects, birds, and beasts. He is also present in everyone you meet." Imagine the influence on prejudice and the victimization of others if everyone embraced the concept of nonduality: God, "I am," is present in all sentient beings.

Those who realize that consciousness, "I am," is not unique to human beings often become vegetarians. Both human health and our planet's health benefit when people become vegetarians. In comparison to meat eaters, vegetarians are less likely to be obese or experience chronic diseases, type 2 diabetes, cancer, high blood pressure or cholesterol. According to the Food and Agriculture Organization, livestock farming is responsible for 14.5 percent of all greenhouse gas emissions. No wonder Sathya Sai Baba said, "God did not create animals for people to eat." Because the oneness of God and creation is not embraced by science, nations and individuals callously do to other sentient beings what they would not want done to them.

If you are a vegetarian or have pets, you may be comfortable with the idea that "insects, birds, and beasts," like you, are spiritual beings with souls. If so, you would be in the minority because human minds reluctantly marry self-esteem diminishing beliefs. Human egos want to believe that "man" in the first chapter of Genesis—"God created man in his own image, ... [to] fill the earth, and subdue it. Have dominion ... over every living thing that moves on the earth."[78]—refers to a person's egoic understanding of themselves and others. Instead of inflating human egos, religion should be about love, tolerance, and humility. When reading this quotation from Genesis, realize that there are two "I's"—an egoic "I" that is merely a surface impression of one's reality, and a "heart" that has a nonduality relationship with God and others. Living revealers of the experience of self-realization provide both evidence for and understanding of these counterintuitive concepts. Instead of passing misunderstandings from this generation to the next, Sathya Sai Baba and contemporary Jesus-like teachers provide an opportunity for religions to correct their misunderstandings. When the world's religions correct their misunderstandings, religion will unite cultures and nations instead of driving them apart.

Science's materialism and Christianity's taboo subjects prevent the widespread acceptance of hypnotism's ability to bypass a person's egoic "I" and communicate directly with their real "I" or Atma. Despite atheistic science's denials, proof of the preexistence of souls and reincarnation exists in research findings like those of Helen Wambach, PhD, who discovered that the past-life memories of hypnotized volunteers contained accurate, obscure historical facts that their brain's egoic "I" could not possibly have known. Hypnosis also reveals that, because souls do not want to be confined in a womb for nine months, fetuses do not have a soul until birth is eminent. Paradoxically, a variety of creatures with souls are heartlessly eaten by the authoritarian bullies who oppose the abortion of unwanted, soulless fetuses. Would souls want to incarnate into an unwanted and potentially unloved baby? Only in a spiritually ignorant culture would young, heartless souls be permitted to serve as judges.

Did you find the contents of this book understandable and believable? I did not initially understand or embrace many of the concepts contained in this book. Even though mystical experiences and what seemed like divine guidance motivated my continuing interest, overcoming my prejudices required time and effort on my part. Gradually over several decades, the pieces to the spiritual puzzle formed a harmonious picture that I have tried to describe in the pages of this book. If all this was strange and new to you, this book's contents may be understandable when reread in conjunction with the "For Further Study" section's suggestions. The common themes, especially nonduality, in humanity's ancient spiritual teachings and religious traditions provide evidence of God's influence upon human history. Earth School involves learning through experience. What did you experience after adopting Sathya Sai Baba's morning and evening prayers? Have you experienced occult phenomena by bringing a question or concern to a tarot card reader, by experiencing what your birth information reveals to an astrologer, or by experiencing past-life regression?

Religious and service groups and activities may be of benefit to you as well as others. As Jesus said, "Ask, and it shall be given you. Seek, and you will find. Knock, and it will be opened to you."[79] The truth that lies behind the world's veil of illusion is revealed through your efforts and God's grace.

In Frank Capra's 1937 movie *Lost Horizon*, Ronald Coleman said, "There are moments in everyone's life when [they glimpse] The Eternal." The focus of this book has been sharing glimpses of The Eternal and the insights that explain them. The most significant human experiences are not transmittable with words. God's grace is required to penetrate the veil of illusion cast by human minds. Sathya Sai Baba said, "I am you; you are I; that is the truth. There is no distinction. That which appears so is the illusion. You are the waves; I am the Ocean. Know this and be free, be Divine." How much longer will Western science and Christianity be in the hands of those who ignore and deny the antidotal and empirical evidence in this book? Must the Western world remain a spiritually ignorant place in which to be born?

FOR FURTHER STUDY

I am inclined to take a speculative and philosophical approach to suggesting ideas for further study. I imagine that the reader is either not convinced that they are a spiritual being or want to know how to awaken from the illusion of separation from God. A less superficial look at this book's sources of evidence may turn skeptics into believers.

1. Thousands of near-death experiences provide proof beyond a reasonable doubt of the nonlocality of consciousness and an afterlife. If consciousness arises from brains, consciousness would be local. You can investigate NDEs at the following:

    a. International Association for Near-Death Studies (https://www.iands.org/)
    b. Near-Death Experience Research Foundation (https://www.nderf.org/)
    c. Eben Alexander, MD's books inspired by his NDE while in a weeklong coma in 2008 provide the perspective and insights of an academic neurosurgeon.

2. The first chapter's evidence for an afterlife and consciousness' nonlocality included the following:

    a. Russell Targ's *The Reality of ESP: A Physicist's Proof of Psychic Abilities* contains evidence for the nonlocality of consciousness.
    b. The research findings of Ian Stevenson, MD, and Carol Bowman reveal the reality of young children with the memories and jiva of a recently deceased person.

c. Gary E. Schwartz, PhD's *The Afterlife Experiments* provide another form of evidence for an afterlife and reincarnation.

d. Past-life regression provides yet another form of evidence for reincarnation while providing consistent, repeatable insights into the afterlife. To learn more, read the books by Helen Wambach, PhD; Brian Weiss, MD; and Michael Newton, PhD.

3. Read *Science at the Doorstep to God: Science and Reason in Support of God, the Soul, and Life after Death* for additional science-based evidence.

4. Self-realization is associated with the development of desirable character traits and the absence of personal desires. "Bookish" learning is not as beneficial as realizing from one's own experiences that God is the doer. The following websites, organizations, and foundations help spiritual seekers become finders.

   a. Sri Sathya Sai International Organization (SSSIO)
   b. Sathya Sai Bookstore, Tustin, California
   c. Foundation for Inner Peace and the Foundation for *A Course in Miracles*
   d. *Adding Facts to Faith*, Franklin Loehr's Religious Research Foundation
   e. Gurus with websites and books: Byron Katie, Eckhart Tolle, David R. Hawkins, Lenard Jacobson, Jac O'Keeffe, and Jeff Foster
   f. Book sources and websites for spiritual seekers:

      i. Advaita Fellowship
      ii. Non-Duality Press
      iii. Society of Abidance in Truth
      iv. Vedanta Press and catalog

5. Instead of spiritual practices that ignore Karma and spiritual growth concerns, Sathya Sai Baba recommended *selfless service*. He said, "Consider SERVICE as the best spiritual discipline," and "Dedicate your entire time to SERVICE and the discharge of your duties. Your spiritual practices must not be for selfish ends."

GLOSSARY

afterlife   Where the soul goes and what happens after death.

apparition   A visual image of a discarnate spirit, a ghost.

astrology   Apparent ability to derive a person's tendencies and circumstances from the positions of the sun, moon, and five most easily seen planets.

Atma   The spark of God, divinity, that is the self, within one's innermost reality.

aura   Uncommonly seen light radiating from the Atma within living beings.

avatar   God in a human body to improve human knowledge and behavior.

Brahman   God, All That Is, eternal ocean of formless, primary consciousness.

channeling   A medium receiving information from a discarnate or distant source with spiritual ears or by allowing their vocal cords to be used while in a trance.

confirmation bias   The detrimental effect of attitudes and beliefs on objectivity.

consciousness   Awareness. Consciousness is unique; we experience it directly. What gives monarch butterflies and past-life memories prebirth knowledge?

darshan   Seeing and being in the presence of a great person.

dharma   One's (as a spiritual being) morally "right conduct."

discarnate   Spirits (souls) without a body.

divination   The use of a supernatural means of obtaining information.

272

duality	The single location in time and space perspective of egoic human minds—here versus there, me/you, then/now, this/that, etcetera.
ego	We are not our ego (sense of I and my), but our ego assumes that we are.
empathy	Sensitive to and able to understand the thoughts and feelings of others. Empathy makes the golden rule a more effective guide.
Enlightenment	1650–1800, period when science embraced a reductionistic and materialistic view of the universe, physicalism, and human reason replaced revelation as our best source of knowledge. Also, a synonym for self-realization, the realization of the Atma within the heart of all beings.
esoteric believers	Have the uncommon, esoteric awareness of God's unity or oneness with creation revealed during mystical spiritual experiences.
evidence (three types)	**Antidotal evidence** involves personal testimony. **Empirical evidence** is obtained by observation or experimentation. **Logical evidence** works with the scientific method to reveal nature's secrets and with confirmation bias to ignore the evidence for God, souls, and an afterlife.
exoteric believers	The common dualistic and materialistic understanding of reality experienced by those who have not had mystical, spiritual experiences.
God	The consciousness of the whole ocean and each wave.

guru	Spiritual teacher who has ideally achieved self-realization.
heart	Where Sathya Sai Baba said you can feel your soul. Do you feel love, empathy, and concern for others; or anger and even hate? Is your soul "near the end" or "just started"?
inner voice	Source of guidance and assistance from within.
intuition	Awareness without knowing how.
jiva	Person, the "I" consciousness associated with the body, mind, and senses.
Karma	Cause-and-effect consequences (seeds) of past actions.
liberation	We achieve freedom, "liberation," or **moksha** in Sanskrit, from the cycle of rebirths, reincarnation, when we achieve self-realization.
materialism and materialistic	Words that usually refer to excessive interest in property and possessions, materialistic but in this book, usually used to refer to the philosophical belief that "reality" does not contain nonmaterial aspects like God and souls.
maya	A jiva's worldly illusion of the material world of desire and ego due to ignorance of one's spiritual nature and the veiling power of the mind.
medium	A psychic who communicates with disincarnate spirits.
metaphysics	Embraces the concepts and phenomena contained in this book, which mainstream science regards as unscientific, **metaphysical** thinking.

mind	Casts the veil of illusion, maya, and creates the ego with its thoughts and desires, but can also penetrate maya and free us from the cycle of rebirths.
mystical	Spiritually relevant nonlocal information.
nonduality	**Advaita**, not two in Sanskrit. Oneness, the primary experience and teaching of God's prophets, avatars, and achievers of self-realization: *The Ocean's* all-inclusive perspective in which *waves* are not separated by time, space, or distance: quantum entanglement.
nonlocality	Not confined to a given location in space and time. If consciousness was merely a material phenomenon, psychic abilities would not exist.
OBE	**Out-of-body experience** or **astral projection** is the ability of souls, consciousness, to leave the physical body and return.
occult	A derogatory label that marginalizes those with knowledge of and experience with mystical and psi phenomena.
paradigm	A scientific discipline's understanding of their portion of "reality."
paranormal	Not compatible with a materialistic understanding of reality.
parapsychology	The study of psi phenomena—occult methods of obtaining information.
prophet	God's divinely inspired servants and messengers.
psi and ESP	Abilities that suggest connections, interconnected consciousness, between people and things outside the usual limits of time and space.

psychic	Those whose spiritual senses—clairvoyants, mediums, remote viewing, etcetera—reveal consciousness's independence from matter.
revelation	The information—provided by prophets like Jesus, and avatars like Sathya Sai Baba—that provides insight into our underlying reality.
sacred	Spiritually significant and worthy of worship.
samadhi	Experienced when the worldly illusion, maya, is removed, revealing the always present (but invisible to the physical senses), unchanging, radiant field of consciousness that projects the visible physical world of duality.
self-realization	Awakening from the worldly dream, maya, to a level of consciousness that is prior to the ego's awareness. See *samadhi*.
soul and spirit	Our essence (underlying reality), which is neither born nor dies and continues in an afterlife when the physical body dies.
spirit guides	Discarnate spirits assigned to provide incarnating souls with guidance.
supernatural	Not compatible with an atheist's understanding of reality: supernatural.
Vibhuti	Sathya Sai Baba manifested Vibhuti, "sacred ash," which appeared to flow out of his fingertips. He "prescribed" Vibhuti to treat health problems and used Vibhuti to remind devotees of the stupidity of ignoring their underlying reality when the "I" that they think they are will become a corpse which reduces to nothing more significant than ash.

ENDNOTES

1   Lincoln Barnett, *The Universe and Dr. Einstein* (New York: Signet, 1964), 58.

2   Ibid., 22.

3   Elizabeth Syoboda, "Why Is It So Hard to Change People's Minds?" (June 27, 2017). This article originally appeared in Greater Good, the online magazine of the Greater Good Science Center at UC Berkeley. For more information, visit greatergood.berkeley.edu.

4   Max Planck, *Scientific Autobiography and Other Papers* (New York: Philosophical Library, 1949), 333–334.

5   Genesis 2:7.

6   *Webster's Dictionary* definition of prima facie evidence.

7   Brian L. & Amy E. Weiss, *Miracles Happen: The Transformational Healing Power of Past-Life Memories* (New York: HarperCollins Publishers, 2012), 43.

8   Michael Newton, Memories of the Afterlife, Life Between Lives Stories of Personal Transformation (Woodbury: Llewellyn Publications, 2009), xiii.

9   Ibid., 95.

10 Dean Radin, Supernormal: Science, Yoga, and the Evidence for Extraordinary Psychic Ability (New York: Random House, Inc., 2013), 116.

11 Hilton Deakin, Some Thoughts on Transcendence in Tribal Societies (Adelaide: E. Dowdy, 1982), 31–32.

12 John 17:21.

13 Acts 17: 27–28.

14 Mathew 18:3.

15 Andrew Newberg, The Spiritual Brain: Science and Religious Experience (Virginia: The Great Courses, 2012), 102.

16 "John Glenn Says Evolution Should Be Taught in Schools," May 20, 2015, http://www.Huffingtonpost.com/2015/05/20/john-glenn-evolution.

17 Luke 17:21.

18 John 14:12.

19 Seth Borenstein and Janie Harris, June 21, 2018, Associated Press Obituary: *Animal Ambassador, Koko the gorilla used smarts, empathy to help change views.*

20 One-eighth of a diopter along one axis.

21 Yasmin Anwar, "Emoji fans take heart: Scientists pinpoint 27 states of emotion," Berkeley News website, September 6, 2017, https://news.berkeley.edu/2017/09/06/27-emotions/.

22 Jeremy Adam Smith, "Can the Science of Purpose Help Explain White Supremacy?" This article appeared in Greater Good, the online magazine of

the Greater Good Science Center at UC Berkeley on August 22, 2017. For more information, visit greatergood.berkeley.edu.

23 Robert Emmons, "Three Surprising Ways That Gratitude Works at Work." This article appeared in Greater Good, the online magazine of the Greater Good Science Center at UC Berkeley on October 11, 2017. For more information, visit greatergood.berkeley.edu.

24 Luke 12:5.

25 Thessalonians 5:18.

26 Philippians 2:3–4.

27 Herb Taylor, The Herbert J. Taylor Story (Downers Grove: InterVarsity Press, 1968), 38–44.

28 Henry Van Dyke's poem "Thoughts Are Things."

29 Vivian Laughrey, "A Profile of Inspiration, Hazel Denning, Ph.D.," Perspectives magazine (February 1988), 13–14.

30 Ibid.

31 Ibid.

32 Robert Skutch, Journey Without Distance, The Story Behind A COURSE IN MIRACLES (Mill Valley: Foundation for Inner Peace, 1984), 33–34.

33 Ibid., 54–56.

34 Kenneth Wapnick, Absence from Felicity, The Story of Helen Schucman and Her Scribing of A Course in Miracles (Temecula: Foundation for A Course in Miracles, 1991), 5.

35 First edition of A Course in Miracles, Volume Three, Manuel for Teachers (Farmingdale: Foundation for Inner Peace, www.acim.org, 1980), 73.

36 Robert Skutch, Journey Without Distance, The Story Behind A COURSE IN MIRACLES (Mill Valley: Foundation for Inner Peace, 1984), third page in unnumbered foreword.

37 "What is Self-Realization?" Definition from Yogapedia website, November 22, 2018, https://www.yogapedia.com/definition/5840/self-realization.

38 First edition of A Course in Miracles, Volume Three, Manuel for Teachers (Farmingdale: Foundation for Inner Peace, www.acim.org, 1980), 77.

39 Ephesians 2:8.

40 Peter 1:11.

41 A. C. Bhaktivedanta Swami Prabhupada, translator, BHAGAVAD-GITA AS IT IS, abridged edition (Los Angeles: Bhaktivedant Book Trust, 1976), 83–84.

42 Exodus 3:14, King James Version's (KJV) use of the word "that" preferred for this quote.

43 Exodus 4:12.

44 Aldous Huxley, *The Perennial Philosophy* (New York: HarperCollins Publisher, 2009), vii.

45 Nisargadatta Maharaj, *I AM THAT, Talks with Sri Nisargadatta Maharaj* (Durham: Acorn Press, 1996), 199.

46 Ibid., 137.

47 Ibid., 222.

48 John 14:2.

49 David R. Hawkins, MD, PhD, POWER VS. FORCE, *The Hidden Determinants of Human Behavior* (Carlsbad: Hay House Inc., 1995), 54.

50 Phyllis Krystal, *Sai Baba, The Ultimate Experience* (Los Angeles: Aura Books, 1985), 40.

51 Ibid., 70.

52 Ibid., 126.

53 Ibid., 90.

54 Mark 1:14.

55 Mark 16:20.

56 Quoted statements are those of Sathya Sai Baba.

57 Phyllis Krystal, *Sai Baba, The Ultimate Experience* (Los Angeles: Aura Books, 1985), 53.

58 Sathya Sai Baba, January 14, 1995, Poornachandra Auditorium discourse.

59 Psalms 121:2 and 124:8.

60 John Hislop, *My Baba and I* (Prasanthi Nilayam: Sri Sathya Sai Books & Publications Trust, 1985), 29.

61 Ibid., 30.

62 Joy Thomas, *Life Is a Challenge, Meet It* (Beaumont: Ontic Book Publishers, 1991), i–ii.

63 John 4:8.

64 Evening of May 18, 1968, discourse in Bombay, India, *Sathya Sai Speaks, Volume VI* (Brindavan: Sri Sathya Sai Education Foundation, 1983), 219.

65 November 23, 1997, birthday discourse titled "I Am I," *Sathya Sai Newsletter, USA 28*, no. 6 (Arcadia: Sathya Sai Book Center of America, 2004), 5.

66 Ibid., 4.

67 Christin Lore Weber, *A CRY IN THE DESERT, The Awakening of Byron Katie* (United States of America: Miracles Whole Health, 1996), 25–26.

68 John 15:12.

69 Sathya Sai Baba, July 7, 1990, Gurupoornima discourse in Poornachandra Auditorium.

70 Galatians 6:7.

71 Sathya Sai Baba, Nov. 19, 1990, Sathya Sai Fifth World Conference, Hillview Stadium.

72 Ibid.

73 Ibid.

74 Luke 17:20–21.

75 *Sathya Sai Speaks, Volume VIII*, 195.

76 *Sathya Sai Speaks, Volume VIII*, 163.

77 *Sathya Sai Speaks, Volume IX*,137.

78 Genesis 1:27–28.

79 Mathew 7:7.

CONTRIBUTORS

This book, which seemed too challenging to write almost forty years ago, has been written thanks to the generous assistance of others. In the order in which they appear in this book, I want to acknowledge those who helped to make this book possible. Physicist Russell Targ's generous permission to use his book, *The Reality of ESP: A Physicist's Proof of Psychic Abilities*, has hopefully enabled me to reveal the nonlocality of consciousness. Helen Roberts and her daughter, Barbara Costelloe, have been incredibly supportive and helpful. We exchanged many emails that provided insights and content for this book. The taboo against knowing that we are incarnating spiritual beings prevents appropriate interest in the Loehr-Daniels life readings and the Religious Research Foundation's books. Before Dr. Daniels's four thousand years of effort are lost to humanity, a large publisher or foundation should purchase the Religious Research Foundation's copyrights and reveal Dr. Daniels to the world. Prior to asking Trudy Philpot Kieschnick for her assistance, I did not know Armand Marcotte had predicted her marriage to an older, spiritual man with a daughter and three sons. I am appreciative of the assistance provided by psychic Kathryn Leeman and my daughter Jennifer Young when they read and corrected my version of events. I am also appreciative that my sister-in-law Karen Marie, my daughter Jennifer, and Doctor Christopher Hair read large portions of my manuscript and provided helpful insights and suggestions. The primary contributor to this book has been Sathya Sai Baba. I believe he orchestrated the experiences that brought me to his ashram. He, or something, has been motivating and helping me to write this book and publish it in 2025. Why 2025? My pendulum confirms my inner voice's answer: 2025 is 99 years after

Sathya Sai's birth in 1926, and 14 years after his death in 2011. At 14, He began his ministry. The numbers 108 and 9 (1 + 0 + 8 = 9 and 9 x 9 = 81 or 8+1 = 9 and 2 + 0 + 2 + 5 = 9) are Hinduism's most sacred numbers.

ABOUT THE AUTHOR

Doctor William K. Dorrance grew up in and near San Diego, California. After graduating from Grossmont High School in 1961 and UC Berkeley's School of Optometry in 1967, he served in the US Air Force as an optometrist. A self-employed optometrist from 1971 until 2011, when he retired, Dr. Dorrance was voted Favorite Optometrist in 1999 by the readers of Riverside County's largest newspaper, *The Press-Enterprise*. Dr. Dorrance's service activities include:

- President of the Moreno Valley Rotary Club in 1976–1977
- California Optometric Association's Director of Continuing Education, 1979 and 1980
- President of the Orange Belt Optometric Society in 1982
- Moreno Valley Chamber of Commerce Board of Directors, 1984–1986
- President of the Parapsychology Association of Riverside in 1988
- Member and President of Moreno Valley's Redevelopment Project Area Committee 2002–2005
- President of Toastmasters Club 2169 in 1990–1991 and 2003–2004
- As Moreno Valley Rotary Club's youth services director for fifteen years, he served as liaison with Moreno Valley High School's Interact Club and shared The Four-Way Test by conducting an annual speech contest among high school contestants who incorporated into their speech The Four-Way Test of the things we think, say, or do.

1. *Is it the truth?*
2. *Is it fair to all concerned?*
3. *Will it build good will and better friendships?*
4. *Will it be beneficial to all concerned?*

www.ingramcontent.com/pod-product-compliance
Lightning Source LLC
Chambersburg PA
CBHW030910120626
46554CB00001B/94